ROSE WINDOWS

Painton Cowen

ROSE
WINDOWS

Chronicle Books
San Francisco
A Prism Edition

On the title page:
Virgin and Child with rose, from
the Laon east rose window

to my parents

and all my friends who have made this book
possible, particularly Ted Matchett and Guy
and Piera de Vogüé. I would also like to
thank Anne and Alan Nero, Jean-Pierre and Dinx
Rosetti, Surgeon Captain E. C. (Buster) Glover,
RNVR, Roger Godfrey, Lavinia Merton, Peter Lund,
my sister Caroline, the directors of many of the
Departmental Archives in France, and many
others who have helped in differing ways. To Tad
Mann and Quentin Neill I would like to express my
special thanks for their magnificent art work.

For permission to quote, acknowledgment is due to
Faber and Faber and to Harcourt Brace Jovanovich,
for T. S. Eliot's *Four Quartets*; to Elisabeth Chase
Geissbuhler, for her translation of Auguste Rodin's
The Cathedrals of France; and to the representatives
of the late Dorothy L. Sayers, for her translation of
Dante's *Paradiso*, published by Penguin Books.

The photographs in the plate sections are my own,
with the exception of 17 (Washington DC), which
is by Irwin Wensink.

CHRONICLE BOOKS
870 MARKET STREET
SAN FRANCISCO, CALIFORNIA 94102
A PRISM EDITION

Text © 1979 Thames and Hudson Ltd, London
Photographs © 1979 Painton Cowen

General Editor: Jill Purce

Library of Congress Cataloging in Publication Data
Cowen, Painton.
    Rose windows.

    "A Prism edition."
    Bibliography: p.
    Includes index.
    1. Rose windows.   2. Christian art and symbolism.
    3. Glass painting and staining, Medieval.   4. Cathe-
    drals.   I Title.

NK5308.C64   748.5'9   78–23286
ISBN 0–87701–121–4 (cloth)
ISBN 0–87701–122–2 (paper)

Filmset in Great Britain by Keyspools Ltd,
Golborne, Lancashire
Printed and bound in the Netherlands
by Smeets Offset, Weert

Contents

Let us make a thing of beauty
That long may live when we are gone;
Let us make a thing of beauty
That hungry souls may feast upon;

Whether it be wood or marble,
Music, art or poetry,
Let us make a thing of beauty
To help set man's bound spirit free.

Edward Matchett

The Glaziers' Dream, 1978. Ink drawing by Quentin Neill

Light into darkness

A present from the past

The ability to create beauty is God's greatest gift to man. And the appreciation of beauty – whether man-made or natural – is not only a joy but an active call to something much greater than oneself. At rare intervals in our lives we may experience moments of magic, when a person, a place, a view, an object or a situation seems to transfix us, and we suddenly see the world in a quite different light. Such moments are often accompanied by an equally sudden 'inner expansion' and the realization that there is much more of life to be experienced, much that is unfulfilled. However unexpected the moments may be, they have a feeling of the Absolute about them. They are rare and elusive but leave us with a sense of awe and wonder which we feel is our birthright.

The Gothic cathedrals have imparted something of this experience to many people. Their towering heights, accentuated by the slender ascending pillars interweaving in the vaults overhead, enclose a space that seems to be held under a spell by the tensions of its stone structure, and into this arena is poured light of almost infinite shades of colour, sparkling jewel-like in the sun or glowing quietly in the light of overcast skies.

A valuable piece of writing has come down to us which expresses how one individual, Abbot Suger, felt in 1144 on entering the first Gothic building, the abbey church of Saint-Denis, built to his own specifications. He saw the jewels and coloured glass in his new church as possessing the ability to transform 'that which is material to that which is immaterial. ... Then it seems to me that I see myself dwelling, as it were, in some strange region of the universe which neither exists entirely in the slime of the earth nor entirely in the purity of Heaven; and that, by the grace of God, I can be transported from this inferior to that higher world'.[1]

Suger's Gothic Saint-Denis was certainly an architectural innovation, even though it included a number of features which had already been in use in certain churches in England and France. At Cluny, for example, flying buttresses had been introduced to support the top sections of the walls and vaults of the choir, and at Durham the first rib vault had been achieved by 1104. Cluny had also already introduced pointed arches into its Romanesque structure. Stained glass had appeared in Europe at least a hundred years prior to Saint-Denis, in comparatively small windows in selected parts of certain churches. But when Suger combined all these developments into a single building the effect was magical. No longer did the building convey the massive weight and solidity characteristic of the Romanesque; a new lightness had been found, suggesting a new-found energy, a restless upward striving, as though towards the very vault of heaven.

This energy is symbolized in light. Flying buttresses enabled much of the weight of the vault to be transferred to the ground outside the building, and instead of the painted stone walls of the Romanesque there appeared at Saint-Denis huge areas of glowing coloured light. It was as if matter had been conquered; and light took full advantage of the victory by flooding in in every shape and colour that the architects and glaziers could devise. Nearly every Gothic church built after that date aspired to be the image of the New Jerusalem of St John's Revelation, whose walls had foundations that were studded with precious stones; this finds its quintessence at Chartres and, in miniature form, at the Sainte-Chapelle in Paris.

Within these images of paradise, which sprang up during the thirteenth century all over France, we frequently find the ultimate jewels – rose windows. They are suspended between floor and vault, as if between heaven and earth, a single beautifully cut jewel containing countless others. They seem almost unearthly, dimensionless, aspiring to something even greater than the cathedral itself. The great rose windows of Paris and Chartres take the breath away with their spectacular webs of glass, lead and stone: a perfection brought about by geometry, which, as Rodin says, 'speaks to our hearts because it is the general principle of things'.[2]

The nineteenth-century French architect Eugène Viollet-le-Duc had such an experience while looking at the south rose window of Notre-Dame de Paris, and in that moment he knew that it was his destiny to help save France's unique and priceless medieval heritage. War, neglect and vandalism had taken their toll over the centuries, and rebuilding and restoring what was lost and damaged became to Viollet-le-Duc a vocation. His work – along with that of many other restorers – is often maligned, but it has to be recognized that without his researches and efforts there would not be much left of many of the great churches and cathedrals in France.

In spite of damage and restoration, the great rose windows can still impart something of the wonder that they must have generated at the time of their creation. This is primarily through the powerful and spectacular *form* which can be generated within a circle, and in which modern designers still find endless possibilities of expression.

The arrival of rose windows in the cathedrals is something of a mystery. They appeared quite suddenly around the year 1200 and within fifty years had diffused right across France. A few appeared in England, Italy, Spain and Germany; but they remain essentially a French phenomenon, and it is around Paris that we find the greatest gems. In all three early large cathedrals around Paris the largest possible rose windows were incorporated from the first on three sides, and in the case of Laon possibly on all four. The reasons for this insistence upon the rose window can be sought in the language of symbolism and in the background of the age.

A symbol of truth

One of Abbot Suger's most important contributions to Gothic architecture was the extensive application of typological iconography, the placing of a New Testament subject next to one from the Old which seems to prefigure it: for example, Jonah and the whale alongside the Resurrection. At Chartres, the north rose with kings, priests and prophets faces the south rose filled with the twenty-four elders of the Apocalypse. This is a typological transformation that takes place across the church: that is across the church as a building in *space*, but also through the Church in *time*.

The building itself is the best guide to this dual role by virtue of its layout, orientated around the end of the Incarnation by its division in *space* into two sides, north and south, which correspond to the division in *time* between Old and New Testaments. Between the two lies the nave forming the Latin cross, derived from the equal-armed Greek cross of many early

The idealized Gothic cathedral – as envisaged by Viollet-le-Duc – was never achieved. Six of the seven spires and the three rose windows are built on the three façades facing north, south and west. The north was generally associated with the Old Testament, the south with the New, and the west with the Last Judgment

Christian churches. The word 'nave' itself betrays a deeper meaning, as it is derived from the Latin *navis*, 'ship': the Ark of the Old Testament that formerly saved all life from the Flood and has become typologically transformed into the Church of the New. The Ark thus becomes a sort of metaphysical vessel that carries mankind through time, and the rose windows on either side to the north and south are the stars that guide its course.

But there is another Ark, the Ark of the Covenant, or the Law of God given to Moses in trust for mankind. These two Arks are essentially related; for the

Ark of the Covenant symbolizes Knowledge that has to be carried through history. When Christ underwent the trials of the Passion the veil of the Temple was rent in twain, indicating the turning-point in human history at which the Mysteries of the ancient world were no longer to be withheld. They had served their purpose: 'It is finished.'

The rose window as an eternal symbol transcends words. Inside the cathedral we are aware of stone, light, colour and shadow, all manifest in dimension and proportion within the measure of man; they emphasize man's presence on the earth, and the verticality of the nave, choir and transepts suggests an aspiration to something greater. The surrounding stained-glass windows relate stories and parables, the lives of saints and all history relevant to the spreading of the Word of God. But in the rose windows, dimension and measure seem to disappear; it is as though they could be infinitely large or infinitely small. They represent an eternal truth – that of the Logos, the Word itself. In Christianity, Christ is the Logos. He is at the centre of each of the three rose windows at Chartres, each one representing His threefold nature: as a child in the north, resurrected in the south, and in judgment in the west. Each of these directions inside the building symbolizes time, the north being *past* (the Old Testament) the south *present* (the New Testament) and the west *future* (Last Judgment and the creation of New Jerusalem).

Through the Logos all three become fused in an eternal present; and in the rose window, by virtue of its very form, this realization takes place on the deepest level of human consciousness. Rose windows are, to use the term popularized by C. G. Jung, mandalas. Their radial and predominantly fourfold form is that which spontaneously appears in dreams and in art as an expression of the human aspiration towards wholeness and coherence: 'a pattern of order which like a psychological viewfinder marked with a cross on a circle – or a circle divided into four – is imposed on the psychic chaos so that each content falls into place and the weltering confusion is held together by the protective circle'.[3]

Rose windows thus symbolize man's highest aspirations: to know God's order, to become at one with Him, and ultimately to become co-creators with the Creator. As mandalas they perform the first task imposed on those who set out on this quest; they enable them to obey the injunction of Psalm 46: 'Be still and know that I am God.'

The way of the Christian mystic involves study, thought, contemplation and action; it seeks ultimately to understand more fully the teachings of Christ, particularly the words 'I am come that they might have life and that they might have it more abundantly' (John 10:10), life finding its greatest expression in action. For this reason Christian mysticism is 'remarkably and refreshingly earthy, human, passionate and worldly', as William McNamara describes it: a way of discipline that seeks as its goal 'the perfection of charity and not, as in the case with other mystics, a mysterious means of acquiring transcendental knowledge'.[4]

The first requirement of mysticism is to seek the soul through purification, to become 'perfect as your Father in heaven is perfect' (Matthew 5:48). This is symbolized in the Virgin Mary, who is generally portrayed at the centre of north rose windows. She represents the sum of all the past, the culmination and quintessence of the Old Testament, of all that went before Christ. The perfect geometric disposition of the panels in the window invites the beholder to reflect in the mind the order perceived by the eyes: to become still and at peace with oneself and with the world before acting. In this sense the rose window could be said to be the key to one's own soul, and the rest of the cathedral the key to perceiving a world transfigured by the Word.

But there are dangers here. The anonymous medieval writer of the *Cloud of Unknowing* forewarns his readers that a man ignorant of the soul's powers may easily be deceived in spiritual understanding: mysticism seeks Grace, not as the fruit of effort, but rather as a gift from God. The agent of Grace is the Holy Spirit, which descends to the Virgin Mary as a dove in the north rose window at Chartres, where she is holding the Christ child. As a mandala of exquisite beauty this rose teaches the first requirement of mysticism: an openness that is innocence, 'as little children'. But Grace is also the means of protection for the ignorant soul against evil, against 'the world, the flesh and the devil' as the liturgy and St Paul put it. The mandala form is relevant here also: it symbolizes what Jung called individuation, the process through which individuals and society might 'become whole', and the imbalance in Western culture be rectified: an imbalance brought about by an inability to acknowledge and cope with the unconscious, resulting in a heavily one-sided development of the personality, no knowledge or expression of one's real self, and a constant objectivization and projection of one's own imbalance on to objects and situations outside oneself or on to images that appear from the unconscious. But Jung also pointed to the dangers of misguided individuation, an ignorant release of the powers of the soul. Christianity's fight against the Devil and all his works can at this level be seen to be above superstition as a fight against the 'terrors' of the unconscious, a battle ultimately between sanity and insanity, between knowledge and ignorance.

Jung noted that mandalas tended to appear in situations of psychic confusion and perplexity. In medieval imagery this could be said to be illustrated in the 'psychic confusion' of the Last Judgment, portrayed in the west roses at Chartres [27, 29] and Mantes [65], with the polarization of good and evil above and below and Christ at the centre as mediator. And the twelfth and thirteenth centuries were certainly a time of psychic confusion: the fanaticism of the Crusades, the struggle between faith and reason in the Church and the universities, the growing heresies, the increasing conflicts between Church and State (exemplified by the murder of St Thomas of Canterbury): all contributed to this confused state of the soul of the age. These were events going on over most people's heads, yet all became familiar with the ruthless and dreaded Inquisition. And yet, before this tragic era of the Church's history reached its zenith in Spain and in the Albigensian crusades, cathedral building was well under way, with rose windows appearing all round Paris and then rapidly spreading elsewhere. In Jungian terms they would seem to be an expression of the group unconscious of the age, for Jung saw the spontaneous and even unconscious production of mandala form in art and architecture as the creation of 'vessels', into which each person (artist or beholder) projected his or her psyche, and which could in return initiate a healing or restorative process.

The radiating form and pattern of most rose windows indicate many paths to one centre; and this corresponds to the paths which lead to the real self at the centre of the soul. It is this journey that is the aspiration of the mystic: to encounter the infinite, in a state of innocence, with the real self. Nor is it a passive process, since each step taken inwardly has to be compensated for in the outside world by some action, followed by another period of reflection and then by action again, and so on, like breathing out and in; a harmonization of opposites not unlike the acceptance of *yin* and *yang* in the Tao of Chinese philosophy. In Christianity the equivalent of the Tao is the Way, exemplified by Christ at the centre of the rose window, midway between heaven and hell.

Queen of cathedrals

Paris in the twelfth century was at the centre of a medieval renaissance, acting as a melting-pot for knowledge from all over Europe and much of the Middle East. This spirit was carried through most of the following century, until plague, war and exhaustion extinguished its flame. After the thirteenth century, in the words of the nineteenth-century architectural historian Henry Adams, 'nine churches out of ten were still-born ... church architecture became a pure matter of mechanics and mathematics'.[5]

The church-building activity of this era was prodigious. Henry Adams and Abbé Bulteau estimate that some 80 cathedrals and 500 churches of near cathedral size were started in France alone in the period 1170–1270; and many of these were almost finished within that period. It was an activity that is estimated to have taken up at least one third of what would now be called the Gross Domestic Product. It is a phenomenon that has never really been explained and probably never will be. We can see only that something

The domes of Early Christian and Byzantine churches, with their mosaic and fresco interiors, often choose a powerful radiating design around Christ Pantocrator or the Virgin and Child. They may well have influenced the concept of the giant rose windows that emerged around Paris following the first three crusades. Twenty-four prophets surround Christ in the Kariye Camii at Istanbul (Photograph courtesy of Dumbarton Oaks Center for Byzantine Studies, Washington, D.C.)

prompted people of all trades and classes to undertake a venture that resulted in workmanship and inspiration of a degree rarely equalled in the history of mankind and acted to weld together communities and to embrace generations. Kenneth Clark expresses the Chartres phenomenon in his *Civilisation*:

> ... the faithful harnessed themselves to the carts which were bringing the stone and dragged them from the quarry to the cathedral. The enthusiasm spread through France. Men and women came from far away carrying heavy burdens of provisions for the workmen – wine, oil and corn. Among them were the lords and ladies pulling the carts with the rest. There was perfect discipline and a most profound silence. All hearts were united and each man forgave his enemies.[6]

And when they had completed their cathedral – or the greater part of it, since few have really been completed – the people must have had a sense of achievement that was inexpressible in words. David Macaulay in his superb book *Cathedral* gives us a glimpse of this:

> Huge banners had been hung from the triforium, and all the candles on the piers were lit. As the choir began to sing, the building filled with beautiful sounds and the people, most of them grandchildren of the men who laid the foundation, were filled with tremendous awe and a great joy.
>   For eighty-six years the townspeople had shared one goal, and it had at last been reached.[7]

The twelfth-century renaissance can be compared in originality and energy to that of Florence some 250 years later, for it has left an indelible mark upon Western culture. The early Crusades brought back from the Middle East much Greek and Arab knowledge and inspiration, particularly in the realms of mathematics, building, poetry and philosophy. Aristotle's works had been rediscovered and were integrated with a separate stream of Arab-modified Greek and Jewish thought which had developed in Spain; and some of the monasteries – notably Cluny – had even been studying the Koran. A common language – Latin – linked the entire scholastic community. Bishops, clergy and scholars from France, England, Italy, Germany and Spain often changed places for a time, bringing about a diffusion and modification of knowledge.

Of all the schools which studied and taught the knowledge of the age, one of the most original and influential was that which belonged to the cathedral at Chartres. Its work reflects the characteristic twelfth-century combination of innovatory excitement and respect for tradition:

> We are as dwarfs mounted on the shoulders of giants, so that we can see more and further than they; yet not by virtue of the keenness of our eyesight, nor through the tallness of our stature, but because we are raised and borne aloft upon that giant mass.[8]

These are the words of John of Salisbury quoting Bernard of Chartres, probably the greatest of the chancellors of the School. In the 1220s, a

Two of the evangelists on the shoulders of the prophets at Chartres, in lancets beneath the south rose window: St Luke on Jeremiah and St Matthew on Isaiah (from Westlake)

century after Bernard's time, the huge south rose window was installed, above five lancet windows containing the Virgin Mary and the four Evangelists [36], the latter being portrayed as dwarfs – or young men – on the shoulders of giants. A coincidence – or a wish to acknowledge the influence of Bernard and the School? There is no doubt that its work and insights are crucial factors in understanding Chartres cathedral, and all the churches built when the Gothic spirit was active. For Chartres is unique, in that its iconographic programme in glass and stone was probably the most complete of its day, and is still more or less intact.

Friedrich Heer describes the School as 'perhaps the most luminous symbol of the intellectual movement of the twelfth century in all its pristine youthfulness and egregious audacity'.[9] The 'giants' they built on included Plato, Plotinus, Boethius, St Augustine and the Bible. Their free and unprejudiced attitude to the acquisition of knowledge enabled them to develop their Christianity in the light of classical purity, Islamic devotion and Arabian thinking. They followed precisely the advice of the early mystic Hugh of St Victor: to learn all that was possible. From Christian and pagan sources alike they studied the created in order to know the Creator.

Intellectibilitas, writes Heer, was a new word coined at Chartres and reveals its guiding principle: 'God, the cosmos, nature and mankind can be examined, reasoned about, comprehended and measured in their proportions, number, weight and harmony.'[10] One of the School's earliest milestones was Chancellor Thierry's *Hexameron*, or 'Six Days of Creation', built largely on Pythagoras' theories of the meaning of number. It led to an appreciation of God as the form of being in all things: 'All numbers derive from Unity: all things derive from God.'[11] As the twelfth century progressed, the School developed Thierry's concept of the Creation into an understanding of creation in every moment. The works of Plotinus and Boethius were particularly important here in building on the Bible and Plato's *Timaeus* to formulate a concept of nature and wisdom as the creative power of the cosmos; and in Bernard de Silvestris' *De mundi universitate* we meet the goddess Natura as the eternal, fruitful mother of all. As a creative power, Natura became identified (mainly by Alain de Lille, another Schoolman) with the Eros of classical antiquity, which in Christian terms becomes the Love of God. He also saw numbers as the binding power of the cosmos.

The School of Chartres seems to have elaborated a concept of evolution, drawn from all available knowledge, Christian and pagan alike, which embodied the Old Testament, number, geometry, nature, the cosmos, Divine Love and the New Testament. It is essentially the Logos, the Word, of St John's Gospel (John: 1:1) seen in the light of the latest knowledge of the age. St John saw Christ as the Word of God incarnate: or, putting it in another way, as the personification and manifestation of the philosophical concept of the Logos, which in the first century AD was seen by the scholars of Alexandria to be the Creative Principle of the Universe within Absolute Reason, active in all things from stars to snowflakes and ultimately in the affairs of men. This amalgamation of Greek, Jewish and Egyptian thought found its main synthesis and expression through Philo of Alexandria. It was St John who saw the importance of this philosophy, its coincidental timing with Christ's ministry, and the meaning of both for human destiny.

The study of the philosophy of the Logos seems (according to the medieval scholar J. van der Meulen) to have led the Chartres School to see its own work as a constituent of God's order in creation;[12] so that, in accordance with the unfolding plan of evolution, the world was ready to receive new knowledge through the School itself. In so doing the School would have been responding to the promptings of the Holy Spirit, for it saw these studies of the Logos as a basis for the doctrine of Divine Providence;[13] and the agent of Providence would have been the Holy Spirit, Who, as Chancellor Thierry saw, 'loves and governs created matter'.[14]

In the cathedral of Chartres there are two small rosettes high up above the clerestory windows, one in the north transept and the other in the choir [8]. Both portray Christ as the Creator enthroned above the primordial chaos. His left hand holds the globe of the cosmos divided into land, sea and heaven, with the castle of mankind at the centre; His right hand is held up in blessing. It is a direct portrayal of Christ as Logos, the mediator between heaven and earth. The much larger rose windows at Chartres can be seen to be themselves actual expressions of the Logos, one centred on Christ, as the Word made flesh, and the other on His Mother. Each rose window is a *symbol* of love, the universe and eternity, but it is also a *construction* that embodies geometry, number and light; and all these are components of the Logos.

Each of the Chartres rose windows has something special about it (for analysis see pp. 122–26). That of the north transept [6] is constructed according to three sets of superimposed geometry, one of which is based on the Fibonacci series – a mathematical and geometric phenomenon that governs, among other things, the growth and positioning of the leaves and flowers of certain plants. A second geometry incorporates all the major features of the window within a system of equilateral triangles, and a third lines up what is created by the other two. And there is more: for the number 12 that underlies the whole window is the product of 3 and 4, the former symbolizing *spirit* (the Trinity) and the latter *matter* (the Elements). The product, 12, is all the possible combinations of 4 and 3, symbolizing the total infusion of matter with spirit throughout the cosmos – of which the rose window is itself a model. So, too, the agency of the Spirit can be seen in the window as a fourfold or 'four-dimensional' dove, since the Spirit acts continuously through all time and space – it 'loves and guides all created matter', as Thierry put it. And as a symbol of this love the rose is the Eros or Divine Love of the creative power of the cosmos. It is a perfect fusion and manifestation of the philosophy of the School: a thing of great beauty created by man for God.

The Christian embodiment of the ideal of Divine Love is the Virgin Mary. As the mother of Jesus she becomes the Notre-Dame of Christ's Church, and it is to her that most of the great French cathedrals are dedicated. Just as the rose had been the flower of Aphrodite, so too it becomes the flower of Mary. The rose itself is the symbol of love and of union; transferred to the rose window it symbolizes the Love of the Creator. It is a view of the world and the cosmos both *as* and *through* the mandala-rose of wholeness superimposed on the world.

Where shall we begin?

There is no beginning. Start where you arrive. Stop before what entices you. And work! You will enter little by little into the entirety. Method will be born in proportion to your interest; elements which your attention at first separates in order to analyse them, will unite to compose the whole.

In the calm exile of work, we first learn patience, which in turn teaches energy, and energy gives us eternal youth made of self-collectedness and enthusiasm. From such vantage we can see and understand life, this delicious life that we denature by the artifices of our enclosed, unaired spirit, surrounded though we are by masterpieces of nature and of art. For we no longer understand them, idle despite our agitation, blind in the midst of splendours.

If we could but understand Gothic art, we should be irresistibly led back to truth.

Auguste Rodin, *The Cathedrals of France*.[15]

1 **The aspiration of the Gothic was** stretched to its limit at Beauvais, where the vaults reached a towering 66 metres (200 feet). In 1284 the choir collapsed and was rebuilt with modifications. Part of it collapsed again along with the spire in 1573. However, the transepts with their rose windows survive. (Beauvais north, 1537, modern glass by Max Ingrand)

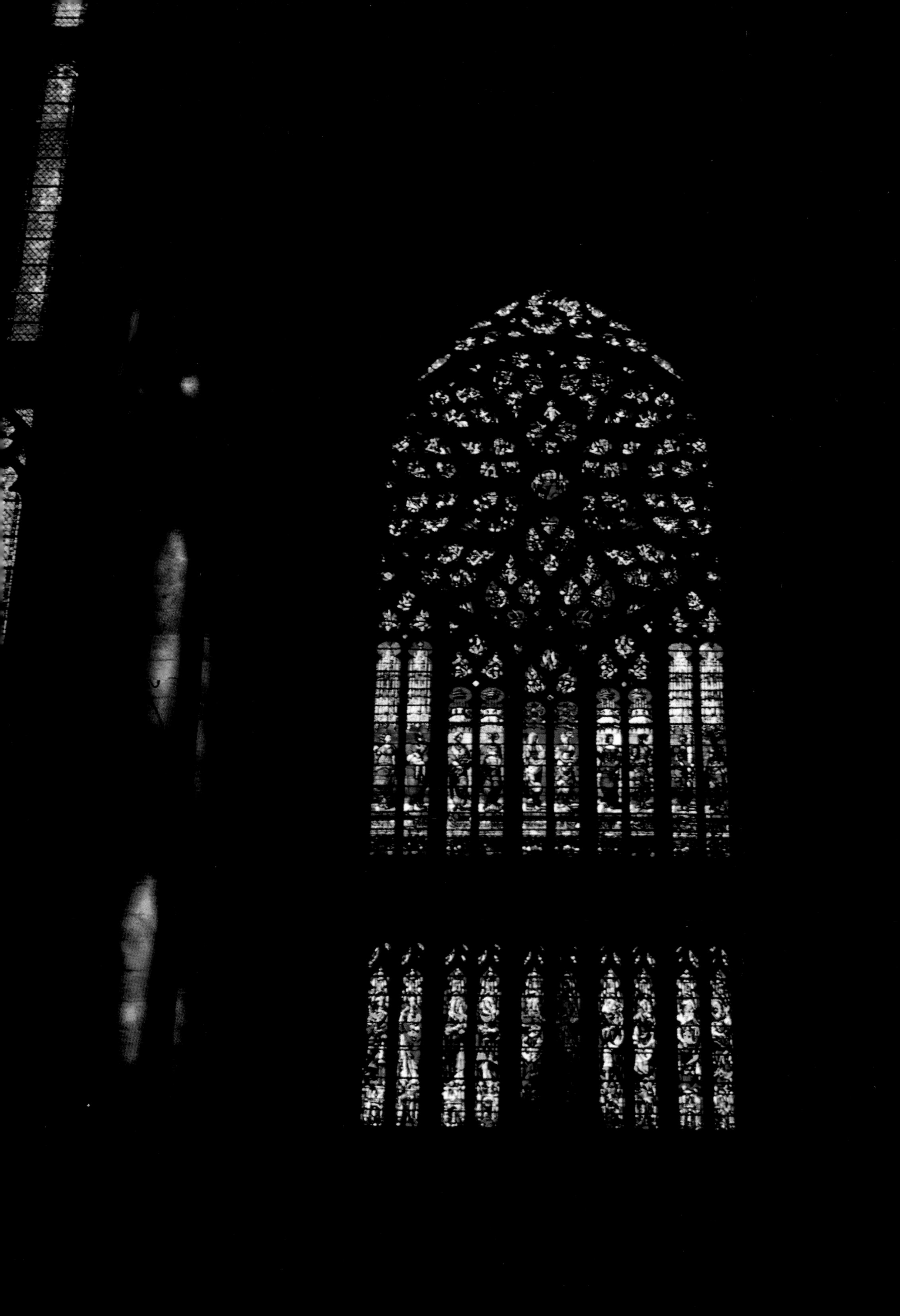

2 **To unite the finite with the infinite
through** the square and the circle is an
aspiration, common to Christian and
Islamic symbolism, which is embodied in
a number of rose windows. (Clermont-
Ferrand south, 14th c., glass restored
1903)

3 **Light,** to the medieval mind, was a
magical substance which contained the
power to transform the soul. (Strasbourg
west, c.1318, glass much restored after
storm in 1840; see also 79)

Overleaf:
4,5 **Colour,** light and the sun often
play strange tricks on the eye: red, in
the great west rose at Reims, strongly
predominates when the sun is out. Thus,
in the sunset, it becomes a consuming
ball of fire evoking the End of Time. The
subject is the Death of the Virgin,
symbolizing the end of the Church as
the End of Time, and here she is
surrounded by the twelve Apostles and
the heavenly choirs. In the outermost
circles are the kings of her ancestry,
while above the rose in the *tiers-point*
Christ, placed between the sun and
moon, receives the soul of His mother.
(Reims west, c.1270, much restored)

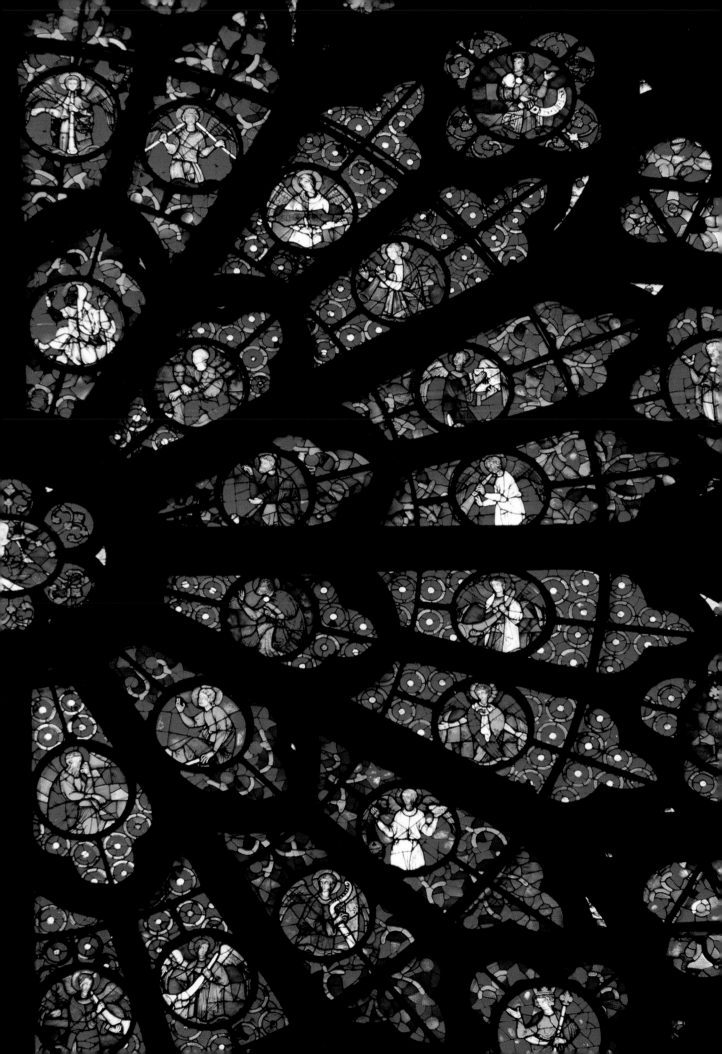

6   **Geometry and** number combine with light and colour in this classic north rose at Chartres – the 'Rose de France'. It is entirely dedicated to the Virgin Mary, who at the centre is surrounded by doves, angels and thrones from the celestial hierarchy. In the twelve squares are the kings of her ancestry – the line of David, as recorded by St Matthew. Beyond are the twelve last prophets of the Old Testament. The fleurs-de-lis are traditional emblems of the Annunciation and of royalty; the window was given by Blanche of Castille, Queen of France. But also we must 'consider the lilies of the field'; for this window is in fact constructed through the number and geometry of the Fibonacci series which underlies the growth of many flowers. (Chartres north, c. 1233; see p. 125)

7   **Perfection.** The doves descending to the Virgin are in fact only one dove, seen from four different directions – above, below and from each side; it symbolizes the omnipresence of the Spirit that 'loves and guides all created matter'. (Chartres north, c. 1233)

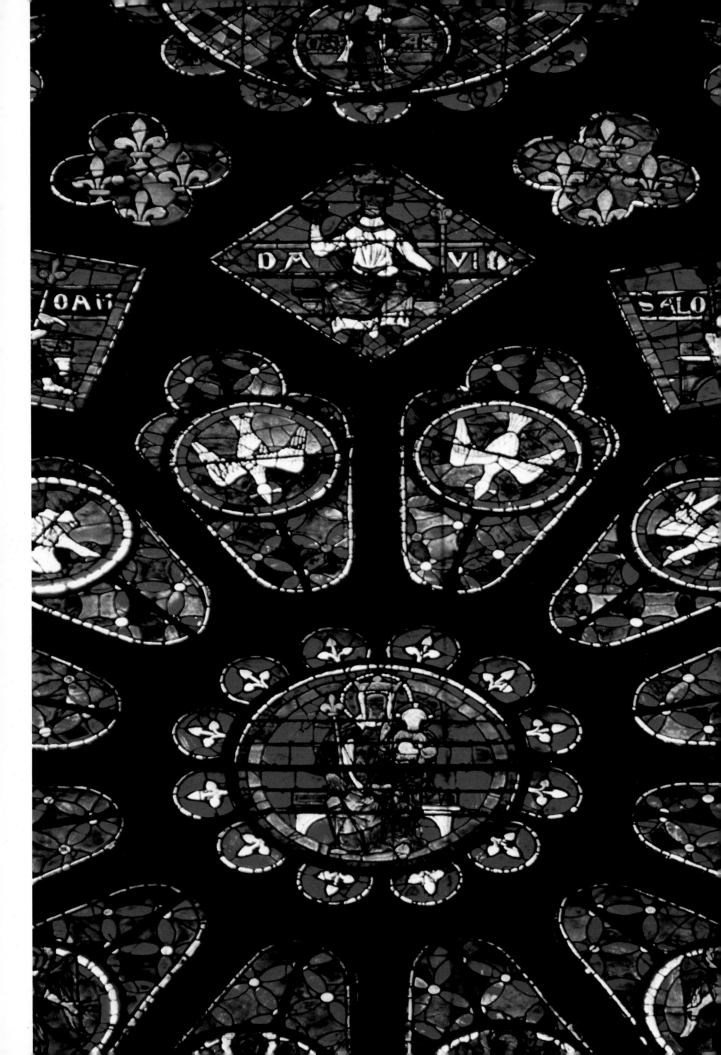

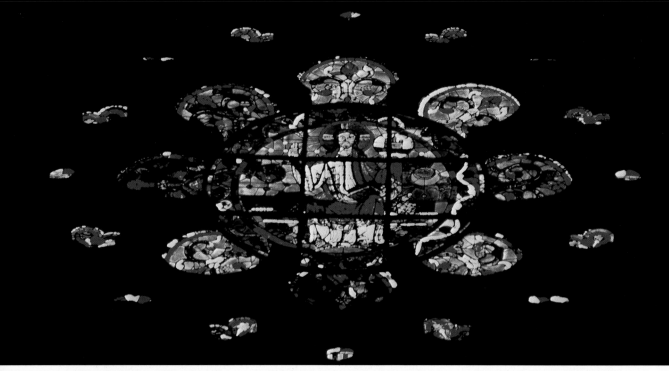

8 **The 'order' behind creation in** the Platonic teaching of the cathedral school of Chartres is symbolized in this portrayal of Christ as the Logos in a small rosette in the cathedral. Seated upon a throne, His feet on a rainbow, He raises one hand in blessing and with the other holds the earth divided into zones of land, sea and sky on top of which is the castle of Mankind. White and yellow stars surround the moon on the right and the sun on the left – six of which are red, suggesting the planets. On His knees is a half-open book – the Word of God, the Logos. (Chartres, mid 13th c.)

9 **The universe is manifested in** the form of every rose window, the concentric layers of which echo the spheres containing the sun, moon, planets and stars. Here in the west rose of Notre-Dame de Paris the 'spheres' contain the Zodiac, time (portrayed as the months of the year), the vices and virtues and the prophets; all surround the Virgin Mary. She is symbol and culmination of all time and space – or the history of the evolving universe, which becomes known in the present in perfected labour through the months. (Paris west, c.1220, much restored; see key on p.134)

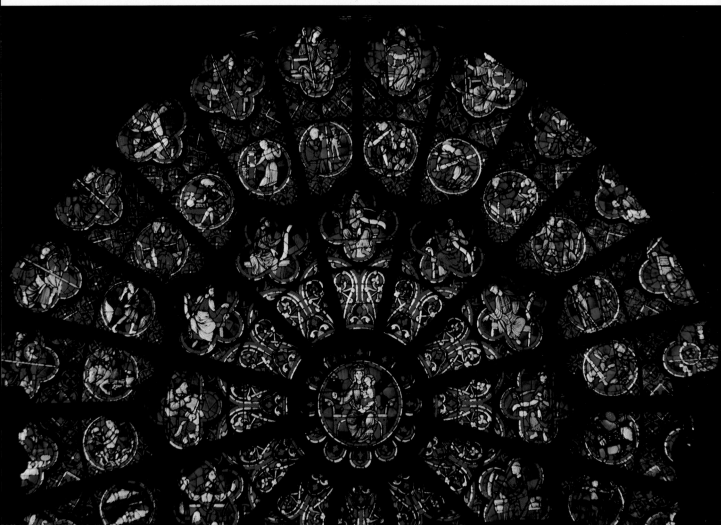

10　**The Word, or the Logos:** resurrected Christ at the centre of the south rose at Chartres, holding the chalice of the Last Supper. (Chartres south, *c.*1227; see also 36, 37)

Overleaf:

11　**The subtle interweaving of** an invisible geometry with the visible creates this magnificent 'Alchemists' Rose', with priests, prophets and kings surrounding the Virgin Mary. (Paris north, *c.*1268; see pp. 127, 135)

12　**The creative 'order' is embodied in** numbers, twelve being the number of perfection, of the cosmos and of Christ. In this south rose at Paris, God was originally portrayed 'in majesty' at the centre, surrounded by the four Evangelists, the twelve Apostles and twenty-four martyrs or confessors. However, the window has been entirely rebuilt twice, in 1726 and again in 1861, and now contains only a few of the (restored) original martyrs and angels. Eight twelfth-century medallions depicting the Legend of St Matthew have found their way into this rose; they are in the small double windows in the second outermost layer, from 2 o'clock to 9 o'clock. (Paris south, *c.*1260, much restored)

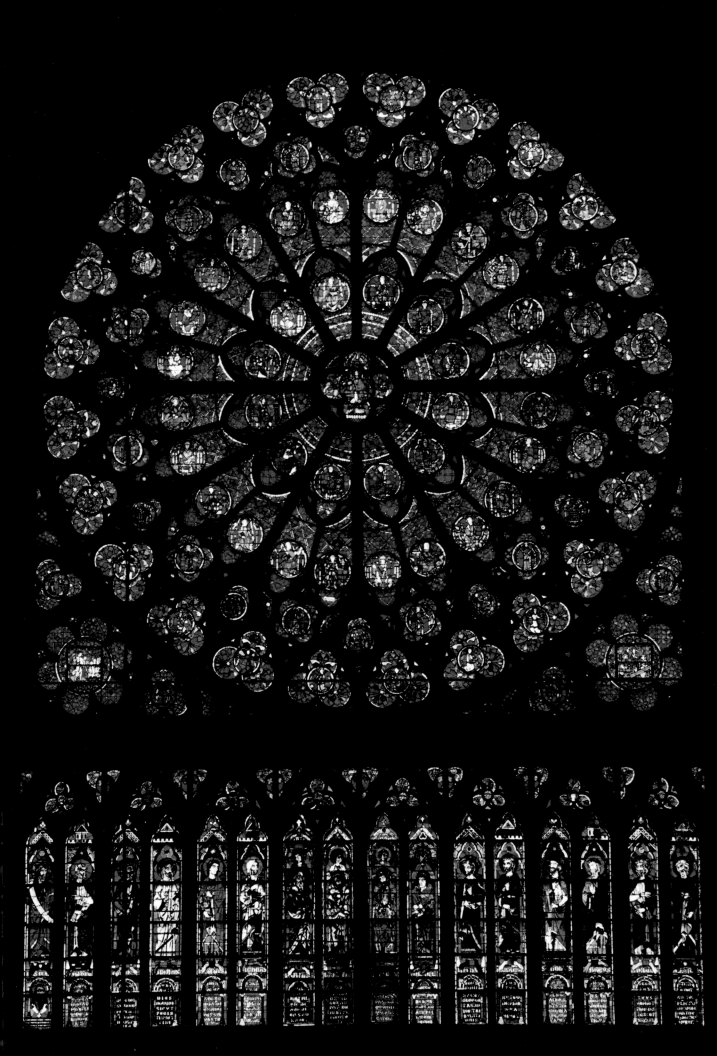

13 Every rose window, from the
largest cathedral to the smallest chapel,
is the symbol of love. Here at Notre-
Dame-en-Vaux an early thirteenth-
century window on the west façade is
placed above three lancets, following
the pattern of Chartres and Mantes.
(Notre-Dame-en-Vaux west, Châlons,
glass mainly 19th c. by Didron)

14 The perfect snowflake of Sées to
many people is the ultimate in delicacy.
It still contains some of the original glass.
The subject is the Mystery of the
Redemption, with six scenes following
the Resurrection. The lancets below
contain various saints. (Sées north,
c.1270, rebuilt 1877)

15 **The rose of Durham cathedral and** its tracery date from the sixteenth century, although it was remodelled in the eighteenth and nineteenth centuries. (Durham, 16th c.)

16 **The marigold of York Minster.** The red and white roses interwoven into the twelve petals commemorate the union of the Houses of York and Lancaster by Henry VII's marriage. (York, c.1515)

17 **The creation is expressed in** the west rose window at Washington cathedral by Rowan LeCompte. (Washington DC, 1977)

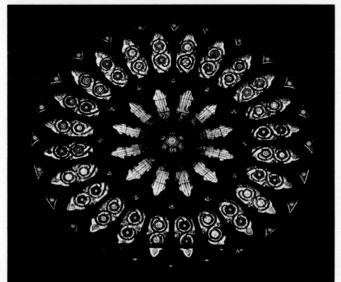

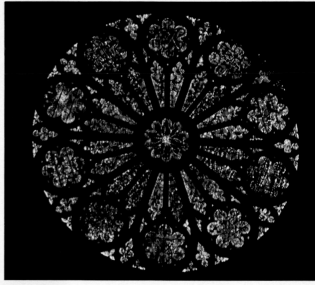

18 **Light and colour** fill the new rose window in Lancing College chapel. With a diameter of nearly 11 metres (33 feet), it is the largest rose window in England. (Lancing College, 1977)

19 **The leaves of the Tree** of Life are for the 'healing of the nations', and the 'Bishop's Eye' at Lincoln depicts two leaves within its circle, and is itself made up of thousands of leaf-like glass fragments. Within the window can also be traced the form of a man, a butterfly, or even two fishes. The leaves are in the *vesica piscis* form, created by equal circles which intersect the rose and touch at its centre. Robert Grosseteste, Bishop of Lincoln 1235–53, was the main exponent of the power of light in nature and the teacher of Roger Bacon. (Lincoln, 13th c.)

The making
From wheels to roses and to flames

Although they are contemporary with the birth of the Gothic, rose windows find their immediate predecessors in the wheel windows of the Romanesque; and these in turn evolved from the simple round holes – or oculi – that often furnish the west façades of even earlier churches. Many of these ancestors of the rose window can be seen in the villages of the French and Italian countryside, particularly in Provence and Tuscany. Some are decorated with an elaborate circumference of carved leaves with animals and faces interspersed, as at Tarascon where a splendid example is accompanied by the four symbols of the Evangelists. The lion, the bull, the eagle and the angel surround the oculus, set high in the gable of the façade, arranged in the favourite Romanesque disposition of a square around the circle [22].

The majority of these early oculi, however, have little or no decoration, and few of them exceed 1 or 2 metres (6 feet or so) in diameter; although during the second quarter of the twelfth century some larger windows began to appear, notably at Coucy-le-Château, Elincourt and Villars-Saint-Paul. This enlargement of the oculus, for aesthetic as well as practical reasons, led to the wheel window, for as the size increased, in came the extra light – but unfortunately so also did the wind and rain. The simplest solution was to add translucent alabastine or a primitive form of glass and to hold it in position within a frame. The most obvious pattern was the most elementary, that of a cross; there is an excellent example of such a window, from the comparatively late date of the mid twelfth century, at Aulnay [24]. Transition to the wheel was then simply brought about by the addition of a few more spokes.

Nothing in religious art is created for its own sake, and the architectural convenience of the wheel motif had to be confirmed by symbolic significance. The similarity of the cross within the circle to the Celtic cross, and even to the halo or nimbus that always surrounded painted figures of saints, was unmistakable. So, too, the Chi-Rho monogram of the early Christian church resembles a wheel – and is in fact often elaborated into one.

Before the wheel evolved into a full-blown rose it developed some marvellous variations and elaborations. The motif itself was firmly established, with hubs, spokes and bosses being carefully carved into the structure. At the height of the Romanesque the spokes were transformed into miniature pillars, complete with bases and capitals, forming a structure that supported the rim on a series of arches – an idea that carried on into the Gothic rose windows of the following century, notably those of Paris. In Italy the *rosoni* are nearly always wheels, and the finest of them are a paean to the concept of the wheel, with tier upon tier of spokes forming vast complex structures that look almost like circular viaducts. The superb specimens at Orvieto [47, 48], Assisi [46, 49–51] and Todi are probably the greatest of these, and evoke the vision of Ezekiel, where 'their work was, as it were, a wheel in the middle of a wheel' (Ezekiel 1:16), and where the four living creatures (which became the symbols of the Evangelists) came expressly to him, the priest.

Chi-Rho monogram mosaic from the baptistery of Albenga, Liguria

20 **The setting sun and the sounds of music: all are part of the dance of the cosmos and of the creative action of the Logos.** This rose at Soissons was originally built in the thirteenth century, but was entirely rebuilt after the First World War by Messrs Gaudin. It features Christ the King surrounded by prophets and Evangelists. (Soissons west, 13th c., rebuilt 1931)

Elevation of the nave at Notre-Dame de Paris, c. 1180. The five-pointed rosettes acted as ventilators for the roof aisles (from Viollet-le-Duc)

With the advent of the Gothic style, around Paris, in the mid-twelfth century, the wheel window took on more elaborate geometrical intricacies to accommodate stained glass, and a metamorphosis occurred: the wheel became a flower. In fact the term 'wheel' continued to be applied long after the transition, probably because wheel elements persisted well into the Flamboyant era. The two forms often coexist in the same window, as at Chartres, where the west rose is externally a massive wheel, but internally has metamorphosed into a perfect flower. It cannot be stated with certainty when the term 'rose' was first used for a window, but it must have occurred fairly soon after the early thirteenth century, when the adoration of the Virgin Mary, whose symbol is the rose, had become well established throughout France.

The immediate predecessor of the first rose window is generally thought to be the wheel on the northern façade of Saint-Etienne, Beauvais [25]. It is in fact a Wheel of Fortune, with carved figures being dragged up one side to pass an ogre-like figure at the top (now, alas, headless) and fall ominously down the other side. The symbolic significance of these Wheels of Fortune is discussed on p. 87; they illustrate an aspect of the early medieval outlook, that life is an endless repetition of night and day, summer and winter, life and death, endless toil and suffering, where all success is transitory. Nevertheless, despite its rather depressing significance, this wheel was to inspire Suger – and the masons of the Ile-de-France – to great works of transformation: from Wheel of Death into Rose of Life.

At Saint-Denis, Suger created a wheel [26] of similar size to that of Beauvais. It is still there today, somewhat restored, placed between the four sacred living creatures that betray its Romanesque origins. The neighbouring cathedrals of Sens, Senlis and Noyon were started soon afterwards; but only the Senlis façade looks to Saint-Denis for its model. Nevertheless, this wheel seems to have set a precedent, for after a delay of about thirty years similar windows began to appear everywhere around Paris. The first really spectacular rose window was constructed in about 1180 at Mantes[65]. With a diameter of some 8 metres (over 24 feet), it is substantially larger than that of St Denis and must be regarded as the first real rose. It still retains many features of a wheel, particularly the enormous, hollow central boss and pillar-like spokes, but these have been reduced in length and the arches expanded to enclose huge panels of glass, each one of which is as large as a moderate-sized medallion itself. Here at Mantes the pillar and arch motif is arranged so that the bases are on the circumference and the arches converge around the centre; in the later roses of Paris they have become reversed, the whole system appearing to support the circumference.

By 1200 the great wave of cathedral and church building was well under way. It was around Paris, on the Ile-de-France, that most experimentation in design took place. At Chartres and Paris itself, the cathedrals were to have giant rose windows on three façades – and on the fourth at Laon. Smaller churches, such as Brie-Comte-Robert, Braisne, Bonneval and Montréal took the idea of the rose/wheel into many charming variations. At Laon the west rose is modelled upon that of Mantes, but its enormous size of some 14 metres (over 45 feet) necessitates a radically different structure [34]. So, too, at Chartres the north and south windows [6, 35–37] have picked up the

Mantes-style circle of semi-circles on the circumference. At Paris there is evidence that there may well have been two Mantes-sized rose windows in the transepts until about 1220; according to Viollet-le-Duc they were dismantled soon after completion. Substantial technical and aesthetic problems appear to have been encountered, both here and elsewhere: at Chartres the west rose is off-centre by about one foot, upsetting the symmetrical aspect of the façade; and at Laon considerable problems arose in the buttressing of the west rose, the solution being camouflaged behind the vast portal.

The next major phase of development in concept and design took place at Paris – again at Notre-Dame, at about the same time as the transept roses were being dismantled. The masterpiece on the west façade is as large a leap in dimensions from the Mantes rose as this was from its predecessors [9]. It dates from about 1220 and measures about 10 metres (nearly 33 feet); but in terms of area of glass it is twice as large as Mantes, since the volume of stone has been pared down to a minimum, leaving a spider's-web frame of great strength. An elaboration of this system was subsequently adopted for the north and south windows in the same cathedral, and it is these – each with twice the area of the west rose – that to many people represent the zenith of the art. The west rose, however, contains the highest ratio of glass to stone of any rose. Structurally it has certainly withstood the test of time: when restorations were carried out on the cathedral during the last century it was found that the only damage to the stonework of this rose had been caused by the installation of the organ a few years earlier. It is built up from two concentric arcades of pillars, which define 12 divisions in the inner layer and subdivide to 24 in the outer, and into which are fitted some 60 panels of stained glass set in iron and lead. It is a masterpiece of design and execution.

In 1216 the cathedral of Chartres, rapidly rebuilding after its destruction by fire in 1194, completed its first giant rose window, that on the west façade [27, 29]. This is the antithesis of the Paris roses, using massive quantities of stone; in fact the whole impression of this rose is that the twelve main openings have been punched through the wall rather than having been constructed within a circle. The 'plate tracery' had been popular in the late twelfth century and can be seen in the rose windows of Lincoln, Lausanne [38, 39] and Laon [28, 30]. The Chartres west rose window, over 14 metres (46 feet) in diameter, is still, to some people, the standard by which all others are judged. It is indeed a triumph in every sense, its carved Béchère limestone tracery creating a wheel that encloses twelve rosettes, while all the main items in the window are defined precisely by geometric considerations (see p. 123). Inside the cathedral, the predominantly red and blue glass colours the twelve suspended stars that surround Christ at the Last Judgment. Nowhere was anyone to attempt anything like this again, whereas the roses of Paris and Laon, and those of the north and south transepts at Chartres, were on occasion taken as models for other cathedrals. Its only close relative is the much smaller north rose at Laon, probably by the same master.

The north [6] and south [35] roses at Chartres, completed in 1226 and 1234, use a much higher proportion of glass to stone than the Chartres west window, but the tracery is still much heavier than the gossamer of the Paris west rose [9] and Reims [66]. At Chartres both north and south windows are designed to take some of the weight of the vaults, and the internal structure is of sufficient thickness to accommodate this. In each window the intermediate layer containing the twelve major lights stabilizes the whole structure by providing it with off-radial members: squares in the north and circles in the south. (Radial windows have an inherent tendency to rotate at the slightest provocation, and this did in fact occur in the south rose at Paris, which was largely rebuilt by Viollet-le-Duc. At Trieste such a movement seems to have occurred during construction, and to have been compensated for in the rest of the structure.) In the massive west rose of Laon, internal stability is provided by enlarging the central eye considerably and constructing the intermediate layer of twelve windows as pentagons – the most stable shape of all.

The builders' change of mind in the 1220s concerning the Paris transept roses, already referred to, is something of a mystery. The present windows [11, 12] are dated at about 1260 and 1268 for the south and north respectively; the timing would seem to suggest that the Parisians were not to be outdone by their neighbours and set to work to design windows that would at least equal those of Chartres.

These two transept roses at Paris are the ultimate in sheer delicacy, and that on the north has remained almost intact since the thirteenth century. Along with the west rose at Reims, these roses have all but lost the characteristic of a wheel in favour of a network of pillars and arches which transmits all the forces and pressures that arise not only internally, from glass, lead and metal fittings, but also to a certain extent from outside the rose. The weakest areas in any rose window are the centre and the perimeter; a well designed system of trefoils and spherical triangles not only compensates for this but at the same time offers the architect plenty of scope for imaginative design. The rim of each rose is a masterpiece of design, as slender as it can possibly be without weakening the structure.

At the same time that the Chartres roses were being completed, new and smaller designs were making their appearance at Reims, Saint-Germain-en-Laye, Saint-Germer-le-Fly and Saint-Denis. Those of the transepts at Reims are built around an enlarged central boss, with fewer spokes more widely disposed and looking like a circle of shields. Each lobe then encloses a window, so that the rose as a whole becomes an aggregation of shields disposed around the centre. It is a development that is pursued even further in the later roses of Sées [14], Rouen, Saint-Quentin and Amiens, where it reaches its greatest expression at the end of the century. And at Reims there also appears for the first time the large *claire-voie* or clerestory window in the form of a spherical triangle, which resolves the space between the Gothic arch and the circle of the top of the rose [5].

At Saint-Germain-en-Laye the rose of about 1240 is mid-way in date and in form between the west rose of Paris and those of the transepts. It is built up of rectilinear tracery similar to the Paris roses, but in style is similar to the transept roses of Saint-Denis; in fact all these windows were probably designed by the same person, Pierre Montereau. Unfortunately the Saint-Germain rose was bricked up at the time of Louis XIV, but Viollet-le-Duc sees it as an important stage in the evolution of the species, which, by placing a circle half-way along each of the radials, substantially increases the stability of the structure.

Reims north

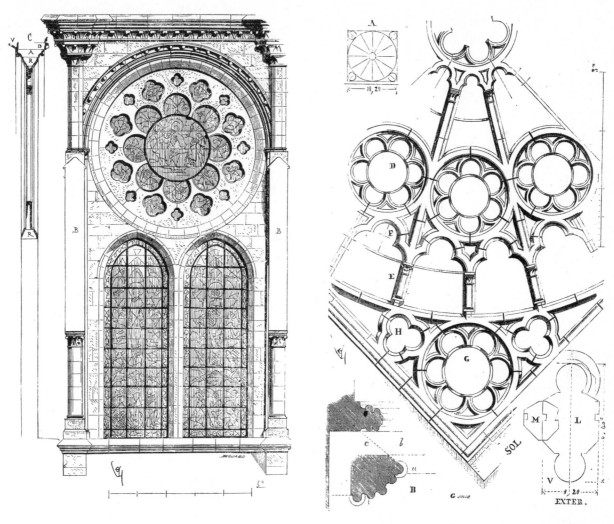

One of the high rosettes at Chartres, above the clerestory windows and just below the vault. Its plate tracery echos the great west rose. Thirty-four of these rosettes lead the eye along the nave to the transept roses and on into the choir, thus linking all the rose windows in the building (from Viollet-le-Duc)

Detail from the rose window in the chapel at Saint-Germain-en-Laye (from Viollet-le-Duc)

The last window in this important line of development is the huge rose on the west façade of Reims [5, 66], which in some ways resembles those of Paris. It is, however, much more robustly built, as indeed is the whole cathedral. Viollet-le-Duc describes it as *inébranlable* – unshakable – an almost clairvoyant insight on the builders' part, since Reims took an unparalleled bombardment during the First World War. The great rose, and much else in the cathedral, survived; this would not have been the case if Paris had been subjected to the same treatment.

The beautiful rose in the north transept of Sées – built about 1270 – is probably the finest representative of an interesting development in design [14]. Its delicate tracery, with hexagonal subdivisions, is reminiscent of a snow crystal. Similar windows can be found on the Calend Portal of Rouen cathedral and at Saint-Germain d'Auxerre. Pentagonal versions exist at Amiens and Saint-Quentin, and an eightfold variant at St Lorenz, Nuremberg. They all attempt to fuse inset medallion windows with the circular form of the rose, but this formula never found its fullest development because of the advent of the Flamboyant rose soon after 1300. At Amiens, for example, the five- and fifteenfold crystalline rose of the north transept has a southern counterpart which is probably the first of the Flamboyant roses [55].

A rare contemporary architectural drawing shows the west façade of Strasbourg cathedral. It shows the linking of the rose window to the portal via the multiple-spired gable: Architect Erwin von Steinbach, 1276

It seems impossible to trace exactly where and when the Flamboyant style was born; but by the mid fourteenth century the style was well established, in rose windows as elsewhere. It is at its best at Amiens, Lieu-Restauré [60–63], Sens [82], Troyes, Auxerre, the Sainte-Chapelle [53, 54] and Beauvais [77]. In all these rose windows there is hardly a straight line to be seen, as the structures are engulfed with weaving and curving stone loops that almost entirely destroy the radial character. Gone is any likeness to either a wheel or a rose. Even the glasswork seems to give the impression of curling flames; the Sainte-Chapelle has a superb example, where fire seems to spread across the rose from the centre. As the fifteenth and sixteenth centuries progressed, many buildings that had been started hundreds of years before were completed with these fiery roses. The Gothic era and its spirit died in tongues of flame.

There are no Flamboyant roses comparable in size with the early roses of Paris and Chartres. On a large scale, curving tracery is successful only when the hardest and most consistent stone is available. Since this is rarely the case, windows after the mid-fifteenth century remain generally small, modelled on the Sainte-Chapelle or Amiens rose. Nevertheless, experimentation and originality are always to be found; and a number of fascinating variations emerged at this time, each a unique gem in itself – in terms of design, that is, the glass work being often somewhat inferior. Some of these – Saint-Bonaventure, Lyon [73], Notre-Dame de la Dalbade, Toulouse [74], Saint-Omer [76], La Rochefoucauld [80] and Saint-Maixent [81] – are illustrated in this book. Two of the most spectacular of these lesser roses are to be found in the transepts of Saint-Ouen, Rouen [57, 58]. Of the two the southern is the more successful, a truly beautiful flower-like construction with six pairs of petals spreading from the centre in jets of stone which endlessly interweave, totally in accordance with the window's subject – the Tree of Jesse.

The patterns of rose windows established on and around the Ile-de-France, in the three hundred years from the consecration of Saint-Denis in 1144, represent the medieval life-cycle of the species. By the sixteenth century that cycle was virtually over.

The Gothic revival of the nineteenth century saw a proliferation of rose windows, but not one that compares with the real thing. Nevertheless, the twentieth century seems to be witnessing another cycle of the rose after a winter of withdrawal, and a number that have appeared since the end of the Second World War have something remarkable about them. At Lancing College in England a rose window [18] has just been completed with a diameter of some 11 metres (36 feet); with over 25,000 pieces of glass, it is by far the largest in England (a position formerly held by Old St Paul's, burnt in 1666, with an east window equal in size to the transept roses of Chartres). In Auckland cathedral, New Zealand, a window has been built in conventional form but with a totally twentieth-century design of glasswork. Probably the finest of all modern rose windows is that of Washington cathedral in the USA [17]. The cathedral was built entirely in Gothic style, using the original building methods, and contains three rose windows, built in traditional form, which exploit to the full the possibilities afforded by modern glass techniques. The west window is an abstract design evoking the Creation and utilizes chipped nuggets of glass to pick up all the available light on winter days as well as to gleam in the midsummer sun. The result is a Creation very much within the words 'Let there be light.'

The rose in the cathedral

From the very beginning rose windows were to cause problems. The troubles and second thoughts encountered at Chartres, Laon and Paris have been mentioned, but the basic difficulty underlying all Gothic roses was the same: how to incorporate a huge circle, a static form, into a design that is fundamentally vertical in its aspiration. Wheel windows fit happily enough into Romanesque buildings, where they harmonize with the underlying tranquillity of the style. On Gothic façades, however, a circle half-way up tends to halt the progress of the eye which the whole of the rest of the building is trying to emphasize.

Perhaps, however, this was what was intended: a moment's pause, suggesting the need for reflection amid all the vertiginous energy unleashed in architecture by the spirit of the age. Certainly, rose windows presented no aesthetic problem to Henry Adams; nor did he see any difficulty over the inevitable conflict of styles:

The quiet, restrained strength of the Romanesque, married to the graceful curves and vaulting imagination of the Gothic, makes a union nearer to the ideal than is often allowed in marriage. The French, in their best days, loved it with a constancy that has thrown a sort of aureole over their fickleness since. They never tired of its possibilities. Sometimes they put the pointed arch with the round, or above it; sometimes they put the round within the pointed. Sometimes a Roman arch covered a cluster of pointed windows, as though protecting and caressing its children; sometimes a huge pointed arch covered a great rose window spreading across the whole front of an enormous cathedral with an arcade of Romanesque windows beneath. The French architects felt no discord, and there was none. Even the pure Gothic was put side by side with the pure Roman. ... For those who feel the art, there is no discord; the strength and the grace join hands; the man and woman love each other still.[16]

Nevertheless, some architects clearly felt the discord and did their best to do away with it. In the early Gothic we see a tendency for rose windows to be placed in squares, or built into the façades with no attempt at integration. At Amiens, in the south transept, a pointed Gothic vault is terminated by a pure semi-circular arch on the end wall, so that the rose fits neatly into it [55]. The rose window is most at home on Flamboyant façades, where the restless intermeshing curves of the whole edifice are carried up through the rose; the work of Martin Chambiges at Sens, Beauvais, Troyes and Rouen provides perfect examples.

The rose window was by no means universally accepted in the early days. Following the consecration of Saint-Denis in 1144, six main schools of Gothic architecture emerged, those of the Ile-de-France, Champagne, Picardy, Burgundy, Anjou and Normandy, to which can be added the builder monks of the Cistercian Order. Rose windows were popular with the first two

The spire that stood over the crossing of the cathedral of Saint-Pierre, Beauvais, from 1570 to 1573

schools, and to a more limited extent in Normandy, but elsewhere they seem to have been admitted only reluctantly. In England, close to the Norman school, there was plenty of interchange of ideas and styles, but rose windows never really established themselves. The original glasswork of Westminster Abbey and of Old St Paul's may well have included roses that could stand alongside their counterparts in France; but English architects generally preferred the long slender lancets and huge walls of glass that are to be found at York, Bath, Gloucester, Salisbury, Wells and Lincoln. The reasons for this are obscure but may consist – apart from taste – in the different quality of light in England, with its longer twilight and weaker full brightness even in midsummer.

As the thirteenth century progressed, and the Gothic architects pushed the vaults to new soaring heights, problems arose concerning the gap created *beneath* the rose. Above the west porch at Notre-Dame de Paris, the problem was solved externally by including a line of huge statues of the Kings of Judah in place of lancets; internally this created a vast expanse of empty wall which is now very largely concealed by the fig-leaf of the organ. The north and south roses in the same cathedral are placed on top of a whole line of lancets which form a wall of glass over 17 metres (nearly 60 feet) high and serves to fill the major part of the difficult rectangle. At Amiens, where the vaults are a staggering 43 metres (140 feet, compared to Paris's 115) the rose windows take up only 10.7 metres (35 feet). On the west façade a line of statues is inadequate, so a sort of external triforium has been added below, while the porch is extended upwards as high as decency will allow. The result is magnificent, even if somewhat contrived and out of balance.

The *pignon* or gable above the door begins to grow at Paris (on the south façade), and by the time the Flamboyant era arrives it has overlapped the lancets; it reaches the rose at Sens, Limoges and Tours, and at Rouen, Troyes and Auxerre it goes even further, right to the top of the rose. These gables are generally beautifully executed and often contain their own little wheels – as at Sées, Bourges and Tours. They represent a further attempt to bring harmony to the whole façade and to integrate the rose window into the sweeping vertical lines of the Gothic. At Paris the rose motif is carried even further, right up into the roof gable, and at Beauvais for three brief years there was a stone rosette in the spire that soared to over 160 metres (nearly 500 feet) before it crashed down in 1573.

In the final count a successful integration is one in which there is total harmony in the exterior *and* the interior. Whether the rose window inside is a spectacular explosion of light and colour or a tranquil, glowing circle of reconciliation, the effect is to a certain extent governed by the quality and positioning of the rest of the glass in the building. At Chartres, for example, the twelve major lights of the west window seem to be suspended like twelve stars in the heavens, and these harmonize perfectly with the three lancets below (or at least they did until the three windows were cleaned during the period 1975–77, and the subtle irregularities in the glass were largely ironed out). The roses of the north and south transepts are perfectly integrated to the lancets of prophets, priests and evangelists below them: in fact they are haloes of light above these carriers of the Word – their source of inspiration and aspiration. At Paris the two webs of roses and lancets in the transepts contain about twice as much glass as those of Chartres but are equally well integrated. These classic windows shine out of the darkness.

Alas, this is no longer the case at most other cathedrals. The ravages of time and man have resulted in the loss of so much glass that the correct conditions no longer exist for viewing those that remain. Lost panels are often replaced with grisaille or even bright glass that creates too much glare for the subtleties of any remaining medieval glass to be fully appreciated. But at certain rare moments the sun still plays patterns on to the stonework in and around the rose, and beautiful effects catch the eye.

At Reims, where much has been lost through war, there is also some of the finest restoration. The west end supports two rose windows, one neatly fitted into the tympanum below the other, and the light from the huge thirteenth-century window above and the modern window by Jacques Simon below blends perfectly with the statues that line the inside face of the wall on either side of the smaller rose [67].

The glass in the rose

Throughout the day, summer or winter, the light is constantly changing, both in intensity and colour, and different windows in the cathedral catch the attention at different times. In fact some windows seem only to come alive at certain moments, often when one is hardly looking. The magic that these windows impart makes every visit to the cathedral a joy, especially when a familiar window surprises us with a new facet.

In the changing light of the day and time of year, the glasswork of the great rose windows is as subtle as elsewhere in the cathedral. Unfortunately it is not easy to see much detail in them, since few are less than thirty feet from the ground. But a good pair of binoculars can be very helpful, and so can a view from the triforium or tribune. Either will reveal that as much care has been taken with these windows as with those nearer to eye-level; even the angels have eyelashes in some, although few people are likely to spot them from the ground!

The art of staining and painting glass expanded considerably in the twelfth century. Large quantities of glass were needed for the new church at Saint-Denis, but previously there had existed in France only a rudimentary craft. Within a few years, however, a number of workshops sprang up around Paris, and Chartres in particular was to become a centre where glass was made for buildings not only in France but in England as well.

Much of the inspiration for this new art came from crusaders and pilgrims returning from the Holy Land. One of the routes passed through Venice and Bohemia, whence came new techniques and materials, and these blended perfectly with the art as it had evolved in France. It was at Chartres, where the river sand was particularly pure, that the finest examples of the art emerged. This glass was to become a legend, surrounded as it was by the 'mystery' of its manufacture. This soon led to the belief that the glass was an invention of the alchemists, which may or may not be true: gold was certainly used in the production of certain shades of red – or ruby – glass. According to the medieval monk Theophilus, glass-making was a rarefied art with closely guarded secrets even in his time (c.1100–55). Details of the methods used in the medieval craft are still very largely unknown – certainly no one has managed to produce anything like it since. There are some

An angel from the early
thirteenth-century rose at
Mantes [65]

contemporary pictures of work in progress but very little indication of what
is actually going on. Similarly, information on the division of responsibility
between designer and executant is equally sparse; in the case of rose
windows one does not know whether the conception stemmed from the
master mason or from the glazier, or whether each inspired the other.

The stained-glass artist's work could always be superficially imitated and
debased by half-knowledge – as any true craftsman knows – and this is what
did subsequently happen to much of the work after the thirteenth century,
when the 'secret' was lost. If there is any mystery attached to stained-glass
work it probably lies in the knowledge of how to work consistently in a
highly creative state of mind and with infinite care and love. There is
certainly much evidence for the pains to which these craftsmen went in
order to attain consistent beauty and perfection.

Theophilus' account is extremely useful, even though it describes glass-
making some years before the advent of the Gothic and before the

workshops of Chartres were well under way. He describes how glass was cast and the ingredients added at crucial moments during the melt, and how, as the twelfth century progressed, the glass was blown to give a much thinner and more easily handled product. The general formula was to combine two parts of beechwood (or fern) ash with one part of river sand, fusing the mixture into a slightly purple-coloured mass (the colour being due to manganese impurities). Metallic compounds were added during fusion to give the required colour: cobalt oxide (from Bohemia) for blue, copper oxide for red, and silver chloride for yellow. In Theophilus' time this was cast flat to give 'pot-metal', but later it was blown into 'muff' glass in a long cylinder which was then cut open and flattened into a sheet. With a red-hot crozing-iron the sheet was cut up and the pieces of glass chosen for their position in the final composition. The design was drawn out on a whitewashed table and the pieces cut and selected so that the flaws in the glass could be exploited to the greatest artistic effect. In fact it is these very flaws, bubbles, grits of sand, streaks and variations in thickness that give the glass its unique light-catching magic.

Some of this glass was shaped and fitted straight into the window, but much of it underwent further treatment with pigment to bring out the highlights, shadows, lines and other details. The pigment was made up of a mixture of iron filings and resin and was painted on to the glass to create the details before being finally fired.

To obtain certain colours and effects the process of flashing was adopted; this consisted of pasting on to the surface of one piece of glass a thin layer of another, often differently coloured, and refiring. It was done particularly with ruby glass, which tended to be too dark when made to a normal thickness. Ruby was therefore often obtained by building up layers of thin red glass on a clear base, sometimes as many as twenty or thirty, with a firing after every application. (One sample of Chartres ruby was observed to have over forty layers of flashing.) An advantage of this method was that the layers could be ground off to the required depth to give a varying tone within the same piece of glass, and even different colours obtained by subsequent staining, although this is rare in medieval work.

Probably the most remarkable form of coloured glass – if indeed it ever existed – was what Theophilus called his 'most precious variety', obtained by 'placing gems on painted glass'. Suger always boasted that real sapphires went into the melt to colour some of the glass for Saint-Denis, but no one has taken this seriously; perhaps in the light of Theophilus' account we should reserve judgment.

After the thirteenth century, stained glass production acquired different and generally easier techniques; the results become less impressive as the centuries pass by. English glasswork of the fourteenth and fifteenth centuries is occasionally superb, as at Fairford or York, although little of it exists in rose windows. The same is true of Flemish glass of the fifteenth and sixteenth centuries, as used at Toledo cathedral in Spain, where there is a very fine fifteenth-century rose at the west end. French stained glass of the fifteenth and sixteenth centuries displays the much cruder colours of bright enamels painted on to the glass; this achieves a high point of its own in the rose windows of Beauvais [77], Sens [71, 72] and the Sainte-Chapelle [53, 54]. In terms of subtlety and light-play, however, these later windows in no way

Head of an angel in the north rose at Lincoln (from Westlake)

approach those of earlier years. In some of the panels of the Sainte-Chapelle an interesting technique is displayed, that of 'Venetian glass', where two colours are mixed into the same piece of glass so that they metamorphose into one another.

Colour. The thirteenth-century Chartres blue glass is legendary. It pervades the whole cathedral as gold pervades Christian mosaic and icons; both seem to symbolize the Divine Light that streams through the whole universe. Other colours become subordinated to it in practically every window, and even when another colour is predominant, blue is nearly always the background. In the thirteenth century red, blue, yellow/gold and white are the most consistently used colours. Green is common although used sparingly; purple is used even more sparingly, although certain windows seem to make a display of it – as in the north rose at Canterbury. Flesh tones are imparted through a type of smoky purple that has frequently darkened to brown. Viollet-le-Duc classifies thirteenth-century colours in stained glass as follows: 4 types of blue, 3 of red, 4 of purple, 2 yellows and gold, 3 greens and 3 shades of white.[17] It would require a sharp eye to detect most of these subtle variations today.

At the height of medieval glass-making, French glass is particularly characteristic, with red and blue being persistently juxtaposed, the blues being tinted slightly green to reduce the heavy purple that this combination can easily bring. White, often carefully placed in thin bands between red and blue, not only outlines the medallions but to a certain extent prevents halation (the mixing of colours in the space between the window and the observer). The subtle use of white can sometimes produce a most dramatic effect; at Tours, for example, it outlines all the other colours in each compartment of the rose, giving an almost explosive quality to the whole window [85].

Generally speaking, in north light a gentler colouring is used than in south light: at Chartres, for example, in the north rose [7] red and blue predominate, with occasional gold, white and other colours, whereas in the south rose [37] white and gold are used slightly more to impart a quite different effect. This is as much due to distribution as to choice of colour, and even on dull days the impression of the south window is much more dramatic than that of the north. This of course is precisely the desired effect: the north side symbolizes preparation and purification, and the south illumination through the joy of the Resurrection.

Because original glass has disappeared from so many medieval churches, it is not easy to analyse this contrast between north and south more thoroughly. Restoration through the centuries has rarely been sympathetic, and little of the tradition has been passed down. Nevertheless, at Paris, despite numerous restorations, the south window displays something of the same contrast, using more red than that of the north; in fact it is a measure of how well the north window was designed that it maintains its tranquillity in spite of all that the restorers have done to its counterpart. In the rare and superb examples of late medieval rose windows at Tours, the contrast between the windows is very largely lost through the amount of daylight that finds its way into the cathedral [64]. Here the more explosive quality of the south rose is achieved by structure rather than colour: it seems to blow itself apart over the head of the man on top of the organ, with trefoils and quatrefoils scattering themselves towards the circumference.

Design. The style and design of the glasswork of the thirteenth-century rose windows naturally has much in common with that of lancet windows elsewhere in the cathedral. Each saint, angel, prophet, king, vice or virtue has very little area in which to express himself, and backgrounds are cut to an absolute minimum. The individual subject is nearly always enclosed within a circle which is itself set into the opening of one petal of the rose, the remaining space then being made up of decorative mosaic or leaf-like ornamentation.

The geometric layout of the greatest rose windows is a triumph of design. In the last part of this book (pp. 122–27) the details of some of the more fascinating and subtle constructional relationships are examined. Most windows rely geometrically upon the cross and circle or radiating pattern, with the rose's predecessor the wheel often making itself felt, even in later windows. Rosettes, and the circle-and-square combinations that are so often found in all medieval illustration and decoration, are natural favourites in rose windows, the windows of Lausanne [68, 69] Clermont-Ferrand [2], Paris and Sées [42] being a few of the many examples. And at Canterbury the design of the rose is almost identical to that of the huge Islamic-inspired system of squares and circles in the mosaic behind the altar. (The inspiration is not only Islamic, for this kind of geometric design harks back also to Celtic patterns and even Roman floor tiles.)

The actual design of the window involved a fourfold cooperation between clergy, master mason, blacksmith and glazier to determine the choice and disposition of the iconographic programme. Then the glazier would proceed according to a fairly well-established tradition concerning the details – such as St Peter always with a large beard, St Paul bald or Melchizedek with the chalice of a priest. Sometimes the characters carry scrolls bearing their names, as in the north rose at Chartres. Choice of colour also followed a traditional pattern, with blue generally as the background against which red, green, brown and purple are set with occasional almost violent contrast. Occasionally red is the background; this is nearly always so whenever Christ or His ancestry is the main subject.

But in spite of the many rules and conventions there was ample scope for individual expression. The glazier drew up the layout and the detail, selecting the glass for its natural characteristics, ran the lead lines round the contours, painted in the detail, and after the final firing fitted each piece into the whole structure. It is fascinating to consider that in creating a rose window over 12 metres or 40 feet in diameter – such as those at Chartres and Paris – there was no way of precisely knowing how the window would appear *in situ* until the project was completed. There may well have been periods of experimentation; but it is nevertheless a measure of the amazing skill, knowledge and intuition of these medieval craftsmen that they worked virtually blind on these vast compositions. However much the design was thought out, drawn up and experimented with, it would have been next to impossible to know in advance how such factors as thickness of stone and the angle of the sun at different times of the day would affect the final colouring. The effect of halation, whereby lighter colours tend to spill over

St Bartholomew, from Laon's east rose window. Early 13th c. (from Florival and Midoux)

Souls being transported to heaven by angels in the Last Judgment window at Mantes. Early 13th c.

Melun, near Paris

into neighbouring darker tones, often results in a substantial change in the overall colouring of the window when viewed from a distance. Halation also influences the overall colour balance, blue being the most problematical colour, often appearing *en masse* to be darker than would normally be expected from each individual piece. Such effects are also more pronounced when the sun is out behind the window – as the window at Reims shows in the photographs, where the colour balance is changed substantially, and red predominates almost violently in the setting sun.

In the final count a beautiful rose window is one which presents a new face every hour of the day and every day of the year. It is like a truly great symphony, never ceasing to fascinate us, of infinite variety within perfect and cyclic order, of irregular rhythms within regular tempi or of regular rhythms within irregular tempi; of light, shade and colour subtly combined or dramatically contrasted. In these grand works of light and geometry the artist becomes a creator of the spheres, at one with the music and dance of the cosmos.

Why did they build these colossal bulwarks, the Cathedrals?

It was to deposit – in safety as they believed – the imperceptible egg, that seed which requires so much patience, so much care: TASTE, that atom of pure blood which the centuries have transmitted to us, and which, in our turn, we should transmit.

All these proud equilibriums, all these accumulations of stone glorified by genius, that rise to the extreme limit where human pride would lose contact with life, with the species, and would totter in the void, all such is but the tabernacle. Or rather – for this shrine is living! – it is the Sphinx, guardian of the Secret.

The secret is virtually lost, since today only a few can reply to the sphinx crouching on all sides of our French cities.

We should know how to respond to the Gothic sphinx if nature herself had not become for us an incomprehensible sphinx.

'The French Countryside',
from *The Cathedrals of France* by Auguste Rodin.[18]

21 **The gaping hole** in the heart of the façade of Saint-Jean-des-Vignes at Soissons is all that remains of the rose window; a memorial to all that has been lost through the futility of war. For Saint-Jean has suffered over the centuries more than most, first in the Hundred Years War, then in the Religious Wars, again in the French Revolution, yet again in the Franco–Prussian War and finally in the First World War. And yet it still stands: a symbol of man's creative as well as his destructive powers, but always looking to a better, brighter world. (Saint-Jean-des-Vignes west, Soissons, late 13th c.)

22   **At Tarascon is an example of an oculus,** predecessor of the wheel window. Richly carved round its perimeter, it is surrounded by the four symbols of the Evangelists, facing the setting sun. (Saint-Gabriel, Tarascon, c.1180)

23   **The ancestor of** the rose window is the oculus, but its parent is the wheel. Here at Barfreston in Kent the circumference of a wheel is enriched with animals, faces and leaves. (Barfreston, c.1180)

24   **The rosette and** its three little arches above the massive Romanesque door at Aulnay is an example of the form that evolved into the rose some fifty years later – that of the circle and the cross. (Aulnay, c.1135–65)

25 The Wheel of Fortune that evolves into the rose of life is beautifully illustrated at Saint-Etienne, Beauvais. People are dragged anti-clockwise around the perimeter past two dragons and a headless ogre with a large club. Such wheels can be said to symbolize the transitory nature of worldly success in an ungodly life (i.e. on the circumference) as opposed to life united with God through the centre. (Saint-Etienne, Beauvais, c. 1100)

26 The first rose window: this wheel at Saint-Denis is thought by many scholars to be the first rose. It is similar in size to the Beauvais wheel, but was probably the first to be filled with stained glass. The four symbols of the Evangelists – somewhat restored here – can be related to the motif of Fortune via the four fixed signs of the Zodiac (see p. 88). This transformation from the Zodiac to the Evangelists is paralleled in the evolution of the wheel of fate into a rose of life. (Saint-Denis, c. 1144)

**27, 29 On the west façade of Chartres
and** facing the setting sun is the great
rose of Chartres, 13.36 metres (44 feet) in
diameter: externally a giant wheel and
internally a beautiful rose – a
masterpiece of light and geometry.
(Chartres west, *c.*1216; see key and
diagrams on pp. 122–23, 136–37)

28, 30 **In the north transept of Laon** there is another rose of plate tracery, probably by the same master as its big sister at Chartres. The external structure shows the change of mind made by the architect, abandoning what probably was to be a window of lancets. Internally the eight lights feature the liberal arts surrounding the queen, Philosophy. Starting at the top and descending to the right they are: Rhetoric, Grammar, Dialectic, Astronomy, Arithmetic at the bottom, then Medicine, Geometry and Music. Whether this was the original disposition is unknown, since Philosophy, Rhetoric, Medicine and Music were missing when the window was restored by Coffertier. (Laon north, early 13th c., restored 1856; see also 31)

29   See 27

30   See 28

Overleaf:

31 Wisdom is personified in the
central rosette of the north rose at Laon
as a woman seated on a throne –
Philosophy – head in the clouds with the
sceptre of royalty and a ladder of nine
rungs up her front, echoing the nine
spheres of the cosmos and the angels,
or possibly of the nine subjects that
originally comprised the liberal arts in
classical times. (Laon north, early 13th c.,
restored 1856; see 28, 30)

**32, 33   The Logos, as the Word made
flesh through the rose;** as foretold by
Isaiah and communicated to the world
through St John. In the east rose window
at Laon, the Virgin Mary with the Christ
Child on her knee holds out the rose to
Mankind, with St John below left and
Isaiah to the right. In the first circle are
the twelve Apostles, and on the
perimeter the twenty-four elders of the
Apocalypse, each carrying a musical
instrument and a phial of perfume –
symbolizing the prayers of the saints.
(Laon east, early 13th c.)

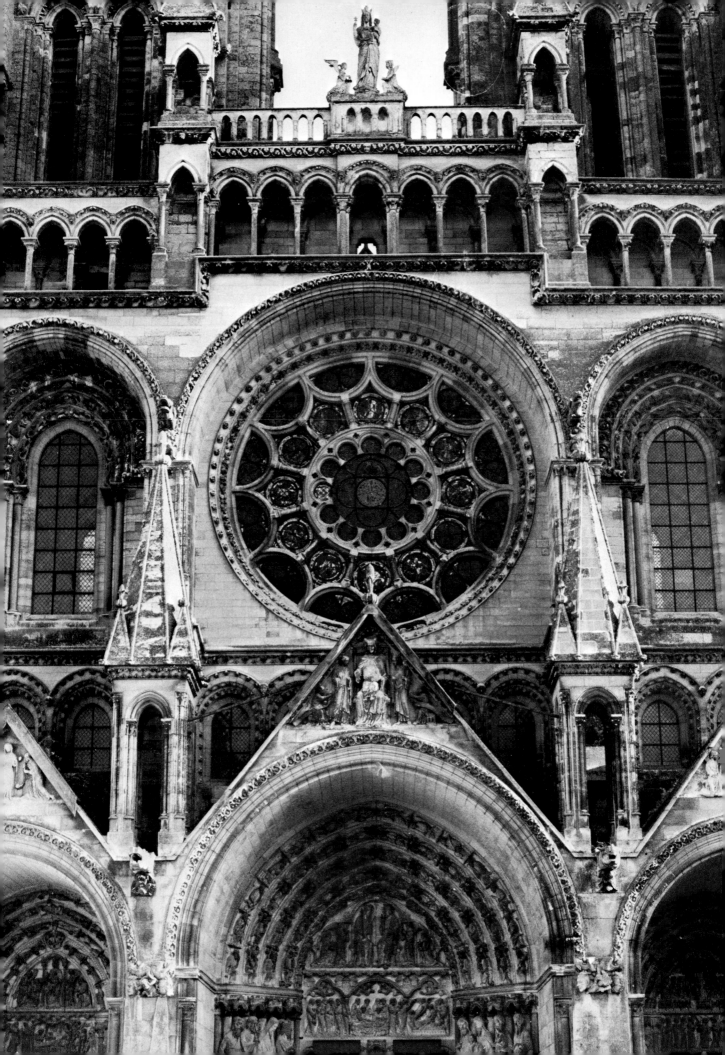

34 **At the heart of** Laon's west façade is the huge rose window identical in structure to that of the east, dominating the composition above the portal of Last Judgment and beneath the enchanting statue of the Virgin Mary attended by two angels. (Laon west, c.1200)

35–37 **Each of the rose windows at Chartres is** a triumph of geometry; this stone flower is centred on Christ at the centre in Glory as depicted by St John in Revelation, surrounded by angels and the four symbols of the Evangelists. In the outer circle are the twenty-four elders of the Apocalypse, each with a crown, a musical instrument and a

phial: the crown symbolizing the martyrs who died for Christ. The south portal underneath the rose is dedicated to the New Testament and the martyrs and confessors who have spread the Word. The window was given by the House of Dreux, whose yellow and black checky arms fill the small quatrefoils. (Chartres south, c.1227; see p.126)

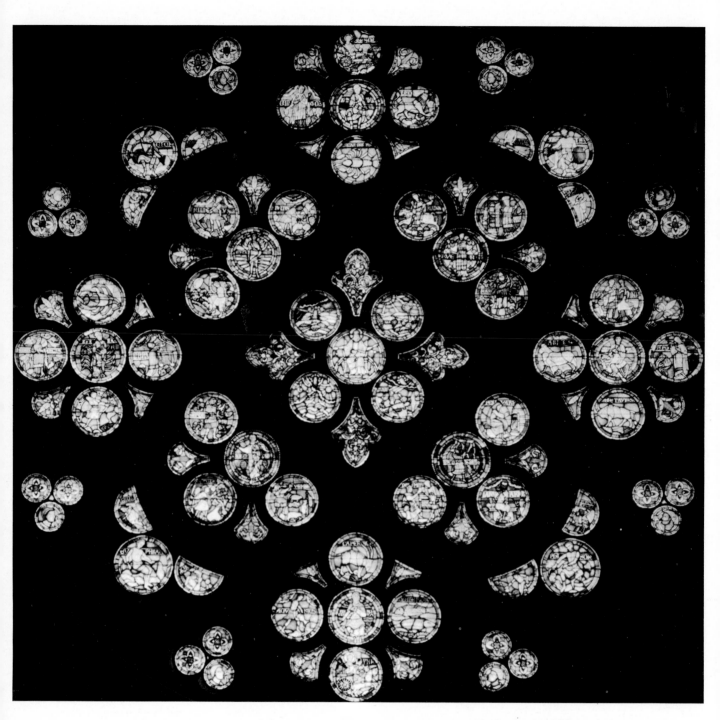

38, 39 **A new world.** Paradise, Time,
Eternity and geometry combine in this
remarkable rose window at Lausanne,
undoubtedly influenced by the School
of Chartres. A full description of the way
in which the squares and circles of the

stonework symbolically interlink with
the subject matter is given on pp.
128–31. It was sketched by Villard de
Honnecourt in 1235 and probably dates
from a few years before this. (Lausanne,
c. 1230)

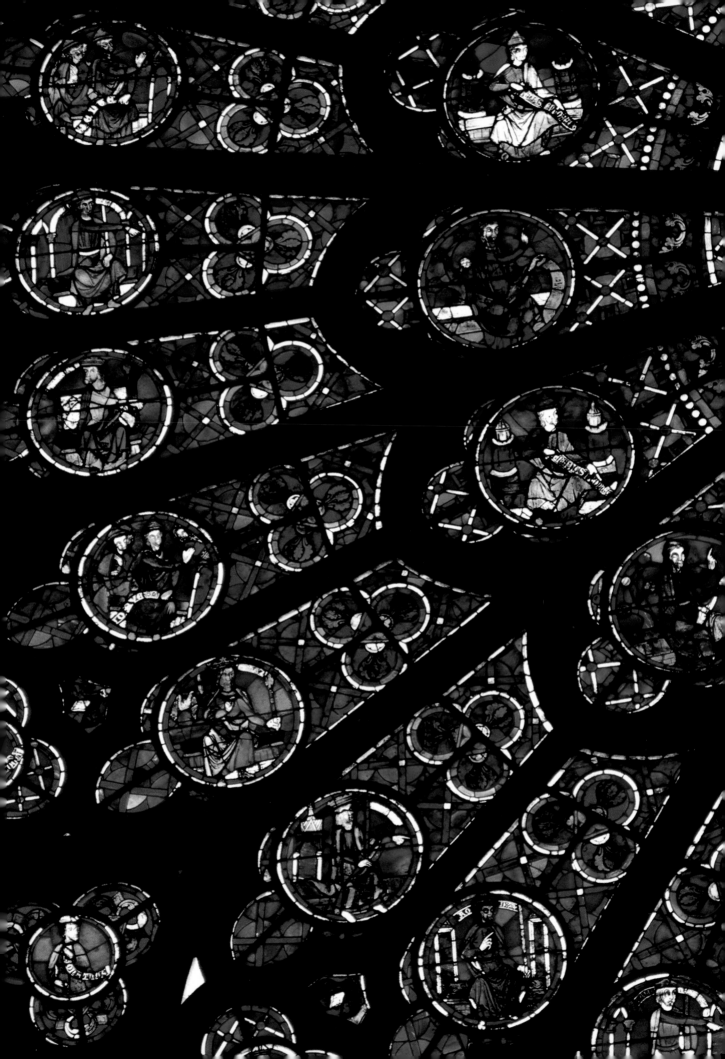

40 At Paris, following the trend set by the delicate west rose (25), the very thin tracery of the north window gives much more room to the glasswork. In this section can be seen the four prophets Elijah, Nahum, Jeremiah and Habakuk (numbers 13, 12, 11, 10 in the key on p. 135), eight other prophets (34–41) and two high priests, Jonathus and Amarias. (Paris north, c.1268)

41 Chartres south rose; see also 36, 37. (Chartres south, c.1227)

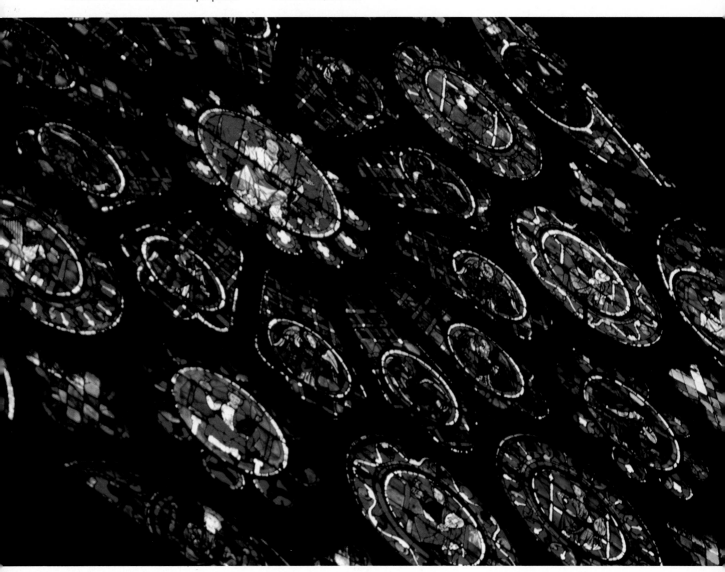

Overleaf:

42 The most delicate traceried roses appeared in the mid thirteenth century. Those of Paris became models for a number of other churches and cathedrals – particularly the south window, as for example here at Sées. (Sées south, c.1270)

43, 44 By the fourteenth century, tracery evolved into many imaginative designs. At St Katharina, Oppenheim, two roses were built into the south side of the nave, one on a threefold geometry and the other on five. By the fifteenth century the cult of the rose was well established, and roses completely surround the gable of one of the windows. (St Katharina, Oppenheim, c.1434)

45 New flower-like forms, such as the south window of Saint-Ouen, illustrate the inventiveness of the late Gothic 'Indian Summer'. (Saint-Ouen, Rouen, 15th c.)

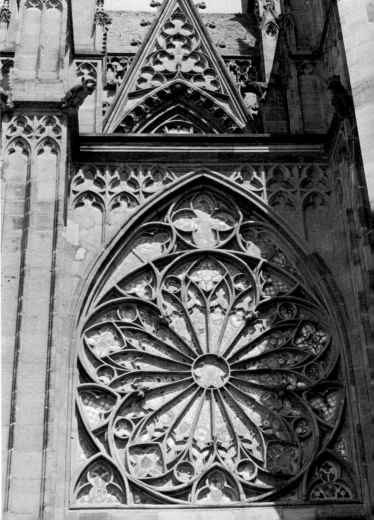

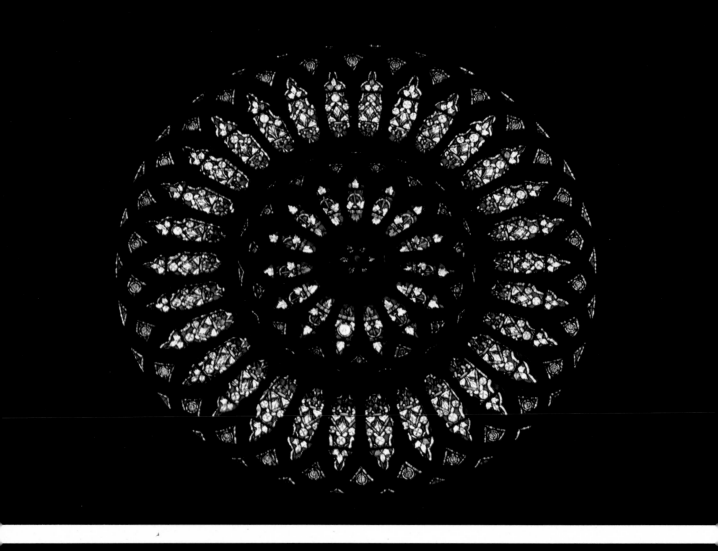

**46   But in Italy the wheels grow bigger
and more beautiful.** Here at Santa
Chiara in Assisi an intricate double
layered wheel has been filled with glass
to give a remarkable three dimensional
vortex effect. (Santa Chiara, Assisi,
c. 1257–65; see also 51)

47, 48   **The rosoni on the façades of
Italian churches are often** filled with
plain glass, but at Orvieto every space
and crevice is occupied. This unique
twenty-two-spoked wheel is carved into
the west façade of the cathedral to
capture the evening sun. At the centre
is the head of Christ; the square
containing the wheel and four of the
early Church Fathers is made up of fifty-
two heads – presumably one for each
week of the year. (Orvieto, 14th c., by
Andrea da Cione, alias Orcagna)

49 Highly decorated simple wheels or rose windows can be found in many parts of Tuscany – there are two like this one on the same building. (San Francesco, Lower Basilica, Assisi, after 1250)

50 Wheels within wheels. Surrounded by the four sacred living creatures, this beautiful wheel on the façade of the Upper Basilica of San Francesco faces the rising sun – exactly the opposite of most other wheel or rose windows. (San Francesco, Upper Basilica, Assisi, c.1250)

51 The wheel finds its greatest expression at Assisi; apart from the three wheels at the Basilica there are three more at the cathedral, three at San Pietro, and this magnificent specimen at Santa Chiara. (Santa Chiara, Assisi, c.1257–65; see also 46)

52 In Italy, where the Gothic style of Northern Europe was reluctantly admitted, the most 'French' cathedral is that of Milan. This almost Flamboyant rose is in the apse, and built with an interlocking tracery of mouchettes. (Milan, 15th c.)

53, 54 **Before the** mid sixteenth century, Gothic architecture in England and France experienced a last inspired burst of energy. The rose of the Sainte-Chapelle is one of the greatest examples of the period. It replaced the thirteenth-century original which may well be the one illustrated in the Duc de Berry's *Très Riches Heures* (under the month June). A full description of this Apocalyptic window is given on pp. 138–40. (Sainte-Chapelle, Paris, 15th c.)

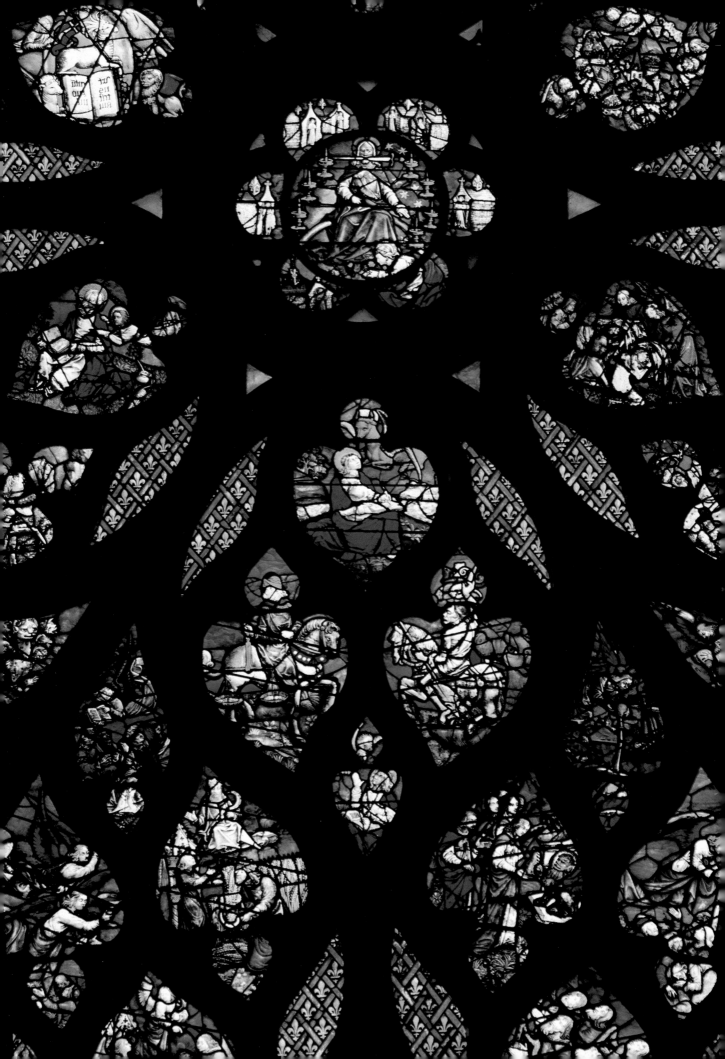

55 **Flamboyant** rose windows became widespread in France after 1450, and this superb example at Amiens may well have been the first of them. It is in one sense still a Wheel of Fortune, with the figures being dragged up one side only to be dropped on to a spike on the other. The whole window is framed with roses. (Amiens, c. 1400)

56 **Rose windows in France had evolved from** wheels, but it was only after years of experiment that they managed to become totally integrated into the general style of the façade. The Flamboyant roses were more easily accommodated, and the lozenge-shaped window of Tours cathedral is one of the most successful. (Tours west, c. 1500)

Overleaf:

57 **The flowing forms of the rayonnant style.** The five-pointed star multiplies to fifteen petals enclosing the *coeur céleste* or Celestial Heart, the pentacle symbolizing in this instance the Crucifixion. The window would also seem to symbolize the macrocosm, with the sun-stars enclosing the angelic hierarchy, and the centre encapsulating the seven lights or suns. The deep red angels at the top may well be the Seraphim – conveyors of Divine Love from the *coeur céleste*, while the blue and gold Cherubim impart Divine Wisdom; the remainder are possibly the Lower Angels. This symbolism of coloured angels belongs more to the Renaissance than to the Gothic. (Saint-Ouen north, Rouen, c. 1440)

58 Opposite in the south transept of Saint-Ouen is the six-petalled rose in the form of a Tree of Jesse, with the Kings of Judah disposed through the interweaving rayonnant tracery, while the doves of the Spirit radiate Light from the six petals and the twelve sub-petals. (Saint-Ouen south, Rouen, c. 1439)

59 **Some rose windows are** neatly fitted into lancets – as is the case with this small example in the nave of Strasbourg; the ring of rosettes is mounted on top of a Last Judgment scene, with angels descending from the rose. (Strasbourg nave, 14th c.)

60–63 **Unforgettable** as it plays with the light is this beautiful and abandoned Flamboyant rose at Lieu-Restauré on the Ile-de-France. (Lieu-Restauré, 15th c.)

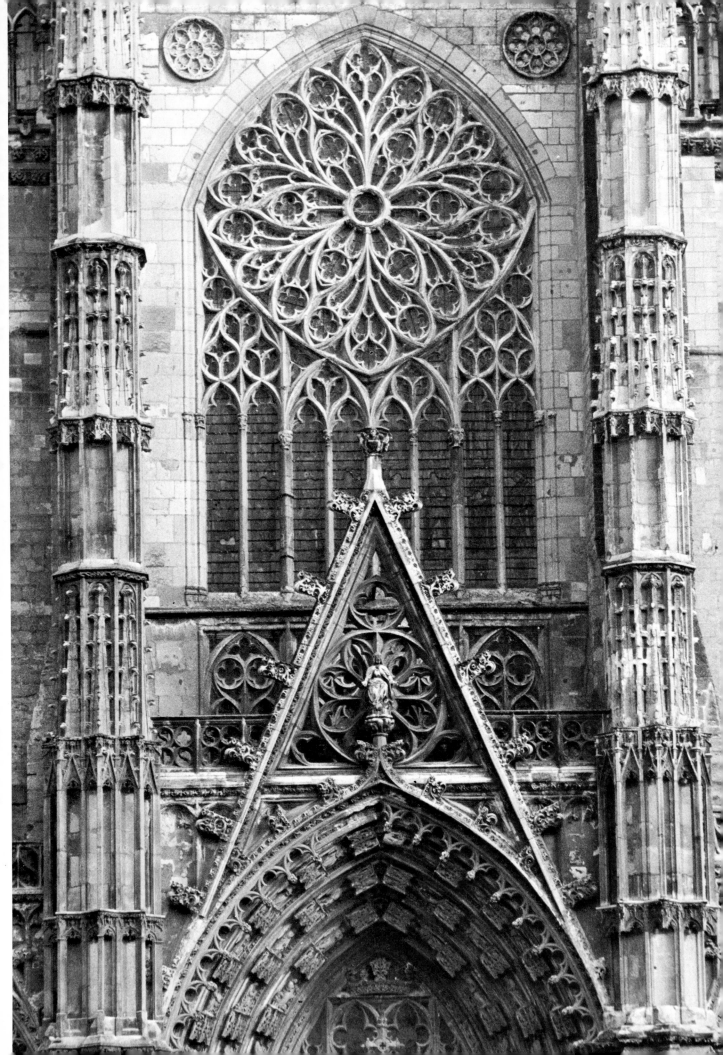

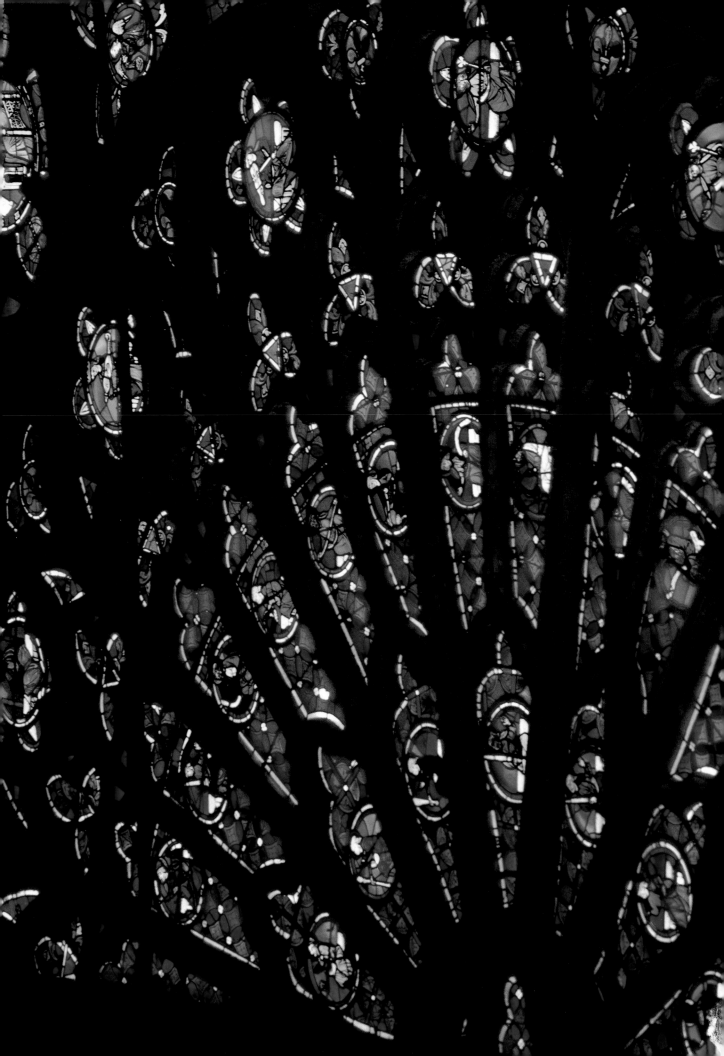

The meaning

Purification: wisdom

'Everything in medieval symbology has hidden meanings: that is, showing men one thing and inviting them to see in it the figure of another.' Thus Emile Mâle very neatly supplies the clue to understanding medieval iconography. In the rose, and in the rose window in particular, there is a mass of symbolism which is as simple or as complex as each individual chooses to make it. Like the flower which the Buddha held up as the sum total of one of his sermons, the rose window is a symbol in itself by virtue of its form, and at the same time presents other symbols – showing men one thing and inviting them to see another. Both the image and its content combine to act as a bridge to deeper meaning; they enable us to see at a glance something which words can only transmit over a period of time.

In any church building, iconography is the key to the Christian view of the world as a *transformed* reality: the truth of the Old Testament revealed in the light of the New. This remains so when the imagery is obscure or even pagan. Medieval philosophers, theologians and cathedral builders translated Christianity into terms appropriate to their age, both in words and in images in glass and stone. They looked back to its roots, particularly to ancient Greek thought and the early Church Fathers, and combined what they found with the knowledge of the day. As at Chartres – where the intellectual light shone most strongly, and they built 'on the shoulders of these giants' – the contemporary view of the cosmos and of life was grafted on to traditional Christian iconography. Thus any set of three rose windows generally portrays the Glorification of the Virgin Mary, the Resurrected Christ and Last Judgment. But within this scheme can be seen a less obvious and deeper meaning, for as mandalas the windows possess the power to bring about a change in thinking, to break down the habitual patterns that govern everyday consciousness. They can open the mind to a new reality, and this is often accompanied by a profound inner peace and reconciliation with oneself. Such an act requires a sincere commitment which Rodin describes as the learning of patience, 'which in turn teaches energy'.[19]

The limitations of the 'everyday' state of consciousness are described by Plato as being due to the grossness of man's senses, a condition that inhibits the Music of the Spheres from making itself heard. But if man could be transported back to his original state, then he would hear the Music again, and in hearing it he could understand nature's deepest secrets. In Christian theology the parallel to this musical image is the Garden of Eden and the Paradise to come: through Christ and His teaching lies the way to a world in which man, in harmony with nature, creates the Eternal City – the New Jerusalem.

In the Gothic cathedrals Christian iconography is infused with classical learning, particularly that of Plato, and with the metaphysics of light that was derived from St Augustine and John Scotus Erigena. All this combines in the architecture and in the iconography to illuminate and lead the way to the Order behind creation: that is, to the Logos.

Before we embark on the wider aspects of symbolism it is important to consider the iconographic programmes of the early cathedrals around Paris, where the rose window evolved; these remain the basic patterns for

64 **Throwing light and colour in every shape and form to every corner of the cosmos,** this south rose at Tours is probably the last of the great windows built, within Henry Adams' 'magic 100 years' of the Gothic after 1170. (Tours south, mid 13th c.)

Philosophy, head in the clouds, holds an open book of learning and a sceptre (now broken). From west portal, Laon (from Viollet-le-Duc)

iconography elsewhere. In *north* windows it is the Virgin Mary who is usually found at the centre, surrounded by the priests, prophets and kings of the Old Testament – as at Paris and Chartres [6, 11]. There are variations however: the Creation at Reims, the childhood of Christ at Soissons, and the seven liberal arts at Laon [28]. In *south* windows Christ is nearly always portrayed in Glory after the Resurrection, and it would seem from this disposition of north and south that the Crucifixion is the dividing point in time. In the *west* Christ presides over the judgment of souls, with saints being led off to heaven and sinners to hell; nowhere is this better illustrated than at Chartres or Mantes [27, 65]. In the west rose at Reims, the Death of the Virgin – the end of the Church of Notre-Dame – again symbolizes the End of Time [4, 5]. Into this fundamental pattern are fitted the iconographic details, different in each church, but nearly always to be found in the same relative positions: priests, prophets and Old Testament characters in the north; Apostles, twenty-four Elders of the Apocalypse, signs of the Zodiac, martyrs and confessors in the south; and the angelic choir, division of souls, vices and virtues in the west. In the rare *east* rose window at Laon there is – almost predictably – an amalgamation of New and Old Testaments, with the Virgin surrounded by prophets, apostles, and the twenty-four Elders [32, 33].

The north rose at Laon [28] features the liberal arts, and would appear at first sight to be outside this scheme, but in fact this points to the integration of classical learning into Christian iconography. The seven liberal arts were originally nine at the height of the Roman Empire, medicine and architecture having been dropped by the Middle Ages. At Laon and Chartres, the seven arts taught in the cathedral schools comprised music, arithmetic, geometry, astronomy, dialectic, logic and grammar. In this rose they are joined by medicine, and all are personified as women surrounding Philosophy, the summit of all learning [31]. They are a good example of Emile Mâle's 'hidden meaning'. For Philosophy is the personified Divine Wisdom, Hagia Sophia, to whom in the Byzantine world great churches were built. By

Philosophy in a bas-relief on the west portal of Notre-Dame de Paris. 13th c.

The wheel of learning, with the seven liberal arts, encircling Philosophy, is represented as a circular temple. Socrates and Plato, whom she teaches, are placed beneath her, while the three heads on her crown may represent the knowledge of past, present and future (from Herrad of Landsberg, *Hortus deliciarum*, 12th c.)

Sketches of carvings of the liberal arts from the west porch at Laon: geometry (top), astronomy (centre) and music (bottom) (from Viollet-le-Duc)

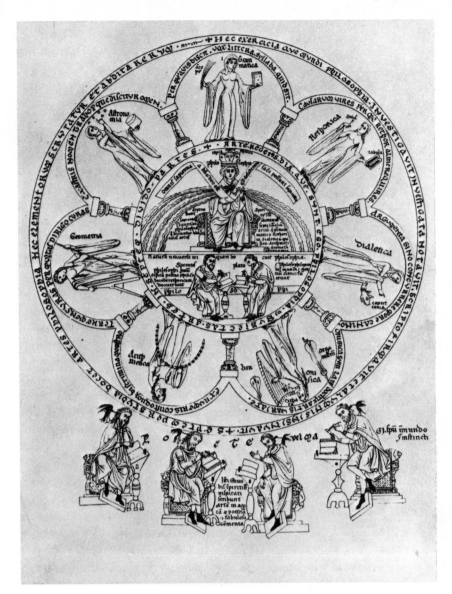

the Middle Ages she had been equated with the Virgin Mary, who, to St Bernard, was herself the embodiment of all knowledge and wisdom. Vincent of Beauvais saw in the liberal arts 'a quickening power, and to each of the liberal arts there is a corresponding gift of the Spirit'.[20] They recall the biblical Seven Pillars by which Wisdom 'hath builded her house' (Proverbs 9:1). There is an interesting double meaning here: firstly, an architect in the Middle Ages had to be well versed in the liberal arts before he could be entrusted with building a cathedral: and secondly the Temple of the Spirit is seen in Revelation as being built *within* every man. So too the gifts of the Spirit have a double meaning, outer and inner, the former being charismatic or possibly miraculous (about which St Paul had much to say to the Corinthians) and the latter being gifts of character and moral and spiritual endowments.

Hidden meaning resides in the iconography of a window; there is also meaning in its *form* – its function as a wheel, a rose, a model of the sun, or of the universe, or otherwise. In the east window of Laon [33] meaning is concealed in form in yet another way. Geometrically the window is made up from twelve pentagons which surround the centre – an echo of the fifth of the Platonic solids, the dodecahedron, the twelve faces of which are pentagons. In the *Timaeus* the four elements earth, fire, air and water, are represented by the solids of the cube, the pyramid, the octahedron, and the icosahedron. They make up matter, which is manifest in time. The fifth element, ether, could be said to be represented by the dodecahedron, 'the whole spiritual heaven', which is eternally manifest.[21] In this Laon rose the iconography confirms this in Christian imagery as the Eternal Mystery, the amalgamation of the Old and the New.

There is a three-dimensional implication in many rose windows, the dodecahedron or sphere of heaven at Laon being a good example. But in some windows this is generated by purely visual means, as in the rose/wheel of Santa Chiara at Assisi [46] and all the rose windows at Chartres. In fact, the north window at Chartres itself [7] tells us explicitly that its image is supposed to be imagined in three dimensions: the four images of the dove descending to the Virgin Mary are so disposed as to give the impression that they come from all directions; one from in front of the plane of the window, one from behind and two from the sides. These are four aspects of *one* dove – as there is only one all-embracing Holy Spirit.

The mandala aspect of any rose window helps us to understand this three-dimensionality and suggests its 'cosmic' significance: the two-dimensional form represents a three-dimensional image which with the imagination takes us to a four-dimensional reality. According to Jung, the healing effect of mandalas, induced by the state of wholeness that they invite, is that they enable us to think and imagine outside time. In Jung's philosophy the process of individuation is achieved by balancing four energies, symbolized in mandala form. In medieval alchemy he found many parallels to the images produced by his patients from the unconscious: in particular, the four elements present themselves as a quaternity which reflects the ordered state of the universe or macrocosm. Within the mind, the elements become qualities of consciousness: thought (air), emotion (water), intuition (fire) and sensation (earth). When all four are held in balance within the psychological viewfinder of meaning, then life is enjoyed in its fullness.

There is one superb rose window exhibiting this quaternary aspect, at Lausanne [38, 39; see pp. 128–31], where knowledge of the world is combined with speculation and myth to present what is without doubt one of the most amazing creations of the medieval mind. As an *imago mundi* – or image of the cosmos – it is a tour-de-force of symbolism contained in a geometric framework that is both real and symbolical. At the centre is the Creation, immediately surrounded by the four seasons and the twelve months of the year, beyond which are the twelve signs of the Zodiac and the four elements [68, 69]. At the edge of this world are the four rivers of Paradise and the creatures that inhabit these remote corners, and outside are the eight winds of heaven. Everything in this cosmos is a part of one totality, of the everyday world cyclically repeating itself through the seasons, yet within an almost transcendent world represented as Paradise. It is a rose that may well have received its physical inspiration from the west rose at Chartres and its philosophical impulse from the School; it is known that a number of canons from Lausanne visited Paris in the period 1222–24, exactly when both Paris and Chartres were in the midst of designing and building their great windows. Another source of inspiration may well have been the reports of Prester John's kingdom in the East, where a land of milk and honey, ruled over by a Christian king, contained the four rivers of Paradise which gushed forth gold and jewels 'at regular intervals, three times a year'.[22] Emile Mâle, however, sees the rivers of Paradise – represented as turning their urns towards the four points of the compass – as 'symbols of the Evangelists who flooded the world with their teaching, like four beneficent streams'.[23]

The universe; turning to one

Every rose window is a symbol and image of the Creation and the created universe. The layers of concentric circles that comprise the great early roses are idealized models of the universe, of the earth at the centre of the spheres. The number varied according to the model that was being considered: Plato's universe had eight, whereas that of Aristotle had as many as fifty-six. In the simpler systems the spheres contained the planets, the moon and the stars, but in the more elaborate models angels, archangels, the elements and even moral qualities had spheres to themselves. In most schemes the outermost sphere was the Prime Mover, beyond which lay the Empyrean of God.

The School of Chartres is known to have possessed a copy of Macrobius' commentary on Cicero's *Dream of Scipio*, which contained the Neoplatonic scheme of the cosmos, based on Pythagoras. It saw Plato's eight spheres of the planets and stars but had an additional three: the world Soul, Mind and the Supreme God. These eleven spheres recall the eleven layers of the Chartres maze, which Keith Critchlow points out as implying that the scheme is a diagram of the 'shells' of reality. He also points to the connection between the maze and the rose window. (This is considered on p. 98.) The combination of 'image of the universe' and 'symbol of the sun' in rose windows is strongly reminiscent of Pythagoras' image of the universe, with its central fire which the last member of his school, Aristarchus, identified with the sun. The Chartres roses seem to possess only three stongly defined layers and a weaker fourth; at Paris there are at least six.

The meaning of different levels in the mandala-shaped rose window may lie in the interpretation of the functioning of the 'invisible universe', or in other words in the angelic hierarchy. The medieval world saw the spiritual world in terms of a ninefold hierarchy inhabiting the spheres between God and the world, passing on by degrees to the souls of the faithful the knowledge and the energy of the Creator. Such an image was used by Dante in *Paradiso*, where the nine spheres of heaven reflect the nine major regions of hell, approached through the seven stages of purgatory. This physically invisible but spiritually visible hierarchy was coupled to the spheres of the planets and the stars in the following way: (1) the Prime Mover, Seraphim; (2) the Fixed Stars, Cherubim; (3) Saturn, Thrones; (4) Jupiter, Dominations; (5) Mars, Virtues; (6) Sun, Powers; (7) Venus, Principalities; (8) Mercury, Archangels; (9) Moon, Lower Angels.

The hierarchy itself does not actually figure in any of the early rose windows – but they are sometimes sculptured into the portals beneath, as at Chartres. It does, however, appear at Saint-Ouen [57], some two hundred

One of the six-winged Seraphim in the west rose, Chartres, with wings full of eyes

years later; but it may well be that at this late date the essential meaning of the hierarchy had become lost. An equivalent could be said to exist in the 'energy' levels of a mandala structure, which builds up from the centre, the source. This is inherent in the Pythagorean universe with its central fire.

Just as a circle has only one centre, so everything in the universe is subordinated to the one Creator, as the very word 'universe' itself implies ('turned to one'). At Chartres, Christ is at the centre of all of the rose windows as the source of all energy. As the Word of St John, the Logos becomes the sun at the centre of the medieval Pythagorean cosmos. Cardinal Nicholas of Cusa – who was much influenced by the School of Chartres – expresses this idea as follows:

> the universal power of the macrocosm that moves itself and all things is perpetual because it is a round and circular movement, having all movement in itself, just as the pattern of the circle includes all patterns within itself, and man is the microcosm corresponding to this and deriving all knowledge from the central point, which is Christ.[25]

From time to eternity; wheel and rose

The wheel is an almost universal symbol of time, the turning evoking its cyclic nature and the seemingly endless repetition of night and day and year after year. The spokes of the wheel create an image of the sun; and, since the sun's passage through the sky marks out time, the two are related. This image is found in the pre-Christian and Celtic world and in the East, where it symbolizes life and reincarnation. In the Middle Ages the Wheel of Fortune symbolized Fate, and its metamorphosis into a rose seems to occur with the advent of the cathedrals. The wheel also symbolizes deliverance from these cycles, in Christianity through the conquest of fate and in the East through enlightenment.

As a symbol of the Buddha, the wheel represents the passage of the soul through the various forms of existence. Deliverance is symbolized by its transformation into a thousand-petalled lotus. Release and the achievement of Nirvana is sought through training, devotion, certain ascetic practices, through meditation and prayer wheels: OM MANI PADME HUM is the mantra that leads to the lotus, the phrase being repeated to the turning of the wheel. It means: 'God (reverence), the jewel, in the lotus, adoration.'

At Orvieto in Italy the head of Christ is carved on the hub of a 22-spoked wheel on the western façade of the cathedral, a veritable 'jewel in the lotus' [48]. But it also signifies the essential difference between enlightenment in Christianity and in Buddhism; that 'no man comes to the Father but by me'. In the metamorphosis of wheel to rose, deliverance from fate is embodied in the principle of the birth of Christ in the human soul – of which the rose and the rose window are symbols.

Emile Mâle, in *The Gothic Image*, draws our attention to the twelfth-century writer Honorius of Autun, who echoes Boethius in describing fate and fortune thus:

> Philosophers tell us of a woman fastened to a wheel which turns perpetually, so that they say she is sometimes rising and sometimes falling with its movement. What is this wheel? It is the glory of the world which is carried round in perpetual motion. The woman fastened to the wheel is Fortune, whose head alternately rises and falls because those who have been raised by their power and riches are often precipitated into poverty and misery.[26]

The essence of this idea can be seen in what remains of the Wheel of Fortune at Saint-Etienne, Beauvais [25], where people are being dragged round the circumference as though through life, only to descend into oblivion. With the advent of Suger's rose window and the greater examples that were to follow, transformation of the wheel takes place on two very important accounts. The first is that in the rose windows the emphasis is drawn away from the circumference and towards the centre – even though the windows may still maintain a wheel-like structure. Secondly there is the metamorphosis that takes place inside the building, where the wheel becomes a rose of light and colour; nowhere is this better illustrated than at Amiens, where a Wheel of Fortune on the outside of the south façade becomes inside a rose full of fire.

One interpretation of the transition from wheel to rose sees it in terms of Time and Eternity, the rim of the wheel representing time as past, present and future and the centre time as Eternity. Early Christian wheels built on the Chi-Rho monogram impart this message by often being placed between Alpha and Omega, the first and last letters of the Greek alphabet, which echo Christ as 'the Beginning and the End', outside Time but in Eternity, which is eternally present. Christ is portrayed as the Master of Time by being placed at the centre of the rose and sometimes surrounded by the signs of the Zodiac – as at Saint-Denis, Angers [70] Laon and Paris [9]. Here He is also Master of Fate:

> And he had in his right hand seven stars: and out of his mouth went a sharp two-edged sword; and his countenance was as the sun shineth in his strength.
>   And when I saw him, I fell at his feet as dead. And he laid his right hand upon me, saying unto me, Fear not, I am the first and the last;
>   I am he that liveth, and was dead: and behold I am alive for evermore, Amen; and have the keys of hell and of death. (Revelation 1:16–18.)

Christ at the centre of the Zodiac – as in some rose windows – suggests a way of synthesis, a way to unite the higher consciousness with the forces of the unconscious. Astrology at its highest sees the Zodiac as a consistent and thorough framework for embodying knowledge of aspects of a Totality; Jung sees the planets (St John's 'seven stars') as 'symbols of the power of the unconscious'.[27] Christianity has tended to reject astrology, because of the identification of these symbols with polytheism and because of the danger that people will abdicate responsibility for their own fate, taking the easy way out by leaving it to 'the stars'. A more mature view would be to see the signs of the Zodiac as patterns of energy, some of which we know through our own birth chart and others of which we can aspire to know. Hubert Whone echoes Jung and traditional symbolic interpretation when he sees twelve-fold patterns in terms of twelve paths to the centre which correspond for instance to the twelve human types reflected in the signs of the Zodiac: 'Because each being has a unique energy pattern which he acts out to the exclusion of others, his main discipline is to become aware of these others, and to awaken them inside himself so as to become a whole man: this awakening opens the door to his own divinity.'[28]

The word Zodiac originates from the Greek *zodiakos kuklos*, 'wheel of animal figures'. The usual interpretation of the four sacred creatures that often surround Christ (and the early wheel windows) is that of the Word being promulgated by the four Evangelists, who are the typological transformation of the creatures that Ezekiel saw in the fire of the wheel. From another point of view the four creatures are the four fixed signs of the Zodiac – Leo (the lion of St Mark), fire; Taurus (the bull of St Luke), earth; Aquarius (the man of St Matthew), air; Scorpio (the eagle of St John, an alternative symbol for this sign), water – flanking the wheel of fate.

Fate is often portrayed in mythology as a woman spinning, the mother goddess who, in Erich Neumann's words, 'not only spins human life but also the fate of the world, its darkness as well as its light'.[29] She also appears on the tenth card of the Tarot pack, sitting on top of the Wheel of Fortune. After the Middle Ages the Virgin Mary is sometimes portrayed at the Annunciation as spinning; when the Archangel Gabriel departed, it is reported that she continued and finished the work, and it was perfect.

The association with St Catherine gives an interesting insight into the problem of deliverance from the wheel – either as a karmic wheel of

A Wheel of Fortune drawn by Villard de Honnecourt, c. 1225–50, with figures in his typical geometric-based forms. The writing translates: 'Here below are the figures of the Wheel of Fortune, all seven are correctly pictured.' He does not say where this is to be found, but it is interesting to note that it is in rosette form and may be a generalized model

Ves la · ii · testes de sueltes ·

Veset desos les figures de le rvee g
fortune · totes les · vii · ymagenes

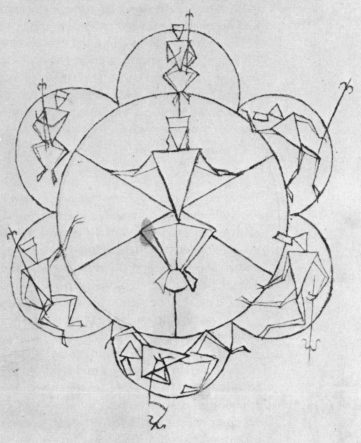

On prent kaus z theule mulue de paiens z fereskume. autre tant
del une cū del autre. z un poi plus del theule de paiens tant come
ses color vainke les autres. destemprez ce ciment vile de linuise-
sen poz faire un vassel pur euge tenir.

On prent une kaus bolete z orpiement se letier on en euge bol-
lans z oile. Cist unnemens est bon por pail ostier.

reincarnation or the wheel of fate in this life. Christianity has always denied reincarnation and maintained that each person has only one life in which he has the chance of fully realizing his talents and bringing about the kingdom of God; to lay the problems of life at the door of a 'bad karma' and do nothing about it is an easy way out. St Catherine is generally associated with the wheel because it was on the wheel that she was tortured. But she has also become the patron saint of weavers and spinners; and Fates are often portrayed as weavers and spinners, as they spin out the destiny of individuals and the world. Weaving is also creation; and the warp and woof that creates the material symbolizes the infinite variety of God's manifest world, and its continuous renewal. The wheel in this spinning aspect reflects the Logos as the creative principle constantly active in the world and the universe. As a 'loom of creation', the rose window shows each person the path to his or her own Soul: deliverance from fate through the realization of Christ working in and through everyone, from the centre of the rose towards the New Jerusalem, 'where all things are made new'. Then fate without God becomes transfigured: fate with God.

A key to nature

The world of nature is one of constant renewal: as Goethe observed of plant life, everything is undergoing metamorphosis. Everything in the cosmos evolves in accordance with the Logos – the Divine Reason – which creates every moment, day after day and year after year from the Creation until the end of time. All life and all nature follows this ever forward-moving Reason; everything, that is, except man, who works against nature rather than with it, polluting and consuming his way to oblivion.

The Gothic cathedrals are themselves 'Mirrors of Nature', as Vincent of Beauvais recorded in the early thirteenth century, and they are also 'Mirrors of Instruction'; tree-like pillars thrust upwards and branch outwards into vaults reflecting the uprising and uplifting power of the creative energy of nature. Everywhere vines, leaves, buds, flowers and thistles burst out, adorning doorways, pillars, windows and choir stalls. And in the rose windows, suspended between earth and heaven, we find the ultimate expression of nature's purpose: love and sacrifice, beauty and metamorphosis.

When the rose dies it leaves seeds for renewal, contained in the chalice-like rosehip. At the centre of the south rose window at Chartres, Christ holds the chalice of the Last Supper [10]; the seeds of His Presence are dispersed across the entire rose of the cosmos – to all mankind and all nature. In the east rose window at Laon, the Virgin Mary holds out a rose to all mankind as it faces the rising light [32]; just as the Buddha was to hold up a flower as the sum total of one of his sermons.

In the Tree of Jesse, a favourite medieval portrayal of Christ as the Tree of Life, Jesse can be seen at the base of the stem and the Virgin Mary as the shoot above the royal ancestors disposed along the stem. At the top is Christ as the flower, surrounded (in a lancet window at Chartres) by seven doves symbolizing the seven gifts of the Holy Spirit. These Jesse windows nearly always take the form of long lancets – as at Chartres, Saint-Denis, Le Mans or Carcassonne – but there are at least two examples where the idea has been transformed into a rose window.

At Paris the west rose [9] can be seen as a kind of Jesse window, where the branches of the tree interweave among the medallions leading to the Virgin Mary at the centre. The lineage of Christ has been replaced by the signs of the Zodiac, the labours of the months and the vices and virtues. This iconography is unlikely to be entirely authentic, as the window has undergone many restorations, but it can nevertheless be interpreted as a replacement of the lineage of Christ by the Way to Him through a path of toil, an understanding of time, of the seasons, of astronomy and astrology coupled with a virtuous life. The much later south rose window at Saint-Ouen, Rouen, is a more orthodox Jesse Tree, with Christ at the centre of kings and patriarchs amid the branches of the vine [58]. In this window the tree grows towards the centre, but the lines of the stone tracery and the shapes of the petals create exactly the opposite effect by giving the impression that everything is thrown out from the centre in great pulses of energy: a magnificent evocation of the creative force of nature.

Every one of the Gothic buildings and rose windows that bloomed out of the twelfth-century 'renaissance' individually reflects the forms of nature; what is astounding is that (as both Mâle and John Ruskin point out) the whole epoch of church-building, from Saint-Denis to the sixteenth century, is itself a season of nature. Buds and shoots decorate the early buildings, flowers and leaves adorn the middle era of high summer, and vines, fruit and thistles mark the autumn of the late Gothic; then, in Ruskin's words, 'The Renaissance frosts came, and all perished.'[30] Rose windows followed this cycle, budding in the twelfth century, flourishing in the thirteenth, and consumed in the flames of the fourteenth and fifteenth.

Numbers and geometry of creation

Every rose window is a direct expression of number and geometry – of light in perfect form. At Chartres all of them are divided into twelve segments, the number of perfection, of the universe, and of the Logos. The scholars at Chartres were clearly fascinated by number and its derivative geometry, not as ends in themselves but as keys to understanding nature. They studied Pythagoras to whom geometry was divine and numbers eternal – since all else perished. The fascination of numbers had already entered Christianity with St Augustine, who saw the divine wisdom of the world reflected in the numbers which were impressed in all things. Numbers and geometry represented order; the word *kosmos* means in Greek literally 'order'; so study of the cosmos involved a study of number.

Churches had been built on geometric principles since early Christian times; numbers were more of a medieval preoccupation. Geometry and arithmetic were traditional studies, but with the discovery of Euclid's *Elements* by Adelard of Bath (who was connected to the Chartres school) the subject inspired a new enthusiasm. Moreover, numbers had by the Middle Ages acquired a metaphysical significance of their own, and according to Mâle were thought to be endowed with occult power. They consequently found their way into nearly every aspect of cathedral building, from the numbers of pillars in the choir to the ratio of the levels in the triforium and layout of the façade and, inevitably, to the division of the rose windows.

The numbers one to eight were the most important, together with the all-important number twelve, and each had a geometrical equivalent. *One* represented the unity of all things, symbolized by the circle and its centre; *two*, duality and the paradox of opposites, expressed as pairs across the centre; *three*, the triangle, stability transcending duality; *four*, the square, matter, the elements, winds, seasons and directions; *five*, the pentacle, man, magic, and Christ crucified with five wounds; *six*, the number of equilibrium and balance within the soul, symbolized in the Star of David or Solomon's Seal; *seven*, the mystic number, of the seven ages, planets, virtues, gifts of the Spirit and liberal arts; *eight*, the number of baptism and rebirth, implied in the octagon; *twelve*, that of perfection, the universe, time, the apostles, the Zodiac, the tribes of Israel, and the precious stones in the foundations of the New Jerusalem.

Twelve and twenty-four are the most common numbers in rose windows, particularly in south transepts. Five- and eight-fold roses (and their multiples) are generally to be found on the north side, but it is difficult to make a rule about this. Thus, at Paris, there are sixteen huge petals in the *north* face [11], twelve in the *south* [12]; the same is true at Rouen; but at Clermont-Ferrand [2] and Tours [64] there are sixteen-petalled roses in both transepts. Much more convincing is the placing of five-fold windows in the north facing six (or twelve) in the south – as at Amiens, Sens and Saint-Ouen, Rouen [57, 82].

Rose windows use geometry in three different ways: *manifest*, *hidden* and *symbolic*. All three can be interconnected, linking the symbolic with the real in describing the creative order of the Logos. Otto von Simson points out that it is in design rather than in measure that geometry is generally used in the Gothic cathedrals, reflecting the truth that in the world of numbers everything is relative. In this sense the rose window becomes symbolic of the infinite, dimensionless and all-embracing operation of the Love of the Creator – active from the atom to the galaxy; somewhat akin to the Islamic representation of God in geometric form, which through endless weaving patterns expresses His creative aspect which is infinite.

In the rose window it is primarily this visual *manifest* geometry that makes the most immediate impact upon the eye; the web of complexity and precision within which every space is defined by a yet smaller geometric figure – a trefoil, quatrefoil, rosette, or spherical triangle. And within these elaborate looms of tracery at Chartres, Paris, Laon and Tours can be seen an even finer pattern woven into the glasswork – the red and blue mosaic diaper symbolizing the activity of the Creative Word right down into every fibre and corner of the cosmic rose.

Behind this visible frame is the equally precise *hidden* geometry. In the greatest rose windows it defines the exact position of nearly every major feature, relating the radial elements to the concentric divisions and all to the centre. The eye probably unconsciously picks up these relationships just as it does with the inner geometry of Renaissance painting. In another sense, hidden geometry would seem to be at work in many aspects of cathedral building, for the sketchbooks of Villard de Honnecourt show many geometric forms drawn within people, animals and buildings alike, and his interest in triangles as the basic component echoes Plato's *Timaeus*. These

'Here is the window of the Church of our Lady of Chartres', says Villard. Note the difference beteeen this drawing, c. 1125–50, and the actual window [29]

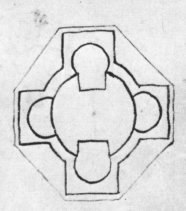

Jestoie une fois enhongrie la v ie mes martir
jor la iii io le pauement dune glize de si fatte
maniere.

books include two sketches of rose windows, one of Chartres and the other of Lausanne; both for some unknown reason are inaccurate.

In many of the world's religions, *symbolic* geometry is used as a kind of shorthand: circles, squares, triangles and stars, for example, are used to embody a meaning much more profound than they have in, say, a traffic sign or an advertising logo. Squares and circles, particularly, seem to have almost universal significance in symbolizing the finite and the infinite, earth and heaven, or matter and spirit. In Sufi thought, the centre, radius and circumference of a circle symbolize respectively Truth, the Path to Truth and the Law. In Christianity the equivalent is Christ as the Way, the Truth, and the Life, which in terms of the rose window are the path to the centre, the centre and the circumference as the wheel of life. The centre is then the point of balance, the still point, the 'point of intersection of the timeless with time', to use T. S. Eliot's words.[31]

In many rose windows, the finite and infinite are united through the placing of the circular part within a square, as at Paris, Clermont-Ferrand, Sées and many others. When the number twelve is defined within the rose, the union of heaven and earth is symbolically complete. At Lausanne the combination is exploited to the full.

Since early Christian times the circle has signified eternity, God, worship, perfection, the year and heaven. And it is for this reason, according to Vitruvius, that some ancient temples are round, representing the form or figure of heaven. As a symbol of the Temple of Spirit within man, the rose window symbolizes the unity of all things, when opposites are reconciled through the centre. A small rose window in the choir at Auxerre cathedral has the vices and virtues disposed in opposition to each other (like the antithetical signs of the Zodiac). St Thomas Aquinas at the end of the thirteenth century followed Aristotle in a concept of a 'Golden Mean' – not as mediocrity but as a genuine third possibility, free of duality.

Faith and Reason were the irreconcilable opposites of the age, at least until Aquinas. But before he posed a solution the cathedral builders were putting forward their version in the form of a symbol, the rose: a lifeline in the confused waters of the age. Many years later St John of the Cross gave voice to the problems of opposites and of paradox, which Eliot echoed:

> In order to arrive at what you do not know
>   You must go by a way which is the way of ignorance.
> In order to possess what you do not possess
>   You must go by the way of dispossession.
> In order to arrive at what you are not
>   You must go through the way in which you are not.
> And what you do not know is the only thing you know
> And what you own is what you do not own
>   And where you are is where you are not.[32]

Avarice, one of the Vices in a bas-relief at Sens, framed within a rosette and set in a square (from Viollet-le-Duc)

SOUL : 'Shall I see my dearest Master, when I reach his throne?

ANGEL : Yes, for one brief moment thou shalt see thy Lord. One moment;
but thou knowest not, my child, what thou dost ask : that sight of the
Most Fair will gladden thee, but it will pierce thee too.'

(Cardinal Newman, *The Dream of Gerontius*.)

The star

Every rose window contains a star, either placed literally in the rose – as at
Saint-Ouen [57] and Sens [71, 82] – or implied through the radiating pattern.
In the language of symbolism stars have many meanings, but they primarily
relate 'to the struggle of spirit against the forces of darkness'.[33] Thus, the
five-pointed pentacle is a symbol of magic, the Pythagorean symbol of
healing, of the Crucifixion, and at a later date of Man, drawn within the
pentacle by Leonardo da Vinci. The six-pointed Solomon's Seal or Star of
David is the star of the macrocosm, of heaven and earth united through
man, the two interlocking triangular symbols of fire and water forming the
perfect union of the conscious with the unconscious.

Every star is a minute point of light in an ocean of darkness, and yet a
blinding sun in its own right. In Christianity the Star of David announces the
birth of the Divine; it is the speck of 'true Light, which lighteth every man
that cometh into the world' (John 1:9). In his gospel St John follows the
opening with the account of the baptism of Jesus in the Jordan;
symbolically, the lowest point on the surface of the earth – the deepest, as it
were, in matter. So, too, the Divine was born at the darkest time of the year
– the winter solstice – and it is in St John of the Cross's 'dark night of the soul'
that enlightenment occurs.

As stars to steer by, rose windows look down on to the nave – the ship or
transfigured ark – and guide it through the waters of time, just as the star
guided the wise men. They point the way for each individual to his own soul
and guide that soul through the maze of life – which at Chartres lies literally
and symbolically beneath the feet. As a symbol and image of the sun, the
source of all light, the rose window acts as a screen between man and the
real sun which would otherwise blind the eyes after a few seconds. Christ
stands before His Father as a screen between the bare soul and the infinite –
between sanity and madness. Gerontius in Cardinal Newman's poem is
allowed but one brief glance at God, but even that is almost too much. As
Eliot put it, 'Humankind cannot bear very much reality.'[34]

Jewelled light

'The light of the body is the eye; if therefore thine eye be single, thy whole
body shall be full of light.' (Matthew 6:22.)

The whole of creation is made manifest through light. As an orb of light
suspended in darkness, the rose window is a perfect representation of the
Creation expressed as 'Let there be light'. It is the universe itself as an
explosion created by light and geometry expanding from a single point at
the centre (reminiscent of the modern Big Bang theory of creation). In the
rose window the Creation would seem to be an explosion re-enacted in
every moment; and as mandala takes one out of time, so the eye of the
mind becomes 'single', concentrated to a point, and 'Let there be light'

becomes an eternal event (in, as it were, a fusion of the Big Bang into the Steady State).

Light to the medieval mind was symbolic of the divine light to which the whole of nature responded. Light was seen to be the principle of order and value. Otto von Simson in *The Gothic Cathedral* paraphrases the thirteenth-century writer Robert Grosseteste:

> Light is actually the mediator between bodiless and bodily substances, a spiritual body, an embodied spirit, as he calls it. Light moreover is the creative principle in all things, most active in the heavenly spheres whence comes all organic growth here on earth and weakest in the earthly substances.[35]

It is in Dante's *Paradiso* that Simson finds the greatest poetical exposition of the medieval metaphysics of light. Some two hundred years before Dante, however, Suger had seen the importance of light in the architecture of the new age, and had filled his new church with glass. Rose windows are a perfect embodiment of Grosseteste's ideas of the light-filled heavenly spheres, and just as the rays of the sun are focused by a glass lens to produce fire, the rose window focuses the light of the soul to a point as though to announce the Fire of the Spirit.

In the Middle Ages, jewels and precious stones were thought to possess occult power – especially that of healing. Traditionally they symbolize superior knowledge; and the twelve stones on the High Priest's breastplate (Exodus 28:17–21) echo this, representing not only the twelve tribes of Israel but also twelve aspects of one truth. These twelve channels can be equated to the signs of the Zodiac, to the twelve Apostles, and ultimately to the twelve stones in the foundations of the New Jerusalem, symbolic of the new City of God built upon the Truth disseminated in twelve different ways.

A whole cathedral filled with the light of jewel-like stained glass could not but evoke the New Jerusalem; as a mandala the rose window would seem to take this further, pointing to man himself as the ultimate Temple of the Spirit. In this direction – as Jung pointed out – lies the secret of healing through faith. The purpose of individuation is to become whole; here again, rose windows are a guide, for each one gives the impression of being filled with thousands of jewels, but is at the same time one perfect jewel; a unique example of multiplicity within unity, evoking the All in the One – a 'pearl of great price'. Being whole in medieval terms would enable a person to receive light – which is why contemporary pictures of saints always include the halo. The rose window's similarity to a halo has already been mentioned, but the word *halo* and *whole* are etymologically related; and so too are *holy*, *hail* and *heal*. They all lead to 'becoming at one with that which is Holy'.

Union: love
The enlightening rose

As the symbol of enlightenment the rose and its Eastern equivalent the lotus are almost universal, and in flowers and cosmic wheels René Guénon finds the imagery widespread, from Japan, India and China to Europe well before Christian times. In Egypt Horus is born in the Lotus of Isis, and further east Brahma is said to reside at the centre of a thousand-petalled lotus, the goal of the patient and thorough adept. And, on Mount Olympus, Eros spilt nectar and, it is said, where it touched the ground roses would grow.

In Christian mystical terms, Angelus Silesius in the seventeenth century sees the rose as the symbol of the soul of Christ, while according to Eithne Wilkins the alchemists of the sixteenth century 'have solid tradition behind them when they call the rose the *flos sapientum*, the flower of those who have the wisdom'.[36] In other words they equate, says Miss Wilkins, the rose with the soul perfected through toil – the weaving aspect of the wheel we saw earlier. A medieval adept, Arnold of Villanova, entitled his treatise on the alchemical Great Work *Rosarium philosophorum*, 'Rose Garden of the Philosophers'.

As a symbol of love and beauty the rose goes back at least to the Isis, Aphrodite and Venus of the Egyptian and classical worlds. In the Middle Ages, St Bernard and the Cistercians bring the rose to the fore at the same time as they elevate the Virgin Mary to almost divine status. The rose becomes symbolic of both human love and Divine Love – of passionate love, but also of love beyond passion. All the subtleties are exploited in the poetry of the age, particularly in the Grail legends. For the mystic, love is the search for union with God. The path of knowledge and wisdom led to Philosophy, portrayed as a woman in the Laon rose, but in the path of faith union is inherent in the rose alone, symbol of a simple acceptance of God's Love for the world. These two paths become fused in the rose of the Virgin Mary – the Queen of Heaven – whom St Bernard saw as the embodiment of Wisdom, Philosophy and Love. This is contemporary with that extraordinary phenomenon of medieval life, the Courts of Love, which elevated womanhood to similar heights with an elaborate set of rules concerning chivalry and the conduct of amorous affairs. Under the Courts' first patron, Eleanor of Aquitaine, romantic poetry of love and adventure finds one of its greatest eras of expression.

The *Romance of the Rose*, written around 1250, is contemporary with the death of the Courts' last patron, Blanche of Castille, and, in the words of Henry Adams, 'the death of all good things'. It echoes the feelings of the time as those of a sadness at the end of an age; an age which saw the rose as 'any feminine ideal of beauty, intelligence, purity or grace – always culminating in the Virgin – but the scene is the court of love, and the action is avowedly in a dream without time or place'.[37] In the *Romance*, the rose is described as being situated in the mysterious tabernacle of the garden of love of the *chevalrie*, or knighthood, to which all men should aspire. Some seventy years later the rose appears in Dante's *Paradiso* – a form of garden of love – where Beatrice presents it to Dante on arriving in Paradise – which is itself constructed as a rose. It symbolizes here perfection and consummate achievement, and ultimately the great mystery of the Trinity and the union of God with man.

Even after 1270 – Henry Adams' date for the end of truly inspired cathedral building – the rose remained as powerful a symbol as ever, and many rose windows were built. But the main stream of mystical inspiration went into writing. Dante's work was the supreme example, but there was also that of Meister Eckhart, Petrarch, and St John of the Cross. The rose, however, follows the cultus of Our Lady, and in the fifteenth and sixteenth centuries she was often portrayed amid roses or in rose gardens. But by this time she has become more human, less of a goddess, someone to whom anybody could pray. It is from this time that the rosary originates, so called because contemporary works of art often feature the Virgin Mary surrounded by garlands of roses, or portrayed in a rose-garden (*rosarium*), from which the word rosary is directly derived. Eithne Wilkins sees the rosary as a kind of moving prayer wheel, bringing about detachment of mind, releasing the spirit through the repetition of prayers, each bead representing a recitation. The prayer itself is dedicated to the Lady of the Rose Garden. The rosary combines 'verbal, mental and bodily prayer to open up the inner world'; its function is

> both physical and spiritual, sensual and mystical. It may glitter, flash and tinkle; it is in some legends 'fragrant' and sometimes literally so; it moves, it is to be continually touched and handled, and it involves the use of exact number, which pertains to wisdom, power and the very nature of being.[38]

Detachment of the mind, moments 'out of time', and paths to the soul have been alluded to earlier in this book. Rose windows and the rosary share this function. It is unlikely that the windows were *deliberately* used in this manner; but when Abbé Suger talks of transcendence through the senses, brought about by light and colour, his words suggest that the effect was known and recognized. The sheer size and strength of form of the greatest of them cannot fail to hold the attention and provoke a moment's reflection in wonder. To the people who first saw them the impact must have been astounding; even in 'sophisticated' people of the twentieth century, with a lifetime's experience of electric light, cinema, television, neon and extensive travel, rose windows still promote a sense of awe, disturbing our image of the world. Such a disturbance, or even a moment of detachment, can be seen as the beginning of a journey of the soul, a journey that is both exciting and perilous. In this sense the petals of the rose symbolize an unfolding mandala or labyrinth along whose path the journey is made.

At Chartres the great west rose window [27] portrays Last Judgment, with the dividing of souls between heaven and hell, a constant reminder to mankind of the perpetual battle between good and evil which is to reach its climax in the Last Days as related by St John in Revelation. This rose window contains an implication which has been generally overlooked. Below the rose is the labyrinth, set into the nave at such a distance from the west door that if the rose were to be 'hinged down' it would almost fit over it.[39] Labyrinths generally symbolize the path of the soul through life, and medieval pilgrims re-enacted this, following the path of the labyrinth in the cathedral on their knees, symbolizing the journey to Jerusalem. The rose window superimposed on this labyrinth suggests the mandala, the viewfinder of meaning, projected on to life, as a means not only of finding one's way but also of differentiating between the forces of good and evil. In the *Divine Comedy* we can see identical symbolism in Dante's journey through the spheres of Hell, Purgatory and Paradise on a journey that, he himself says, could be interpreted in four different ways, one of which was that of the Christian through life. On arrival at the last circle of Paradise, Beatrice offers Dante a rose; so too at Chartres the labyrinth weaves its way

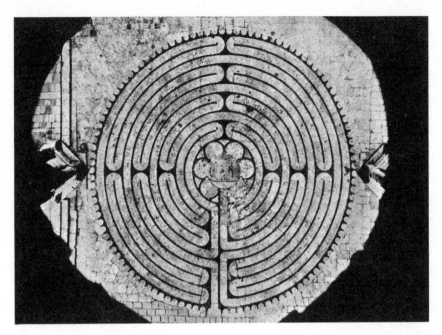

The maze in the nave of Chartres cathedral; with its central rosette, it mirrors the west rose above it

(there is only one path) through concentric circles and at the centre there is a six-petalled rosette into which the path leads: it unmistakably echoes the rosette at the centre of the rose window that overlooks it. At the centre of the rosette there was formerly (according to Keith Critchlow and Malcolm Miller) a metal plate with an image of a centaur or Minotaur – a clear allusion to the Cretan labyrinth, the walls of which were lined with roses.

Having found the way to the centre of the maze – to enlightenment and to the Minotaur – the searcher has to return to reality. In Christian terms it is the Holy Spirit that acts as Ariadne's thread in the labyrinth of life: union with Christ as the bridegroom through the 'mystical marriage' imparts Grace to withstand the dark forest, the leopard, lion and wolf of Dante, evil and mental disintegration, the Minotaurs of the ancient, medieval and modern worlds. H. Daniel-Rops sees the association of the rose window with Last Judgment and Dante in a similar light:

> Like every cathedral, the *Divine Comedy* is built on the human scale. The Last Judgment over the cathedral door warns the soul of its peril, as does the *Inferno*, and then leads it with an escort of saints to the great rose window where the angelic choirs are arrayed about the majesty of God. The poet is himself directed by our Lord Himself to 'rescue those who live on earth in a state of misery and lead them to the state of bliss'.[40]

The rose and the grail

The essence of Christianity is a hidden truth, the 'pearl of great price' that cannot be imparted in words but must be approached by allusion, parable or symbol, or realized in action. Similarly, the essence of the Gothic cathedrals, the reason why they hold such fascination for so many people, the source of the knowledge that built them, are virtually unanswerable questions. Some clues may lie in the background against which the cathedrals were built, particularly at the beginning of Henry Adams' magic hundred years, 1170–1270. For this coincides, in time and place, with the appearance of the various versions of the Holy Grail legend.

Somewhere around 1180, Chrétien de Troyes' *Compte del Graal* was written; this is the first comprehensive account of a legend which finds its origins in the Celtic world and its Arthurian legend or 'Matter of Britain'. By 1270 a number of different versions had appeared in France and Germany, the last of which, Albrecht's poem *Younger Titurel*, features the Temple of the Grail. The parallel between the legend and cathedral building is alluded to in this poem; A. von Scharfenburg suggests that 'Albrecht had in mind the dematerializing and spiritualizing effect of the Gothic and was able to communicate these qualities to his readers, by means of poetry and mysticism'.[41]

In the differing versions of the Grail legend, scholars have seen much symbolism as well as much romanticized fact. But the essence remains hidden, the Grail itself being variously described as the Chalice of the Last Supper, a stone, a bowl, the Philosopher's Stone of the alchemists and even in one theory a glass lens. Most of these suggestions are mentioned in Emma Jung's excellent study; she summarizes the many properties of the Grail as including dispensing food, preserving youth, radiating a sweet fragrance, and discriminating between good and evil.[42] In Chrétien de Troyes' original version the Holy Grail is introduced as 'a grail', suggesting a type of vessel rather than one particular vessel. He describes it as 'being of pure gold, set with precious stones and with such a brilliant light streaming from it that nearby candles lost their brightness'.[43]

Emma Jung sees the chalice at the symbolical level of the medieval mysteries as the vessel of receptivity that 'signifies the whole psychic man (not his ego) as a realization of divinity, reaching right down into matter'.[44] Elsewhere she recounts the poem entitled 'The Heart of Jesus', written by Hermann Joseph who was born in about 1150. Here the Divine Heart of Jesus is seen, in more mystical language, as 'the temple in which dwells the life of the world, as a rose, a cup, a treasure, a spring, as a furnace of Divine Love, ever glowing in the fire of the Holy Ghost, as a censer and as a bridal chamber'.[45]

Wolfram von Eschenbach's account of the Grail, in *Parzival*, begun in about 1197, is probably the most mysterious of all. The Grail itself is seen here to be a stone rather than a vessel, a supreme jewel surpassing in its powers the virtues of all other gems, and guarded by the Knights Templar, whom some people (such as Charpentier in the *Mysteries of Chartres*) see as being responsible for initiating and continuing the building of the Gothic cathedrals. This Grail was supposed to have a number of strange properties. Apart from suspending old age and physical decay, it produced food and drink in any quantity, and most important of all: 'commands are issued by messages which appear round its edge and vanish as soon as they are read'.[46] This brings to mind the Urim and the Thummim, the two gems on the High Priest's vestment by which the will of the Lord was made known; and also Christ's teaching to his disciples when their faith was on trial: 'take ye no thought how or what thing ye shall answer or what ye shall say. For the Holy Ghost shall teach you in the same hour what ye ought to say' (Luke 12:11).

At the centre of all the versions lies the idea that the search for the Grail is a quest, in which the individual sets out to liberate mankind from a spell. In most versions the Grail is associated with the Round Table, King Arthur and his twelve or twenty-four worthy knights. Their quest is to restore the kingdom of the Fisher King, who in some versions is just suffering from old age, but more generally has been wounded and needs healing. The Grail itself appears at Grail Castle; whether as a chalice or a stone, it manifests its powers through light to all who gaze upon it – particularly at Easter. Thus it revitalizes the King from time to time; but all mankind awaits the knight who will finally redeem the kingdom and heal the King by asking the right questions of the Grail. The King can be symbolically related to the true self that resides in everyone; the liberating knight (Sir Perceval or Galahad) is the individual consciousness (ego), groping through the world trying to find meaning, making mistakes, and generally failing to learn from them.

In Robert de Boron's version, *Le Quest du St Graal* of about 1220, the Round Table was

> set up on the advice of Merlin; nor was it established without great symbolic significance. For what is meant by being called to the Round Table is the roundness of the world and the condition of the elements in the firmament; and the conditions of the firmament are seen in the stars and in countless other things; so that one could say that in the Round Table the whole universe is symbolized.[47]

Emma Jung – whose words these are – adds that it reminds us of Charlemagne's table of twelve peers – possibly derived from Solomon's table, upon which was defined the cosmos in three circles of the earth, the planets and the stars. These particular aspects of the Round Table are strikingly similar not only in appearance but in symbolical meaning to rose

The Round Table at Winchester with the names of the 24 knights (as named by Malory) and the Tudor rose at the centre. Originally made in the fourteenth century, it was repainted in the sixteenth

windows with twelve radial divisions and concentric layers; mankind and the elements are shown superimposed on to the same model of the universe – all the individual microcosms reflecting the macrocosm. Edward Matchett sees this archetype in all its fullness:

> Around the table are the knights of chivalry, the disciples, the planets, the signs of the Zodiac, or the entire family of nature and man. It is not idle fancy that forms these and many other different representations, but rather the whole cosmos making initial contact with us through a symbol that is its most potent intermediary.'[48]

Merlin's role in the Grail legend is vital. Not only did he set up the Table but he also symbolizes mankind's return to the knowledge contained in nature, without which service to the Round Table – the whole of mankind – is not complete. The key to understanding lies in allowing nature itself to be the teacher, and to do this man has to learn to be receptive in a way that he has probably not experienced before.

The Round Table on the wall of the Great Hall at Winchester Castle is strikingly reminiscent of an archetypal rose window, and symbolically the two can be seen to be sacred and secular counterparts. Painted in Tudor times, it has 25 divisions, with Arthur at the top. The Tudor rose at the centre is a strange coincidence, for the rose and the Round Table would seem to be a fusion of the sacred and the secular in the service of mankind, the deeds of chivalry ideally – but alas not always – serving a higher ethical goal, even if that service involves personal suffering, since the rose is the symbol of suffering as well as of love.

The kingdom of the spirit

In one version of the Grail legend the temple that houses the Grail is a

> chapel of glass (like the Sainte-Chapelle), but a type of glass that can stretch to any extent. If three enter, the chapel is full and all have room; if ten enter it is full and all have room, and so on to infinity. When people leave, it contracts to the lowest limit of three.[49]

Another version sees the Temple of the Grail as being situated in Paradise, a sanctuary at the centre of the world, an image of the cosmos. This idea of a mandala-shaped 'spiritual beyond' in the shape of a castle may well have originated in the East, particularly from the Parsee sanctuary of the Holy Fire at Siz (Gazat), which was 'the pattern of the royal tomb as well as a sanctuary at the centre of the world and an image of the whole universe'.[50] Another similar type of image was seen in connection with the Lausanne rose window: that of Prester John's kingdom, a land of milk and honey with the secret of eternal youth and four jewel-bearing rivers. Here the Land of the Grail (it was Wolfram von Eschenbach who connected the two) has become the land of milk and honey; it strongly suggests mandala form, with its quaternity of rivers. More akin to a literal idea of a Gothic temple is the chapel of glass, capable of stretching and contracting to any extent, but always returning to a lowest limit of three. The tabernacle of God was, according to the Revelation of St John, to be with man, in the first instance within his own soul, and ultimately in the Christian Utopia of New

Vernon, near Paris

Jerusalem, with its fundamental component of the Trinity, but with the whole of humanity as its potential inhabitants. St John describes it as being 'like unto clear glass', with the foundations of the walls being garnished with all manner of precious stones.

The similarities between all these conceptions of the Temple of the Grail, and their appearance in France before 1200, may well have had much influence upon cathedral building, and particularly upon the design of rose windows, built on a mandala-like quaternary structure, jewel-like, representing Paradise. Emma Jung, interpreting the various versions of the Grail legend in the light of the individuation process, connects the appearance of mandala symbolism in many aspects of the legend to the process of the realization, within the individual, of his own soul. She points strongly to the creation of a 'temple within' symbolized in the Grail, for 'when the soul is dead, then "God is dead" too, since it is only in the vessel of the soul that God's activity becomes perceptible to man. Because he did not ask about the Grail, Perceval no longer understands himself and is cut off from the source of his own inner being.'[51]

Elsewhere she interprets the meaning of the Grail in no uncertain terms: 'A vessel is also a material thing, but it serves the purpose of containing other physical substances. This specific function of the symbol therefore indicates that the image of the Self, Christ, is practically non-existent unless it is realized in the human soul.'[52]

Henry Adams sees parallels between the Grail legend and the cultus of the Virgin Mary in the twelfth century: 'Whilst the "Lancelot" gave the twelfth-century idea of courteous love, the "Percival" gave the idea of religious mystery. Mary was concerned with them both.'[53] Deep wisdom has always been seen as a feminine attribute, appearing in men when they come to appreciate the feminine within themselves – and vice versa. The individuation process, by which a person seeks and succeeds in bringing an inner balance to the psyche, extends this to the successful reconciliation of opposing forces to produce harmony within the mind and consequently in the world around us.

Modern psychology is often seen as a substitute for religion – or, worse, as an explanation of it. But in Christianity there is a depth of wisdom that far exceeds that of psychology and psychoanalysis, and breaking through to the depths of wisdom – the well of one's own being – is the essence of all great art and the secret of all religion.

Rose windows are guides – externally in regard to their position in the churches and cathedrals, and internally in their ability to restore inner and outer harmony. It is thus possible to see the Trinity of the Christian faith in an awe-inspiring light. For between the 'passive' role of God the Father and the 'active' role of God the Son lies the Holy Spirit. It is neither active nor passive but is rather the catalyst or guide through the labyrinth of the unknown: it makes itself known to any sincere searcher for truth, guiding individuals in the language that they know, whether it be poetry, music, architecture or whatever – so long as that work is sincere. It is the key to nature that lies at the balance point between the extremities of activity and passivity at the centre of the rose. It is the Way that leads to union and to the New Jerusalem of all humanity: the way of Love, 'the love that moves the sun and the other stars'.[54]

Abbaye de Beaulieu, Caussade, near Lavaur

But to receive the sun, one must have dwelt for a long while in its thrice-blessed courts. One must have gone to meet it for a while, must have long been its student. As to bad monuments, the sun has nothing to say to bad artists whom the open air of the workyards has not prepared with understanding.

Is it possible that everyone is oblivious to, or mistakes, the sun's gifts? Does it not present the universe with majesty, making everything perceptible and living? Does it not inspire the poet, whether famous or obscure? The sun is responsible for the prosperity of the farmers, the joy of animals, the fertility of the land; and man's thoughts perhaps have their hearth in its light and warmth. For a long time man believed he saw God's truth blazing in its fires, and God wishes us to adore the sun. When it shines, the earth is modelled according to its divine flame.

Thus it is allowed, and, by patience and diligence, it is possible, to understand and feel the geometry of light. In this the spirit tastes repose in silence, drawing from it a new energy and generosity.

Auguste Rodin on Mantes, in *The Cathedrals of France*.[55]

65   Illuminated by the setting sun on the west façade of Notre-Dame de Mantes, this window is the first real rose breaking away from the strictly spoked structure of the wheel. The subject is Last Judgment, strongly reminiscent of the west rose at Chartres, with Christ at the centre surrounded in the innermost circle by angels in adoration and by the Virgin Mary and St John to the left and right beneath Christ. The outermost twelve huge panels depict scenes of Judgment; following the hours of a clock, at 12 is the Bosom of Abraham, here depicted as a white veil enclosing five souls, while the Mouth of Hell (3) has already received three. A demon leads off four unfortunates and among them are a bishop and two kings (2), while others are transported by angels to heaven (4) and (9). St Michael (6) divides the souls who rise from their graves (5) and (7), some of whom ascend to heaven (8), where St Peter guards the gate (10) and four of the Apostles are seated (1) and (11). Unfortunately some of the panels have been interchanged since the nineteenth century (4, 6, 7, 8) and some are new (1, 8, 10). (Mantes west, stonework c. 1180, glass early 13th c.)

66 **The great rose at Reims creates** a
golden crown for the Virgin Mary.
(Reims west, upper rose, c.1260)

67 **A new rose in the tympanum
beneath the coronation of the Virgin.**
Reims was badly damaged in the First
World War, but this exquisite window featuring the Litany of the Virgin Mary is
probably the finest twentieth-century
rose. (Reims west, lower rose, c.1260,
glass by Jacques Simon, 20th c.)

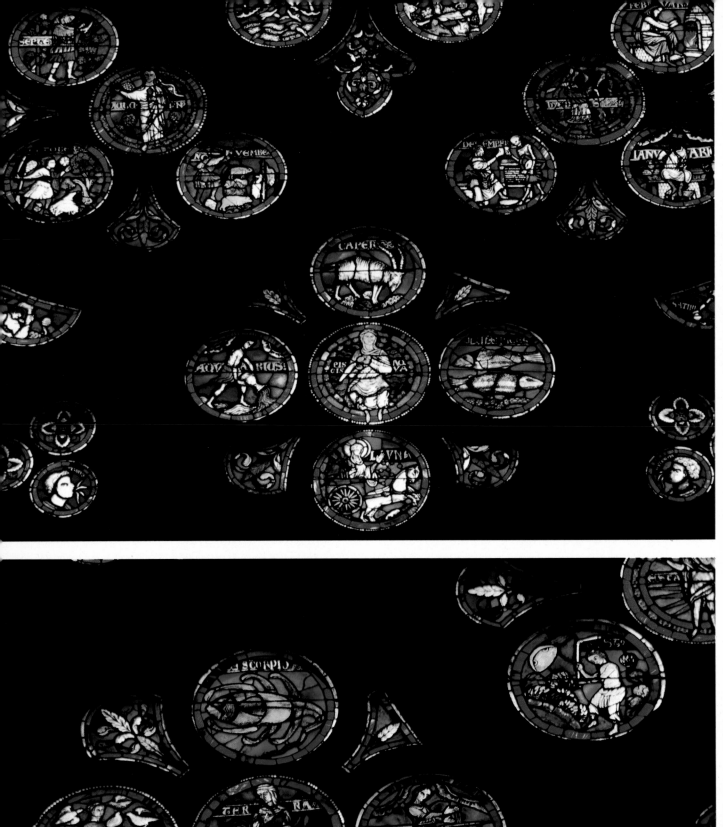
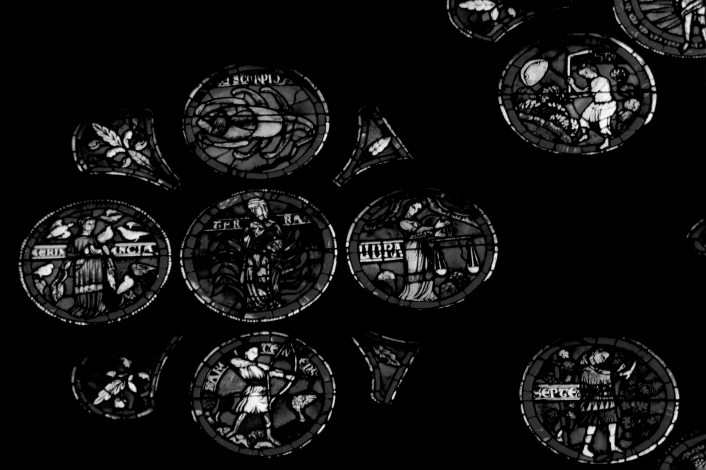

68 The initial creation becomes constant creation, manifest in every rose window as light and colour. At Lausanne the cycle of the year, the signs of the Zodiac and the four elements symbolize the forces of creation eternally acting in the cosmos – and through man when he creates in accordance with Nature. (Lausanne, c.1230, partly restored 19th c.; see key on p.131)

69 Earth is surrounded by Scorpio, Libra, Sagittarius and Aeromancy, who foretells the future from seven doves. (Lausanne, c.1230, restored 19th c.)

70 The Wheel of Life, often containing the Zodiac, at Angers has twenty-four spokes instead of the usual twelve. The signs are disposed through the upper half of the wheel with twelve of the twenty-four elders of the Apocalypse below, each holding a lute and a vase. (Angers, stonework 13th c., glass c.1463)

Overleaf:

71 Generating shapes and forms in patterns of light and colour, the Flamboyant north rose of Sens places members of the heavenly choir inside mouchettes which seem to swim through space. (Sens north, early 16th c., see 82)

72 Sweeping across the cosmos: from the centre of the south window at Sens the mouchettes enclose scenes from Last Judgment portrayed in vivid late fifteenth-century style – intermingled with the arms of Tristan de Salazar, the window's donor. (Sens south, c.1494)

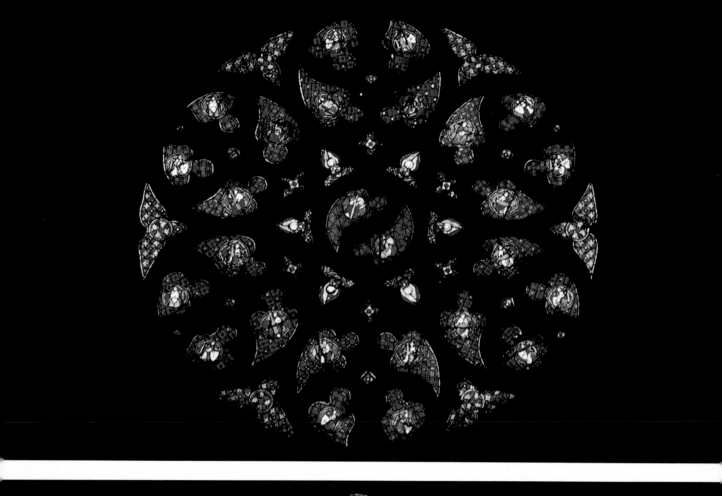

73 **Rose windows seem to generate** motion around their centre in a ceaseless stirring movement. At Saint-Bonaventure this seems to reduce to a Yin/Yang type of arrangement at the centre, recalling the 'breathing' of the cosmos in Eastern philosophy: the balance between active and passive modes of existence. The scene here is Last Judgment, with twenty-four elders of the Apocalypse in six groups of four. (Saint-Bonaventure, Lyon, 15th–16th c.)

74 **Inspired** by the Saint-Bonaventure rose, this window in Toulouse dates from the same period. (Notre-Dame de la Dalbade, Toulouse, 15th–16th c., glass modern)

75 **Tongues of flame,** of the Spirit, the Sun and Last Judgment, at the little church of Houdan near Paris. (Houdan, 15th c.)

76 **The Spirit of Life**, interweaving all creation, transforms stone into coloured glass in the late fourteenth-century rose window at Saint-Omer. (Saint-Omer, late 14th c.)

77 **Bringing the creation into** an eternal present is superbly demonstrated through cyclic form in this late rose window at the cathedral of Saint-Pierre, Beauvais. (Beauvais south, c. 1548; see key on pp. 132–33)

Overleaf:

78 **Every moment** of history is symbolically contained in a rose window. 'The fire and the rose are one', in T. S. Eliot's 'Little Gidding' and in the rose window, fusing all past, present and future into the Eternal Present. As the Alpha and Omega, the beginning and the end, of St John's Revelation, Christ is at the centre of this south window at Sées, surrounded by the twelve Apostles, the four Evangelists and the twenty-four elders. (Sées south, c. 1270, glass restored)

79 **Through light and colour in** concentric bands, the great west rose at Strasbourg suggests the different 'energy' bands of the mandala that focuses the mind to a point at the centre of the window. (Strasbourg west, c. 1318, glass much restored; see also 33)

80 **A myriad forms.** (La Rochefoucauld, 16th c.)

81 **As a 'viewfinder of meaning'** the cross-and-circle pattern of the mandala represents order and healing in macrocosm and microcosm alike. (Saint-Maixent-l'Ecole, 15th c., rebuilt 17th c.)

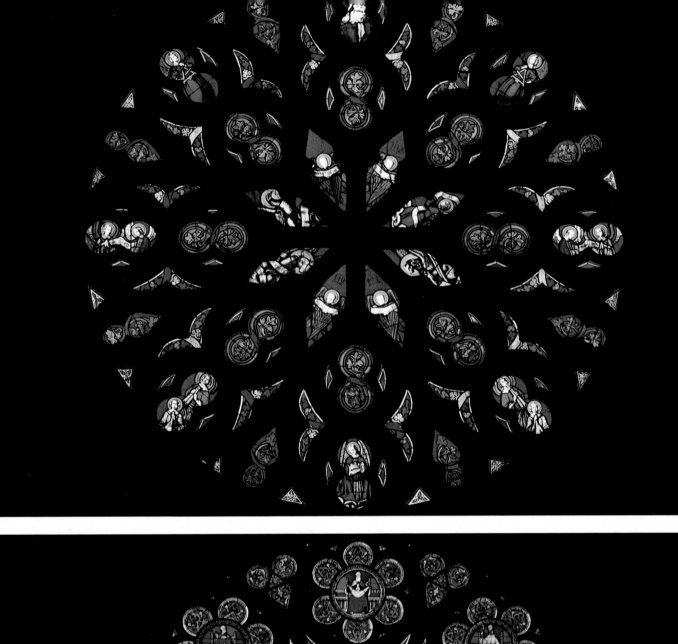

82 **Acting as a vortex** of light, the five-petalled north rose of Sens is a paean to God. All the instruments of Psalm 150 are employed to praise God in His sanctuary. Sixty-two angels play trumpets, psaltery, harp, timbrel, stringed instruments, organs, loud cymbals and high sounding cymbals: all join in the dance of the cosmos. (Sens north, early 16th c.; see 72)

83 **Spiralling to the centre**, this small rose window is in the Chapelle des Bourbon in Lyon cathedral. (Lyon, 16th c.)

84 **Each rose window transmits to** man beauty in light – 'enough to fill the mind with wonder' in the words of Henry Lincoln. This exquisite rose by Henri de Nivelle features incidents from the lives of St John the Baptist and St Stephen. (Lyon west, c.1392)

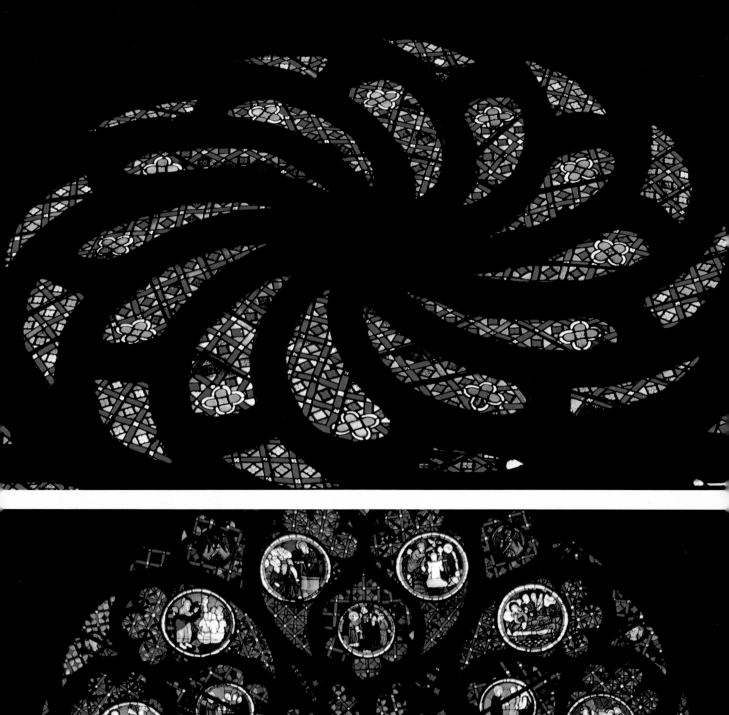

Divine geometry

As the geometer his mind applies
    To square the circle, nor for all his wit
    Finds the right formula, howe'er he tries,

So strove I with wonder – how to fit
    The image to the sphere; so sought to see
    How it maintained the point of rest in it.

Thither my own wings could not carry me,
    But that a flash my understanding clove,
    Whence its desire came to it suddenly.

High phantasy lost power and here broke off;
    Yet as a wheel moves smoothly, free from jars
    My will and my desire were turned by love,

The love that moves the sun and the other stars.

> (Dante, *Paradiso*, xxxiii.1.133–45,
> translated by Dorothy L. Sayers.)[55]

85 **The creative force of the cosmos in light streaming from its centre** illuminates elders, angels, prophets, martyrs and patriarchs – the 'great cloud of witnesses' of the Christian faith. They glow in colour surrounded by haloes of white light in the north rose of the cathedral of Saint-Gatien at Tours. (Tours north, early 14th c.)

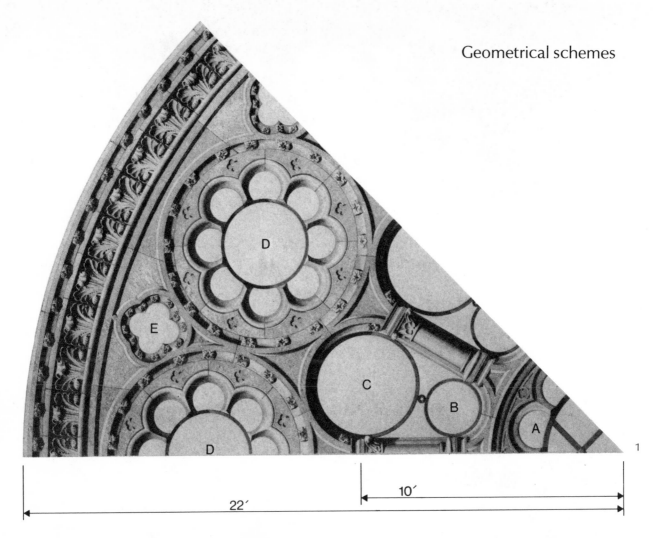

22′

10′

The almost obsessive interest that medieval architects and theologians showed in geometry goes back at least to St Augustine and his concern with Pythagorean and Neoplatonic number mysticism as an expression of divine proportion. He talks about the 'anagogical' function of music and geometry, of beauty realized through figures and proportions. At Chartres, Chancellor Thierry's preoccupation with numbers manifested itself in his geometric representation of the Trinity and led to a trend of almost reducing theology to geometry that disturbed a later chancellor, John of Salisbury. Nevertheless, geometry is at the basis of all Gothic cathedrals, everything being created from basic relationships. The means of proportioning elevation from plans using regular polygons – particularly the square – was a carefully kept secret until the fifteenth century, when Matthew Roriczer of Ravensburg made the knowledge public.

Geometry – and the use of polygons in setting proportions – is fundamental to all rose windows: every one of them involves extremely careful calculation and precise construction. It operates in different ways in different windows, and in the greatest of them the satisfaction is more than visual – it is intellectual and even cosmic in its implications. Four of the greatest windows are analysed here, in order to give an insight both into how the windows were conceived and into the other, secondary geometric relationships that emerge from any perfectly designed window.

CHARTRES WEST [27, 29]

This classic rose window on the west façade of Chartres is more than a triumph of design: it is a 'tour de force, where five separate systems of proportion rhythmically pulse across the wheel, dividing the whorls from the vortex'.[57]

This quotation is from John James' article on the geometry of this window, a superb analysis which will act as the basis of this account. Working from the best drawings and measurements available, James rarely accepted an error of more than ± 2 cm in the work of establishing the relationships within this immense rose. He found it to be built up on two units, measured as shown above in Roman feet of 29.6 cm: one of 3 feet and another of 10 feet, which reduces to $\frac{2}{3}$ and $\frac{1}{3}$ to give $6\frac{2}{3}$ and $3\frac{1}{3}$ feet (an expansion of the number 3, and a division by 3, being a neat echo of Thierry's preoccupation with the geometric configuration of the Trinity). Here are the main features of this extraordinary construction:–

Figure 1
A segment of the rose – from Lassus' drawing of 1842 – shows that the 10-foot unit gives the line of centres of the middle row of lights, and the $6\frac{2}{3}$-foot unit

that of the inner twelve medallions. (The twelve petals of the central rose lie on the 3⅓-foot circle.) These outer two circles also define the masonry joints at each end of the pillar.

Figure 2
The twelve large rosettes D are defined from the 3-foot unit by creating 6 squares of side 12 feet about the centre, and expanding them to a 24-pointed star which then creates the centres and the points of contact of the rosettes.

Figure 3
By interconnecting the centres B to form three squares the inner cornice is defined, and when the squares are expanded into a 12-sided star they meet at the centres of the small outermost lights E. This same star is also tangential to the rosettes *and* to the middle row of medallions C. Finally a hexagon around the star defines the perimeter of carved leaves, and, as John James says, 'With an elegant precision the Master placed the leaf that adorns the centre of each capital on the intersection of the arms of a star. Thus in a splendid consistency the thirds fix both leaf forms, and the three concentric rings of circlets that look like a sunflower.'

Figure 4
There is one final construction from the 3-foot unit that generates the outer circle. Around the 3-foot centre four equilateral triangles are drawn, and the three squares that enclose them are expanded into a twelve-pointed star which arrives at the perimeter on the axis of little lights.

John James takes the analysis even further, finding that a series of 'expanding pentagons' from the central 3-foot unit confirm certain points in the structure, although I find this less convincing. James finds many more subtle interrelationships and the use of a second unit, the *pes manualis*, ⅚ Roman foot; between the two units, 'every minor element and every moulding reflects one or another of the basic measures. In careful geometry everything is made a part of everything else; nothing stands alone. Thus it was with God's universe, thus it should be in man's efforts in praise of him.'[58]

2

3

4

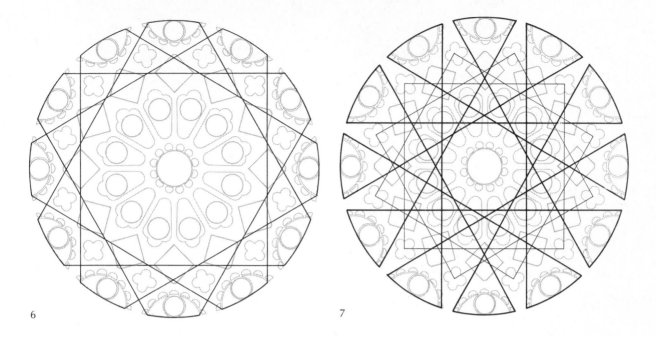

6

7

CHARTRES NORTH [6, 7]

The glorious Rose de France in the north transept of Chartres has been used in this book to illustrate many differing aspects of rose windows; its divine geometry is amongst its finest glories. Everything in the window is generated from the properties of the square within the circle.

The twelve squares set at angles to the radii are the most striking features of this window. They can easily be related to three interpenetrating squares that contain the smaller ones; the eye can pick these up unaided. These squares suggest that there is a very subtle underlying geometry that is based on the spiral, and the eye seems to sense the window's sunflower form that spirals out of (or into) the centre. In fact the set of squares that creates the true spiral geometry is more closely related to the outside stonework. It is the centres of the small outer circular lights that create a geometry of expanding and diminishing squares that takes in the square lights. By joining every second and every third of these the sequence of squares can be drawn, and they very neatly focus down to the central rosette with its twelve little petals (see *figure 5*).

This series of squares can also be related to the Golden Section, for the intersecting points of the two sets of

squares lie on a spiral whose points are governed by the Fibonacci series (a series in which each term is the sum of the two preceding ones). The underlying geometry and mathematics of this relationship is explained in Peter S. Stephens' *Patterns in Nature*.[59] Briefly, the points through which the spiral passes are laid out so that the circular arc between any two consecutive points is 137.5°, which is $360° \times (3 - \sqrt{5}) \div 2$, or $360° \times \phi^2$, where ϕ is the golden section 0.618. 'In terms of the Fibonacci series it approximates 360° times one term in the series [1,2,3,5,8,13 etc.] divided by the term directly after the next succeeding one.'

It is this system that governs the system of growth in a number of flowers – notably the sunflower, daisies and in a related but more complex way the rose. Certainly the Golden Section must have been known to the School of Chartres through their studies of Euclid. Fibonacci (*Filius Bonaci* – 'son of good nature') published his work in *Liber abaci* in 1202 – some thirty years before this window; it was, according to H. E. Huntley, widely known and may well have come to the attention of the Chartres mathematicians.[60]

In this window at Chartres there are

twelve groups of spirals following this law, four of which are drawn in *figure 5*. Thus the lights of the prophets on the outer circle bind into the key points in the structure, pass through the twelve kings, angels and doves to give birth to the Logos at the centre. The Creative Logos of the universe, the law of nature, is followed by man to give perfect beauty.

There are three other structural relationships in this window, independent of this sunflower arrangement. The first two are in *figure 6*, which demonstrates the network of equilateral triangles built up from the semicircles around the edge. They create three interlocking squares around the centre, the corners of which define the centres of the twelve innermost circles. Another system of squares interlinks the twelve little square openings with the twelve quatrefoils – shown by the light lines in *figure 6*. In *figure 7* another system of squares interconnects the outer semicircles to the diagonals of the twelve little squares – yet another demonstration of the subtle nature of this remarkable rose. Further studies on this window may well reveal that, like the west window in the same cathedral, it is built up from units of measure which are equally subtle and ingenious.

8

CHARTRES SOUTH [10, 35–37, 41]

Figure 8 shows a scheme for the south rose window of Chartres. Doubtless there are other schemes more subtle than this, but this one shows some interesting relationships that the eye probably picks up unconsciously. The semicircles around the edge suggest a 'focusing' mechanism which leads the eye to the centre: the thin lines in the diagram drawn from the extremities of

each of the outermost semicircles to a point at the centre of the opposite semicircle define perfectly the central medallion that encloses Christ. (And each one picks up the little quatrefoils en route, thus defining their centres.) Any line drawn from the centre of one semicircle to that of another, five windows away, is tangential to no less than four of the twelve central medallions – a

remarkable alignment! Furthermore, a set of three squares inscribed in the rose is tangential to the middle row of the largest windows. This same system of three squares may well generate further subtle relationships built up from the properties of three squares; but this will have to be the subject of another study.

The north rose window of Notre-Dame de Paris, sometimes called the Alchemists' Rose, is probably the supreme example of a rose window built up from a lattice of invisible geometry. *Figure 9* shows how the geometry creates and defines each concentric layer in a logical progression.

The starting point is the centre of any one of the thirty-two outermost lights. By joining it to another, eight windows away, and continuing the process, an endless line is generated that takes in all of these outer lights. At the same time it creates a series of tangents to a circle which contains the centres of the next layer of thirty-two medallions. A similar operation repeated on this new layer – but this time by joining every eleventh window – creates two interlocking sixteen-pointed stars; and these in turn define the centres of each of the sixteen central windows containing the prophets. From these centres four interlocking squares can be drawn, which in turn tangentially produce the heavy red and gold halo around the Virgin and Child at the centre. Finally a sixteen-pointed star from this circle creates the opening for the central lights – and the size of the openings that form the border of this central rosette.

Thus the geometry relates every part to every other part and the totality to the point of focus – the centre. The window is full of other subtle relationships which the reader can verify for himself with a ruler: a different scheme for example can be created by joining every seventh of the outer windows – or every tenth window in the middle layer.

9

Creation

'The glass in the windows, through which pass the rays of light, is the mind of the doctors, seeing heavenly things as in a glass darkly' (Honorius of Autun). This medieval *imago mundi*, or schema of the Creation and the created, dates from about 1225–35. Its imagery represents the culmination of cosmological speculations that go back to Greece and Rome. Its sources of inspiration can be traced to Pliny, Aristotle, Solinus, Isidore of Seville and the Venerable Bede – and possibly even the Prester John legend. Its immediate source is probably Honorius of Autun, the medieval encyclopaedist, and its scale of conception and construction is clearly linked to the School and cathedral of Chartres; the style of

the glasswork, however, is that of Picardy.

The rose as it exists today contains 105 panels, of which 61 are figured; and of these 17 are replacements dating from 1894–99, when Edouard Hosch restored it from its then dilapidated state. There is some dispute concerning the nature of the original iconography: some observers have suggested that God was at the centre, surrounded by the four Evangelists instead of the Creation. But the more likely scheme is that suggested by Ellen Beer, having 'The Year' at the centre (1) surrounded by light and dark, sun and moon (2–5). This would then have meant that geomancy and hydromancy (prophecy by earth and water) would have had places in the scheme (38, 39), which would be more logical and consistent. It would also mean that things temporal and earthly were always shown within a square, things eternal and celestial within a circle or part of a circle (see also p. 84).

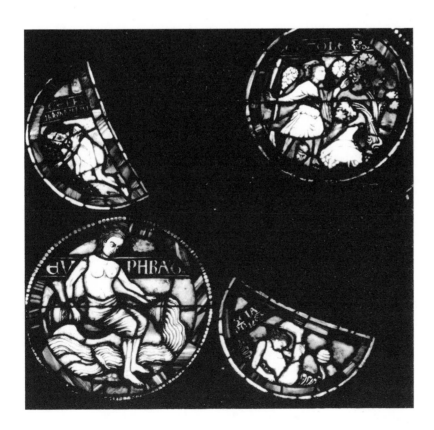

Central portion of the Lausanne rose, depicting the Creation, the Seasons and the Months

Here is the present disposition of the Lausanne rose. Panes asterisked are nineteenth-century replacements.

1 God the Father.*

Matter: in the small square

2 Light and dark.*
3 Land and sea.*
4 Fish and birds.*
5 Animals and men.*

Time: in the four semicircles

6 Spring, a man surrounded by flowers and leaves and holding a flower.
7 Summer, red rays warming the blue sky.
8 Autumn, amid the red and white grapes.
9 Winter, dressed in white and hooded, weathers a storm of icicles.
10 March, wearing a cotton turban-like hat, pruning the vines.
11 April, wearing a toque, flowers in hand, opens the door to his garden.
12 May, on a white horse, carries his falcon to the hunt.
13 June, inaccurately labelled IULIUS, cuts the hay.
14 July, reaps the harvest with a sickle.
15 August, stripped to the waist, threshes the harvest under a baking sun.
16 September, harvesting the grapes.
17 October, tending his pigs while they eat acorns (and hunt for truffles?).
18 November, the month of cattle and pig slaughter.

19 December, raising his glass to death, symbolizes the year that has gone.*
20 January, a double-headed Janus figure, with one half holding up his cup to the bountiful year ahead, the other looking at the year that has passed.
21 February, warming his hands.*

The elements and the Zodiac, formative and beyond time

22 Earth, a woman surrounded with ears of corn.
23 Water, breast-feeding a fish.
24 Air, doing likewise to a dragon.
25 Fire, feeding a salamander.
26–37 The signs of the Zodiac portrayed in usual medieval style; 27, 29, 34 and 36 are replacements.
38 The sun with a fiery halo being drawn across the sky in a chariot.
39 The moon being drawn likewise but with only two horses.
40 Aeromancy, surrounded by seven doves by whom she foretells the future.
41 Pyromancy, foretelling the future from the flames of the fire.

Paradise and the lands of myth

The four rivers of Paradise portrayed as bearded men pouring their waters across the four corners of the earth:

42 The Geon (Nile).
43 The Tigris.
44 The Phison (Ganges).
45 The Euphrates.
46 Ethiopians, with four eyes to help the accuracy of their archery.
47 Gangaridae, inhabitants of the Ganges who supposedly lived off the sweet smell of fruit – and died in the presence of any foul odour.
48 Acephali, creatures with no heads and with eyes in their bodies.
49 Cynocephali, dog-headed men, thought to live in India.
50 Pygmies, also thought to inhabit India, here fighting a crane.
51 A Satyr, a small hook-nosed creature with horns and goat-like feet.
52 Sciapodes, creatures that lived in the desert and had only one foot, which they used as a sunshade.*
53 Cephi, elusive creatures detectable only by their human-like footprints.

The eight winds of the cosmos

54 Auster, the south wind.
55 Euroauster, the south-south-east wind.
56 Subsolanus, the eastern wind of the Levant.
57 Vulturnus, the south-east wind.
58 Septentrion, the north wind.
59 The north-west summer wind.
60 Zephyr, the west wind.
61 Austerozephyr, the south-west wind.

BEAUVAIS SOUTH [77]

A much later, more traditional representation of the Creation was chosen for this cathedral. It is nevertheless full of subtleties and hidden meaning and exploits to the full the opportunities offered by the concentric structure of this Flamboyant rose. It portrays the Creation according to Genesis in the innermost six petals and then a sequence of stories starting with the Temptation in the Garden of Eden and continuing up to the beginning of Exodus, where the wandering Israelites receive manna from heaven. Here is a brief description:

1 At the centre, God the Father, represented as an old man with a long white beard, white halo and yellow nimbus.
2 The sun, moon and stars in classic fifteenth- and sixteenth-century style, the sun and moon with faces and the stars five-pointed.
3 The creation of birds.
4 The creation of trees and plants; represented as a pristine forest.
5 The creation of animals; sheep, an ox and a deer identifiable.
6 The creation of fish; an eel and a mullet join the others swimming towards the centre.
7 The four winds of heaven.
8, 19 The Celestial Paradise: in the angelic realms, two red and green, elegant young men (seraphim) can be seen close to the stars.

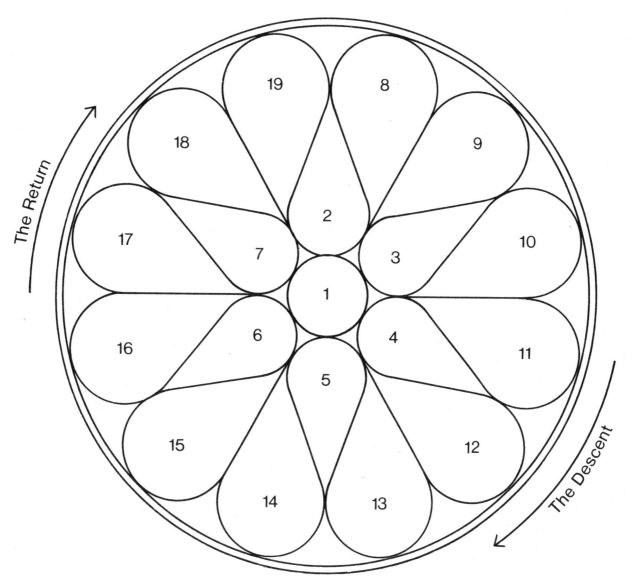

The Return

The Descent

9 The Earthly Paradise; Adam relaxing under a tree while Eve, watched by the snake, offers the forbidden fruit.

10 Adam and Eve being driven out of paradise by an angel with a sword.

11 Adam tilling the ground while Eve spins.

12 The Flood, with a dove bringing three ears of wheat to the ark.

13 The Tower of Babel.

14 Abraham about to sacrifice Isaac; an angel interposes.

15 The benediction of Isaac; Rebecca waiting behind.

16 Joseph being lowered into the pit by his brother Reuben.

17 The burning bush; Moses learns how he will deliver the Israelites into the land of Canaan.

18 Manna, in flakes white as snow and large as saucers, falls from heaven to the Israelites in the desert.

19 See 8.

The window relates the Creation, but symbolizes man's intimate connection with nature. The right side of the rose represents the descent of mankind from the angelic and spiritual realms, from Paradise, through disobedience to his lowest point in matter which destroys all but the most faithful, Noah and his sons. The attempt to build the tower of Babel symbolizes the futility of trying to reach heaven without faith. The return is initiated, however, through Abraham's act of faith, and thereafter his descen-dants move up the left side of the rose through trials and tribulations until manna from heaven in the desert begins to echo the conditions under which man received food in paradise.

Throughout the window the motif of nature – of constant creation – is present: the angels above the firmament de-scend to Paradise and send down man-na into the desert; the birds in panel 3 look to Paradise and seem to be flying out of the trees underneath them; the deer seems to await the moment when he can spring into the forest.

The glasswork is known to be by either Nicholas le Prince or Nicolas le Pot; façade and stonework designed by Martin Chambiges and Michael Layle, c. 1500.

Roses for the Queen
of Heaven

PARIS WEST [9]

The west rose at Paris is dedicated
to Our Lady, although it is not certain
that this was originally so. It has undergone numerous restorations, particularly in the sixteenth and nineteenth
centuries, when some of the panels
were completely renewed. Those
marked * are sixteenth-century restorations, those marked ** are nineteenth-
century, and those marked (n) are modern.

The upper half of the outer circle
contains the virtues, and the corresponding vices are in the next inner
layer; in the lower half of the outer
circle are the months, corresponding to
the zodiac signs in the inner layer. The
innermost layer contains twelve
prophets. At the centre is the Virgin.

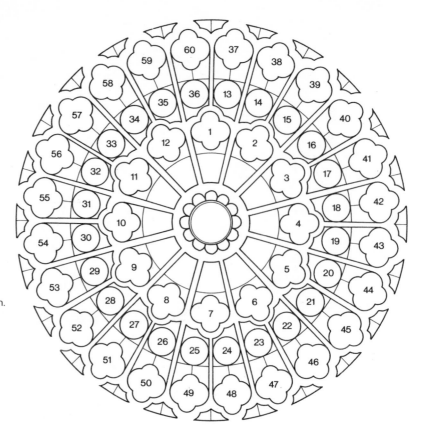

1 Prophet (n)	21 Scorpio**	41 Obedience**
2 Prophet (n)	22 Libra**	42 Strength
3 Prophet (n)	23 Virgo	43 December (n)
4 Prophet	24 Leo**	44 November**
5 Prophet**	25 Cancer	45 October
6 Prophet*	26 Gemini**	46 September (n)
7 Prophet (n)	27 Taurus*	47 August*
8 Prophet*	28 Aries**	48 July (n)
9 Prophet (n)	29 Pisces**	49 June*
10 Prophet*	30 Aquarius	50 May (n)
11 Prophet (n)	31 Pride*	51 April (n)
12 Prophet (n)	32 Folly (n)	52 March**
13 Anger**	33 Lust**	53 February (n)
14 Despair**	34 Avarice	54 January**
15 Ingratitude**	35 Inconstancy (n)	55 Humility**
16 Discord**	36 Idolatry**	56 Prudence**
17 Rebellion**	37 Patience**	57 Chastity**
18 Cowardice	38 Hope (n)	58 Charity
19 Capricorn*	39 Gentleness	59 Perseverance
20 Sagittarius**	40 Peace**	60 Faith (n)

Built on the geometry of the number 16, this rose window is the ultimate in sheer delicacy, the ratio of stone to glass having been reduced to an absolute minimum. The underlying geometry is as spectacular as the rose itself (see p. 127), and shows many fundamental and subtle relationships.

The rose portrays the Old Testament, with prophets (p) in the innermost circle, kings (k) and judges (j) in the next, and kings and high priests (hp) in the outermost. They all surround the Virgin Mary who, with the Christ child on her knee, represents the culmination of history before the coming of Christ.

The sixteen primary and thirty-two secondary divisions of the rose are further subdivided by the ironwork to give nearly 700 panels made up of an estimated 50,000 pieces of glass. The subjects marked with an asterisk in the following list have undergone some restoration.

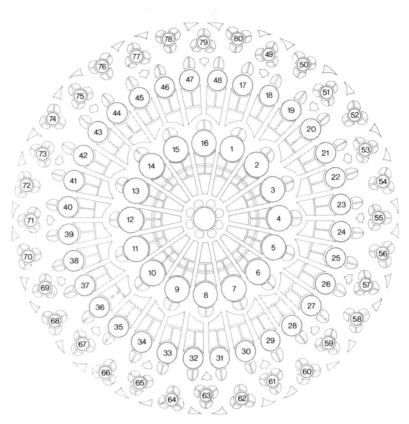

1 Micah (p)
2 Jonas (p)*
3 Malachai (p)*
4 Daniel (p)*
5 Zachariah (p)
6 Ezekiel (p)
7 Pharaoh's Dream*
8 Zephaniah (p)*
9 Elias (p)*
10 Habakuk (p)
11 Jeremiah (p)
12 Nahum (p)
13 Elias (p)*
14 Ageus (p)*
15 Isaiah (p)
16 Hosea (p)
17 Solomon (k)*
18 Jair (j)*
19 Othoniel (j)*
20 Joachaz (k)
21 Hezekiah (k)*
22 Samuel (j)
23 Hely (j)*
24 Ahialon (j)
25 Jeroboam (k)*
26 Asa (k)
27 Joram (k)
28 Ochosias (k)

29 David (k)*
30 Moses (j)
31 Abraham ?*
32 Ahiud ?(j)
33 Nadab (k) (modern panel)
34 Amon (j)*
35 Aod (j) (modern panel)
36 King*
37 Ahaz (k)
38 Joshua (j)*
39 Amasias (k)*
40 Abimelech (j)
41 Jephtha (j)
42 Abdon (j)
43 Josaphat (k)
44 Joas (k)*
45 Judge ?
46 Saul (k)
47 Ozias (k)
48 Deborah (p)*
49 Achias (hp)
50 Zadok (hp)*
51 Eliachim (hp)*
52 Azarias (hp)
53 Manasses (k)
54 Achitob (hp)*
55 Meraioth (hp)
56 Joachaz (k)

57 Saraias (hp)*
58 Aaron (hp)
59 Zedekiah (k)*
60 Heli (hp)
61 Amarias (hp)
62 Achitob (hp)
63 Zadok (hp)
64 Jehoiada (hp)
65 Abiathar (hp)
66 Azarias (hp)
67 Amarias (hp)
68 Jonathus ? (hp)*
69 Jeddoa (hp)*
70 Bocci (hp)*
71 Achab (k)
72 Achimelech (hp)*
73 Jechonias ? (hp)
74 Phineas (hp)
75 Sellum (hp)
76 Ozi (hp)
77 Eliacim ? (hp)
78 Zaharias (hp)
79 Helcias (hp)*
80 Josias (k)*

In the bottom left panels outside is the death of Antichrist. And on the right Antichrist decapitates Elias and Enoch.

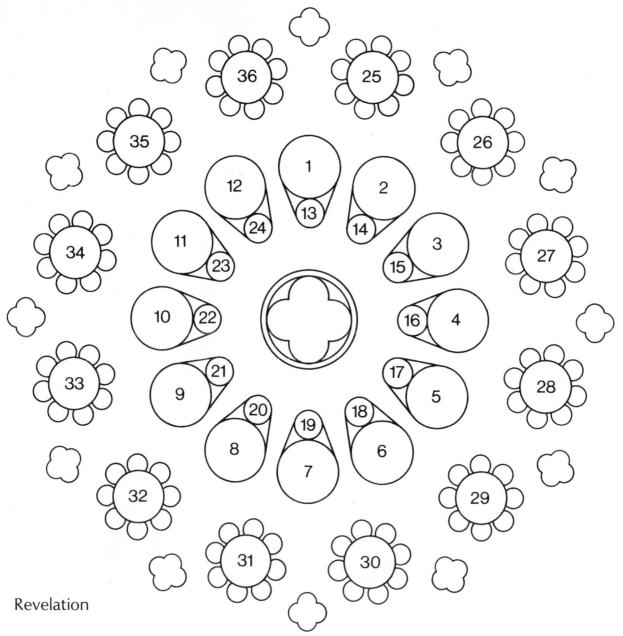

Revelation

CHARTRES WEST [27, 29]

The west rose of Chartres, probably the greatest and most widely acclaimed rose window of all, features the Last Judgment. The end of the world was predicted to occur in 1200 by St Hildegard of Bingen; even though it did not happen, the idea remained prominent in medieval iconography and appears vividly in a number of west rose windows.

Here at Chartres the rose of 1216 portrays Christ at the centre showing the wounds of the Crucifixion. He is surrounded by twelve small lights containing eight angels and seraphim and the four symbols of the Evangelists: The lion of St Mark (22), the bull of St Luke (16), the eagle of St John (13) and the angel of St Matthew (19). Above and below Christ in the outer lights are the souls divided by St Michael (7), the good ascending to the bosom of Abraham (1), while the bad are led off by devils (6 and 30) to another devil who gloats over three souls roasting in the flames of the mouth of hell.

The twelve apostles are arranged in pairs in windows 3, 4, 5, 9, 10, 11, and in 10 St Peter can be identified holding a huge green key. Above Christ are six-winged cherubim carrying the instruments of the Passion, the Cross (36) and the Spear (25). The dead can be seen rising from their tomb, as prophesied by St John in Revelation, and looking to Christ (28, 29, 32, 33). To the left of St Michael are three souls being led off by an angel (8), while an envy-green-faced devil waits for others (7). To complete the scene, angles blow huge curved trumpets (26, 27, 34, 35), and two cherubim, second in rank to the seraphim next to God, with eyes in their wings and containing all knowledge, look down (1, 2).

The 'Bosom of Abraham' and the 'mouth of Hell', which looked at upside-down reveals a veritably devilish face. Both from the Last Judgment west rose at Chartres

The fifteenth-century rose window of the Sainte-Chapelle in Paris is one of the most remarkable Last Judgment windows ever devised. It is a replacement of an earlier thirteenth-century window which would have been contemporary with the building itself, and in the *Très Belles Heures* of the Duc de Berry the Sainte-Chapelle is depicted with this original rose.

The iconographic programme of the existing window is thought to be the same as the original, although the style of the imagery pertains to the fifteenth century. It is not a generalized scheme of Last Judgment as in the case of most other windows (as for example at Chartres), but is an illustration of the main features of the whole of St John's Revelation – from chapter 4 right up to the New Jerusalem of chapter 21.

Of the eighty-five major panels, nine are complete nineteenth-century restorations (marked with an asterisk) and a further nine are fairly extensively restored (double asterisk). The numbering of the panels in the diagram follows the order of the description in Revelation.

1 At the centre is Christ enthroned on a rainbow surrounded by seven golden candlesticks and the seven churches of Asia. In His mouth is the sharp two-edged sword. His hair is white as snow-white wool, His eyes flame like fire and His face like the sun in full strength. Above His right hand are the seven stars (1.11–16).

2 Some of the twenty-four elders with musical instruments (4:4–10).

3 Twenty-four elders together with the angel of St Matthew and the lion of St Mark (4:10).

4 God on his throne with the closed book of seven seals (5:1).

5 More elders, the bull of St Luke and the eagle of St John (5:5).

6 The book is given to the lamb (5:6).

7 The lamb with seven horns and seven eyes opens the book. Note the 4 Evangelists' symbols (5:7).

8 The elders, with harps and phials of perfume, prostrate themselves (5:8–10).

9 Angels chanting (5:8–12).

10 Opening of the first seal, with the angel of Matthew (6:1).

11 A man on a white horse with a bow and crown (6:2).

12 Opening of the second seal, with St Mark (6:3).

13 A man on another horse (not red, as in the text) with a sword to take peace from the earth (6:4).

14 Opening of the third seal, with the bull of St Luke (6:5).

15 Another horseman (his horse not black as in the text) carrying the scales to measure the wheat and barley (6:5).

16 Opening of the fourth seal, with the eagle of St John (6:7).

17 The pale horse with the grotesque figure of Death, armed with a javelin and vipers. He is emerging from the huge green mouth of hell with its red eye. Beneath the horse in the mouth can be seen the 'Venetian' two-toned glass representing the flames (6:8).

18 Opening of the fifth seal (6:9).

19 The souls of the martyrs under the altar of Christ (6:9–10).

20 The souls being arrayed in white robes by angels (6:11).

21 Opening the sixth seal: 'The great day of his wrath'. The ruin created by earthquakes, the sun with a black sackcloth of hair, and the moon turned to blood (6:12–17).

22 Angels holding back the wind from the land and the ships of the sea (7:1).**

23 The multitude before the throne of God, in white robes carrying palms (7:9–12).**

24 The lamb before the throne, between the four sacred living creatures (7:9–12).

25 St John and an elder (7:13).

26 Opening the seventh seal (8:1).

27 The seven angels before God being given seven trumpets (8:2).

28 An angel giving incense to the altar (symbolizing the prayers of the saints) (8:3).

29 The prayers of the saints reaching God (8:4).

30 An angel taking the altar fire and casting it upon the earth (8:5).

31 The sounding of the first trumpet. Hail and fire descend (8:6–7).

32 The second trumpet; a burning mountain descends into the sea (8:8–9).

33 The third trumpet; the star Wormwood falling on to the waters (8:10–11).

34 The fourth trumpet; sun, moon and stars darkening, and the eagle as the angel crying Woe, Woe, written beneath it (8:12–13).

35 The fifth trumpet; the star falls from heaven, the key to the bottomless pit, and a huge locust (9:1–6).

36 Locusts as horses prepared for battle, with heads like men, hair like women and tails like scorpions (9:7–10).

37 Abaddon or Apollyon, the angel of the bottomless pit (9:11).

38 The sixth trumpet (9:13).

39 The four angels of the Euphrates unbound (9:14).

40 Some of the two hundred thousand thousand warriors destroying a third part of humanity (9:16–19).

41 An angel (on a rainbow) giving St John an open book (10:1, 8).

42 The heads of the seven thunders (in a blue cloud) and St John being forbidden to write (10:3–5).

43 St John measuring the Temple of God with a reed (11:1).

44 The two witnesses are put to death – with a turbaned figure looking on (11:3–11).

45 The resurrection of the witnesses and their ascension (into the blue clouds) whilst the lookers-on are amazed (11:11–13).

46 The seventh trumpet; the elders prostrate themselves before the throne (11:15).

47 The woman clothed as the sun, the moon under her feet and twelve stars in her nimbus (12:1).

48 The dragon with seven heads and ten horns and a 'third part of the stars' (12:3–4).

49 'War in heaven'; St Michael conquers the dragon (12:7–8).

50 The dragon persecutes the mother of the man-child; but she has wings with which to fly into the wilderness (12:13–14).

51 The beast with seven heads comes out of the sea (13:1).

52 The dragon gives power and authority to the beast (13:2–3).

53 Adoration of the dragon (13:4).

54 The beast makes war against the saints (13:7).

55 Adoration of the beast (13:8).

56 Another beast with ram-like horns calls down the fire from heaven (13:11–14).

57 The lamb on Mount Sion with the 144,000, redeemed (14:1–5).*

58 The angel announces the hour of Judgment (14:6–7).

59 Two angels, one announcing Babylon is fallen, the other carrying the wine of the wrath of God (14:8–11).*

60 The time of harvest. The son of man with a sickle on a white cloud (note the Venetian glass in the red and white spirals of the pillar on the right) (14:14–16).

61 The gathering of the grapes with the sickle (14:17–18).*

62 The elect singing the song of Moses (15:2–4).*

63 One of the four beasts gives the seven angels the vials of the wrath of God (15:5–7).*

64 The first vial is poured upon the earth (16:2).*

65 The second vial is poured upon the sea – which turns to blood (16:3).

66 The third vial is poured upon the rivers and streams (16:4–6).**

67 The fourth vial is poured upon the sun, scorching men (16:8).**

68 The fifth vial is poured upon the seat of the beast – a *fauteuil Dagobert* – his subjects gnawing their tongues for pain (16:10).

69 The sixth angel pours his vial upon the Euphrates (16:12).*

70 Unclean spirits like frogs, coming out of the mouth of the dragon, subsequently go to the great battlefield of Armageddon (16:13).*

71 The seventh vial is emptied, as a yellow liquid, into the air (16:17).

72 The great earthquake and hailstones as heavy as coins (16:18–21).

73 The seven-headed beast carries the whore of Babylon with a golden cup in her hand (17:3–5).**

74 A mighty angel casting a great millstone into the sea (18:21).

75 'Faithful and true', the king of kings on a white horse, with two other warriors behind (19:11–16).

76 The kings of the earth making war against the beast (19:19–20).

77 The seven-headed beast and the two-horned beast being cast into the lake of fire burning with brimstone (19:20).

78 The angel with the key of the bottomless pit binding the dragon Satan for a thousand years (20:1).

79 The New Jerusalem, coloured fine-gold, an angel at each door, with all manner of stones in the walls and the lamb on the throne in its midst (21:10–24).

God in Majesty is in the right-hand trefoil outside the rose, and opposite is the beast with seven heads. Unfortunately both these panels are extensively restored. The rest of the window contains the royal arms (80, 81, 83) and the initials of Charles VIII (82, 84, 85).

Fallen angel, Lyon north

Source References

1 Quoted by E. Panofsky, *Meaning in the Visual Arts*, London 1970, p. 162.

2 Rodin, *Cathedrals of France*, translated by E. C. Geissbuhler, London 1966, p. 35.

3 C. G. Jung, *Collected Works*, vol. 10, Princeton and London 1964, p. 803.

4 W. McNamara in *Transpersonal Psychology*, London and New York 1975, p. 411.

5 H. Adams, *Mont Saint-Michel and Chartres*, New York 1959, p. 100.

6 K. Clark, *Civilisation*, London and New York 1969, p. 56.

7 D. Macaulay, *Cathedral*, London and New York 1972, p. 77.

8 Quoted in R. L. Poole, *Illustrations of Medieval Thought and Learning*, New York 1962, p. 102.

9 F. Heer, *The Medieval World*, London 1974, p. 112.

10 Ibid., p. 114.

11 N. Haring, 'The Creator and the Creation of the World According to Thierry of Chartres and Clarenbaldus of Arras', *Archives d'histoire doctrinale et littéraire du moyen-âge*, vol. XXII (1955), C. 36, p. 196.

12 J. van der Meulen, 'A Logos Creator at Chartres and its copy', *Journal of the Warburg and Courtauld Institutes*, vol. 29, p. 90.

13 M. M. Marcia, 'The Logos as a Basis for a Doctrine of Divine Providence', *Medieval Studies*, vol. v (1943), pp. 75–101 ; J. M. Parent, *La Doctrine de la Création dans l'école de Chartres*, Toronto 1938.

14 Van der Meulen, op. cit. note 12, p. 88.

15 Rodin, op. cit. note 2, p. 9.

16 Adams, op. cit. note 5, pp. 38–39.

17 See E. Viollet-le-Duc, *Dictionnaire raisonné de l'architecture française du XIe au XVe siècle*, 10 vols. Paris 1854–69.

18 Rodin, op. cit. note 5, p. 56.

19 E. Mâle, *The Gothic Image*, translated by Dora Nussey, New York 1958, p. 14.

20 Ibid., p. 24.

21 Plato, *Timaeus and Critias*, translated by Desmond Lee, Harmondsworth 1965, p. 74.

22 J. K. Wright, *The Geographical Lore of the Time of the Crusades*, New York 1965, p. 265.

23 Mâle, op. cit. note 19, p. 15.

24 K. Critchlow, 'Chartres Maze', in *Architectural Association Quarterly*, vol. 5 no. 2, pp. 11–21.

25 Quoted from E. Wilkins, *The Rose Garden Game*, London and New York 1969, p. 86.

26 Mâle, op. cit. note 19, p. 96.

27 C. G. Jung, *Letters*, vol. 2, Princeton and London 1977, p. 260.

28 H. Whone, *Church, Monastery, Cathedral*. London 1977, p. 62.

29 E. Neumann, *The Great Mother*, Princeton 1963, p. 2290.

30 J. Ruskin, *The Works of John Ruskin*, London 1903–12, vol. 11, p. 22.

31 T. S. Eliot, 'The Dry Salvages', *Four Quartets*, London 1944.

32 T. S. Eliot, 'East Coker', *Four Quartets*, London 1944.

33 J. E. Cirlot, *A Dictionary of Symbols*, London and New York 1962.

34 T. S. Eliot, 'Burnt Norton', *Four Quartets*, London 1944.

35 O. von Simson, *The Gothic Cathedral*, New York 1962, p. 51.

36 Wilkins, op. cit. note 25, p. 113.

37 Adams, op. cit. note 5, pp. 272–73.

38 Wilkins, op. cit. note 25, p. 26.

39 See Critchlow, op. cit. note 24, pp. 11–20.

40 H. Daniel-Rops, *Cathedral and Crusade*, London 1927, p. 607.

41 Quoted in P. Frankl, *The Gothic*, Princeton 1960, p. 175.

42 E. Jung, *The Grail Legend*, London and New York 1961.

43 Ibid., p. 122.

44 Ibid., p. 159.

45 Ibid., p. 100.

46 W. von Eschenbach, *Parzival*, ed. H. M. Mustard, New York 1961, introduction, p. xliv.

47 E. Jung, op. cit. note 42, p. 163.

48 E. Matchett and G. Trevelyan, *Twelve Seats at the Round Table*, London 1976, p. 13.

49 Frankel, op. cit. note 41, p. 175.

50 Quoted by E. Jung, op. cit. note 42, p. 107, referring to L. J. Ringbom, *Graltempel und Paradies*, Stockholm 1951.

51 Ibid., p. 222.

52 Ibid., p. 158.

53 Adams, op. cit. note 5, p. 234.

54 Dante, *The Divine Comedy (3): Paradise*, translated by Dorothy L. Sayers, London and Baltimore 1962, p. 145.

55 Rodin, op. cit. note 2, p. 116.

56 Dante, op. cit. note 54, p. 145.

57 J. James, 'Medieval Geometry', in *Architectural Association Quarterly*, vol. 5, no. 2 (1973), pp. 4–10.

58 Ibid., p. 6.

59 Ibid., p. 9.

60 P. S. Stevens, *Patterns in Nature*, London and New York 1976, p. 161.

61 H. E. Huntley, *The Divine Proportion*, New York 1970.

62 J. Harvey, *The Medieval Architect*, London 1972, p. 220.

63 E. J. Beer, *Die Rose der Kathedrale von Lausanne*, Berne 1952.

Further Reading

Aubert, Marcel, *Le Vitrail français*, Paris 1958

Aubert, Marcel, Louis Grodecki et al. (eds), 'Notre-Dame de Paris and Sainte Chapelle' *Corpus vitrearum medii aevi*, Paris 1959

Barber, Richard William, *The Knight and Chivalry*, Harlow, New York 1970

Child, Heather, and Dorothy Colles, *Christian Symbols Ancient and Modern. A Handbook for Students*, London 1971

Clerval, Jules Alexandre, *Les Ecoles de Chartres au moyen âge (du Ve au XIe siècle)*, Mémoires de la Société Archéologique d'Eure-et-Loir, tome 11, Chartres 1895

Cook, Roger, *The Tree of Life: Symbol of the Centre*, 'Art and Imagination' series, London 1974; publ. as *The Tree of Life: Image for the Cosmos*, 'Art and Cosmos' series, New York 1974

Copleston, Frederick Charles John Paul, *A History of Medieval Philosophy*, London, New York 1972

De Wulf, Maurice, *Philosophy and Civilisation in the Middle Ages*, Princeton 1922

Florival, Ad. de, and Etienne Midoux, *Les Vitraux de la cathédrale de Laon*, Paris 1882–91

Frankl, Paul, *Gothic Architecture*, trs. from the German by Dieter Pevsner, Pelican History of Art, Harmondsworth, Baltimore 1963

Fulcanelli (pseud.), *Les Mystères des Cathédrales: Esoteric Interpretation of the Hermetic Symbols of the Great Work*, trs. from the French by Mary Sworder, 2nd edn, London 1971

Gillet, Louis, *La Cathédrale vivante*, Paris 1936

Grodecki, Louis, *Chartres*, 'Musée des grandes architectures' series, Paris 1963

Harvey, John Hooper, *The Master Builders. Architecture in the Middle Ages*, London 1971, New York 1972

Hopper, Vincent Foster, *Medieval Number Symbolism: its Sources, Meaning and Influence on Thought and Expression*, Columbia University Studies in English and Comparative Literature, no. 132, New York 1969

Huysmans, Joris Karl, *The Cathedral*, trs. from the French by Clara Bell, London, New York 1925

Jung, Carl Gustav, Marie-Louise von Franz et al., *Man and His Symbols*, London 1964, New York 1968

Lafond, Jean, *Le Vitrail*, 'Je sais, je crois' series, Paris 1966

Lee, Lawrence, George Seddon and Francis Stephens (contributing eds), *Stained Glass*, London 1976

Mann, Aldon Taylor (Tad), *The Round Art*, London 1978

Matchett, Edward, *Creative Action: the Making of Meaning in a Complex World*, London 1975; *The Journeys of Nothing in the Land of Everything*, London 1975

Panofsky, Erwin, *Abbot Suger on the Abbey Church of St Denis and its Art Treasures*, Princeton 1946; *Gothic Architecture and Scholasticism*, London, New York 1957

Pevsner, Niklaus, *An Outline of European Architecture*, new edn, Harmondsworth, New York 1948

Phenomenon Publications: *The Phenomenon Book of Calendars*, 1973, 1974, 1976–77, 1977–78, 1978–79, London, various dates

Schmemann, Alexander, *Of Water and the Spirit, Liturgical Study of Baptism*, Crestwood 1974, London 1976

Sencourt, Robert, *The Consecration of Genius. An Essay to Elucidate the Distinctive Significance and Quality of Christian Art by Analysis and Comparison of Certain Masterpieces*, London 1947, Port Washington 1970

Sherril, Charles Hitchcock, *Stained Glass Tours in France*, London, New York 1908

Simson, Otto Georg von, *The Gothic Cathedral. The Origins of Gothic Architecture and the Medieval Concept of Order*, London 1956, Princeton 1973

Sitwell, Sacheverell, *Gothic Europe*, London, New York 1969

Swaan, Wim, *The Gothic Cathedral*, London, New York 1969

Warner, Marina, *Alone of All Her Sex: Cult of the Virgin Mary*, London, New York 1976

Westlake, Nathaniel, *A History of Design in Painted Glass*, London 1879–94

Worringer, Wilhelm, *Form in Gothic*, trs. from the German, London, New York 1964

Zaehner, Robert Charles, *Mysticism, Sacred and Profane. An Enquiry into Some Varieties of Praeternatural Experience*, New York, Oxford 1961

Index

NEWS HOUNDS

THE WACKIEST DOG STORIES
FROM AROUND THE WORLD

Ryan O'Meara

The Lyons Press
Guilford, Connecticut

The Lyons Press is an imprint of The Globe Pequot Press.

Illustrations: Patrick Carlson
Text design: Elizabeth Kingsbury

Library of Congress Cataloging-in-Publication Data
O'Meara, Ryan.
 News Hounds : the wackiest dog stories from around the world / Ryan O'Meara.
    p. cm.
 ISBN 978-1-59921-478-8
 1. Dogs—Anecdotes. I. Title.
 SF426.2.O44 2009
 636.7—dc22
                              2008042710

Printed in the United States of America

10 9 8 7 6 5 4 3 2 1

For Jackson.
A dog that changed my life. A best friend forever.

Contents

Acknowledgments

Thanks must go to all the fine people who helped to research and write about some of the amazing canine stories from around the globe that have made this book possible.

Particular thanks go to:

Kim Bruce, for helping me find the time to dedicate to this entire endeavor.

Lynsey Forrester, for putting the love of dogs into words.

Cenydd Phillips, for hunting down tales of our best friend doing what it does best.

Joy Ward, a fine canine author in her own right, for looking to the stars and rounding up a constellation of heavenly hound stories.

My Mom, Dad, and brother Sean, whose encyclopedic knowledge of dogs helped me immeasurably.

John Williamson, for believing me when I said there were an awful lot of people around the world who love dogs and would love to read about dogs.

Chloe and Mia, a constant inspiration whose romping and frolicking keep my mind focused on what owning dogs is all about—sheer, unadulterated fun!

Jackson, without whom my fantastically rewarding career with canines would never have happened.

Finally, thanks go to all the dogs whose antics made a book like this a joy to put together.

Introduction

Did you ever notice when you blow in a dog's face
he gets mad at you? But when you take him in a
car he sticks his head out the window!
—Steve Bluestone

I love dogs—always have—and I wanted one for as long as
I can remember. It was odd, really, because neither of my
parents were ever particularly "doggie" folks. I guess some
of us are just born with a natural love of dogs. And only dog owners truly understand the power and value of how life enhancing
dogs can be.

We love our furry companions for what they are. They can be funny, serious, intuitive, entertaining, loving, loud, silly, and supportive—and that's just their morning routine! When I turned sixteen I got my first dog, Jackson—a handsome yellow Labrador. Jackson changed my life forever that day.

Given that our friend the dog has managed to plant its paws firmly under the table of mankind for more than fifteen thousand years, it stands to reason dogs have gotten into plenty of scrapes, made plenty of headlines, and affected the lives of millions of people.

News Hounds is a compendium of dogs in the news. Marvel at their magic touch, laugh at their clowning, and prepare to be amazed at their incredible antics. And maybe throw your dog a bone next time it gets into a little trouble in your house. While we're only human, they're simply, well, dogs.

Go Fetch, Fido!

My Labrador retriever had a nervous breakdown. I
kept throwing him a boomerang. —Nick Arnette

The canine companions in our lives often manage to brighten up our days with the odd things they find around our homes. From pulling socks and underwear from bedroom drawers to digging candy out of handbags foolishly left unattended, our pets never cease to amaze us.

But the ability of dogs to find random objects goes far beyond picking up knickknacks at inopportune moments. Our canine companions have been trained to sniff out drugs, explosives, pests, and missing people—all to help keep us safe and for the benefit of our society. Their highly sensitive noses and strong tracking abilities make them excellent partners to accomplish feats that humans simply could not, even if we tried. From locating explosives in the snow to discovering lost hikers in the middle of the woods, many lives would be lost if it weren't for our dogs' help.

Some of these dogs make their discoveries by chance: from significant archaeological treasures and old grenades to stolen medals and even brain tumors. Their extraordinary finds would have gone unnoticed if it weren't for their simple curiosity. Other stories do not have such happy endings; sometimes missing people were found too late, and sometimes dogs helped uncover unidentified corpses—or bits of them—and the mysteries remain unsolved.

Read on to learn about some of the incredible things dogs have unearthed, often on purpose, other times by accident. Be inspired, be amused, and most important, find yet another reason why a lot of us consider dogs to be our best friends.

Pint-sized pup digs up mammoth find

How would you feel if you were walking along your favorite route, minding your own business, when you suddenly came across a serving of your favorite food—and it was twice your size? You'd feel pretty darn good! Well, that's just how a dachshund named Daisy felt. The small dog always loved walks on the beach because of all the wonderful treasures she'd find along the way. But one such lucky find surpassed all others in significance and magnitude: a piece of mammoth bone.

The massive bone, about two million years old and bigger than Daisy herself, was half buried in the sand. She couldn't dig the bone up herself, so instead she waited patiently for her owner, Dennis Smith, to find her and help pull it out.

"She just stood there looking at it, so I went over to see what it was. There was about six inches of it sticking in the sand, so I pulled it out. It was obvious that it was some sort of bone and my first thought was that it might be from something like a mammoth," Dennis said.

Apparently this type of fossil is relatively common in Dunwich, England, where Daisy found it. It had been washed up on the shore from the ocean floor and may have been waiting there for hundreds of years before Daisy discovered it. The mammoth is estimated to have reached an adult weight of sixteen tons—truly enormous compared to Daisy's petite frame.

Daisy does enjoy an occasional lamb bone and may have thought that her hidden find would be the best treat ever. Technically, such a fossil would have no nutritional content left. However, this doesn't mean Daisy can't feel proud of herself: It's every dog's dream to have a bone bigger than it is, and this little dachshund managed to make her dream come true.

Border collie calls for help and saves a life

Not all dogs can get a message across to their owner with a meaningful whine, a pitiful look, or a soft bark. Empathic barks may work for movie star dogs, but in the real world sometimes a written note is much more effective.

In 2003 Robert Sinclair suffered an asthma attack at the age of fifty-five and was left helpless, stranded alone in a farmhouse near Falkirk, Scotland, for seven days without food or water. In a last effort to get help, he wrote a desperate note, placed it in a water bottle, and dropped it from the window. Fortunately for Sinclair, a local border collie named Ben found that bottle and took it back home to his owner.

Ben carried the bottle and its cry for help to Brian Besler, who at first wasn't sure what to make of it. Initially he thought it might have been some kind of joke but realized it was genuine and serious when he saw the name.

"Ben found this bottle and came running up to me with it in his mouth," Besler said. "There was a message in it asking for help. I thought it was a prank until I saw the name—Robert's well known 'round here. It said he was ill, he couldn't breathe right, his chest was clogged up, and he'd run out of food and water."

Ben and Besler came to Sinclair's rescue, alerting police and firefighters who rescued Sinclair from the first floor of the farmhouse and transported him to Falkirk Royal Infirmary. The border collie undoubtedly saved Sinclair's life; the medical staff believe that he wouldn't have lived another two days. It was pure luck that Ben had found the bottle with the message in the first place, but the biggest piece of luck was that Sinclair was still alive once he was found.

Labrador has knack for acquiring ax heads

If it looks like a rock, feels like a rock, and is found among other rocks, there's a small chance that it's actually a Neolithic ax head. Of course, humans walking the same path day after day didn't notice it, but one lucky dog did.

Rowan, a black Labrador, seems to have a knack for noticing special rocks. She managed to unearth an ancient stone ax head, estimated to be six thousand years old, in Aberdeen-shire, Scotland. Her owner, Alec Gordon, had been taking his dogs on their usual walk when Rowan picked up the stone. It was only when they stopped and Rowan dropped the stone on her master's foot that Alec was able to examine it closer.

Alec noticed that the stone had what appeared to be edges, so he gave it to a local archaeologist from the National Trust for Scotland. The archaeologist confirmed that it was indeed an ancient stone ax head. It was an unusual find because nothing from that time period had been discovered previously in the area.

People began to farm the land in the Neolithic age, the period in history the ax is estimated to be from, using axes to clear forests and build their farms.

"I think she [Rowan] should become my honorary assistant," the archaeologist said.

Kuri diffuses explosive situation

It's cold, it's snowing, and it's your job to clear snow from the mountainsides with explosives so that it doesn't cause an avalanche onto the roads below and hurt somebody. The problem is that one of the bags of explosives has fallen, and you can't see it in the snow. If only you could sniff it out or something, right?

In March 2006, a bag of explosives used to clear snow in Snoqualmie Pass, Washington, disappeared while a team from the Department of Transportation was attempting to clear paths. The twenty-five-pound bag of ammonium nitrate fuel oil vanished when the cable it was attached to became unhooked and the bag fell off.

The team faced a conundrum. It couldn't use a snow-blower to work through the snow, because that might set off the explosives, releasing a force equivalent to eighteen pounds of TNT and potentially injuring someone or damaging property. So the workers decided to call in a professional.

Kuri, a border collie from New Zealand, is trained to locate missing people and objects in avalanches. It wasn't the best day to look for something in the snow—the whiteout conditions of the day made seeing anything on or in the snow nearly impossible. That's when having the extremely sensitive and well-trained nose of a dog comes in handy. Kuri managed to sniff out the bag of explosives and was rewarded with lots of affection.

Without dogs like Kuri, bags of explosives that become dislodged can fall down slopes to the roads below and may detonate at inappropriate places or times, damaging property, infrastructure, or severely injuring people. Kuri really saved the day that afternoon.

Human's best friend "nose" it all

We all know that dogs are clever creatures, but it's not often that a dog succeeds where a doctor fails.

Steven Werner, of Brentwood, St. Louis, had been feeling not quite right for a while and had sought medical advice. He could hear a ringing in his ears and often felt nauseated. After a series of tests and no plausible explanation for his ailments, his faithful golden retriever, Wrigley, began to show a great deal of interest in Steven's right ear.

"She kept turning her head around and sniffing my right ear," Steven said. "After a week or so I noticed it was *always* the right ear. It wasn't a sniff sniff, 'Thanks for the bone.' It was, 'What's inside your head?'"

While watching a documentary on cancer-sniffing dogs, Steven wondered if whatever was in his ear that was so captivating to Wrigley might be the cause of his symptoms. An MRI of his brain finally gave Steven the answer he had been looking for. A rare brain tumor, an acoustic neuroma, was growing just behind his right ear—and it was already the size of a ping-pong ball. Doctors had not even suspected that the cause of his symptoms may have been in his head.

The tumor was removed and thankfully was not malignant. If it had continued to grow, it's very likely that Steven would have suffered a stroke or facial paralysis. After the surgery he lost about half his hearing, and parts of his face will continue to sag for a while. And although he could only cry from his left eye, he cried over Wrigley when he thanked her.

Today trials are being conducted to see if dogs can be trained to detect cancers before they are large enough to be found with traditional diagnostic methods. Wrigley no longer sniffs at Steven's right ear and Steven is expected to have an uneventful recovery. Wrigley, on the other hand, is expected to be spoiled for the rest of her life.

Hound helps locate treat-taking bandit

Everyone knows that a dog's natural ability to find something lost is a fairly easy task. However, this talent can even go as far as locating other dogs when they have lost their way.

Bandit, a sixteen-year-old black Labrador from Boothbay Harbor, Maine, would go by himself to visit his neighbors for treats every day. Two weeks after his long-term companion, a husky named Shadow, passed away, Bandit didn't return one afternoon, and his owners became alarmed. He'd had the same routine for years, so for him not to return home was very unusual. His family was worried that he may have wandered off because he was upset and then somehow was unable to find his way back home. They immediately called animal control, not wanting to face losing another pet so soon after losing Shadow.

A search party was quickly organized. The terrain was steep with swampy areas, and considering Bandit's age, his chances of survival were slim if he wasn't found soon. Enter Lincoln: a young bloodhound in training as a rescue dog for the police and practicing for his American Kennel Club Tracking degree.

This was Lincoln's first real search, and as soon as he had Bandit's scent from Bandit's sleeping spot, he rushed off to visit the neighbors, having no idea about the treat excursions. Lincoln followed the trail through bush and mud, leading down to a low, swampy region where weak cries were soon heard. Bandit was rescued, tired but safe, and Lincoln was one step closer to joining the police.

Lincoln was trained by Jean Conte, who was very pleased with his dog's progress, because before then he had only managed to follow a fresh trail. Today, Lincoln is well on his way to performing many more rescues, and Bandit is back to making his daily treat runs.

Lexi lends a (human) hand

Sadly, sometimes the surprising ability of dogs to find missing things comes too late to save lives. Of course it is always tragic to learn of a person's death, but in many cases just knowing the answer can ease the worry and allow the healing process to begin.

In Ohio, a pit bull named Lexi would often go for adventures in the forests around her home, returning later with newfound treasures—balls, sticks, toys, and on one occasion . . . a human hand. Lexi brought the unique play toy home in November 2005, startling her owners when she walked into the garage with it.

"Yeah, Lexi, she always used to run out and get stuff, like

balls and stuff, and bring them back, but this was the first time she brought back a human bone," said Julius Romero, her owner. "We had the garage door open and she had come in with it, and we were like, 'Wow!' We were all flipping out, and it was scary."

Lexi's grim discovery sparked an investigation of the nearby woods, where the rest of the body and some clothing were found. A forensics team analyzed the age of insects found on the body and estimated the time of death was the beginning of that November. Investigators don't think the man they found without one hand had been the victim of foul play, because a vial of insulin was found nearby. It was believed the man was a diabetic who may have had a hyperglycemic or hypoglycemic episode.

While it's a pity that Lexi hadn't managed to find the man while he was still alive, thanks to her his family may finally find out what happened and get some closure.

Dog finds missing Olympic medals

Some days there are lucky finds indeed—precious objects with huge sentimental value, thought to be lost forever. Even more precious are the honest souls, and their dogs, who return these sentimental objects when we least expect it.

Rowing champion James Cracknell had his two Olympic gold medals returned to him after a dog walking by his house found them in a bush. The dog's owner handed the medals to a neighbor to return to the rower.

It had been four weeks since James Cracknell and his wife had returned to their home in London after a romantic dinner to find their home burglarized. The back patio doors, where the burglar was believed to have broken in, were wide open, drawers had been opened, and rooms were ransacked.

Along with the missing gold medals from Sydney and Athens, other valuables had also been taken including a diamond-studded platinum wedding ring valued at about $16,000, three laptops, an iPod, a camera, and several watches, including a limited-edition Adidas watch worth $1,000.

Mark Murphy, of West London, was accused of committing the burglary. A footprint from the scene of the crime matched footwear found in Murphy's bedroom, and when arrested he was wearing the limited-edition Adidas watch. Murphy also had previous convictions for burglary and attempted burglary.

The medals, won at the Sydney 2000 and Athens 2004 Olympics, could have been very valuable to a collector, but an attempt to sell them would have been suspicious, which is probably why they were abandoned close to the Cracknell home. Murphy had not confessed to breaking into the house and so had not revealed where the medals had been thrown. Without the dog's lucky find, the gold medals may not have been recovered.

Chamonix is champion in missing hiker case

Sometimes the keen nose and steadfast determination of a tracking dog is just what is needed to find people who get lost in the woods, before it's too late. Some dogs happen to be in the right place at the right time when they find missing people—others, like Chamonix, have been specially trained for the job.

Shaun Green spent three nights lost in the freezing Rocky Mountains before the search party finally located him. He had planned to go camping for only one night after being dropped off on the National Forest Service land by a friend, but when he didn't return at the expected time the next day, his friend reported him missing.

All-terrain vehicles and dogs were called in for the search party, but they were unable to find Shaun until three days later, when a yellow lab named Chamonix caught the camper's scent. He was found three hundred yards away from the four-wheel-drive road, a mile away from where he was expected to be picked up.

Justin McLean, the dog's owner, was with Chamonix when they first saw Shaun. He called out from one hundred yards away but got no answer from the limp body and feared he may be dead. Shaun was slumped over a rock and initially unresponsive. When Justin called out again and Shaun's leg twitched, he couldn't believe his eyes.

"All of a sudden my heart jumped one hundred feet. Everyone stepped it up a bunch of levels. It was not expected," he said.

Fortunately, Shaun was still alive, through very hypothermic. He was evacuated by helicopter to Longmont United Hospital, where he recovered. Shaun's family was extremely thankful that Chamonix had been able to find him and requested that she get a big hug for doing so.

Family dog helps father find son

It's a terrible nightmare for any loving parent: It's freezing out and your barefoot two-year-old toddler wanders out of the house through the backdoor. That sort of adventure is almost certain to result in death and eternal guilt if the child is not rescued in time.

Fortunately for the family from Kingston, Massachusetts, their yellow Labrador was on hand to help the worried father find his son. Once the child was discovered missing, it took the father and his dog only thirty minutes to find him, huddled on the frozen ground. He was still conscious but very cold.

The child was flown to Boston Medical Center for treatment. When the boy was reported missing, officials from the police and fire departments were called in to assist with the search, in addition to a highly trained K9 tracking unit.

Still, it was the humble family dog that located the child before the trained professionals had even arrived at the scene. Perhaps he had been there to see the toddler wander off, or maybe he had better luck finding him because he already knew the child's scent. Or it simply could've been that special, indescribable bond between a boy and his dog.

Missing person case solved by canine

For a dog there's a fine line between a good bone, important evidence, and a person's remains. Fortunately in Blue's case, he stayed on the right side of that line. The dog and his owner were walking along the edge of some woods one afternoon when Blue suddenly pulled off his leash and ran into the trees. His owner quickly followed and found Blue sniffing around and concentrating hard on something in the leaves.

"It looked like he was messing with a—it looked like a rock, a white-color rock. As I got closer to it I realized it was a human skull, and then I noticed there were other bones laying all around the area," said Blue's owner, who didn't want to be identified but said that it really was Blue who had done all the detective work.

Blue had discovered human remains. Later, the coroner determined that the bones belonged to Brent Lee Ratliff, a twenty-nine-year-old man who had been reported missing during the summer of 2007. He was identified by his dental records. The cause of death was never determined, but at least his family was able to know his fate and give the man a proper burial.

Dog involved in airport drug bust

Drug-sniffing dogs at airports all over the world patrol areas containing baggage, packages, and passengers for illegal imports and dangerous substances. Drugs, explosives, and quarantine risks are routinely sniffed out by dedicated dogs that work hard for the benefit of the community.

Glory, a young black Labrador, is one such dog working hard at Sydney Airport, Australia, to keep unwanted substances out of the country. In 2004 she made a big discovery—a significant importation of cocaine. She had picked out a suitcase as a source of interest, and when the owner of that suitcase was identified and questioned, customs officials found two packages of cocaine strapped to his legs. The Portuguese man faced a fine of up to $750,000 or life in prison.

Drug-sniffing dogs in Australia, like Glory, are trained in Canberra to detect a variety of substances in cargo, mail, vessels, vehicles, packages, bags, and on people. Some of their other successes have been locating cocaine concealed in letters and books, heroin hidden in shampoo bottles, and undeclared explosives on boats. Police are allowed to stop and search anyone a drug-sniffing dog reacts to positively, and have used drug-sniffing dogs to patrol music festivals, major events, and generally reduce the level of drugs available on the street.

Nifty training helps track noxious amphibians

Nifty, a Belgian Malinois, was the first dog ever to be trained to detect the toxic cane toads that are breeding out of control in Australia. The introduced toads are slowly hopping across the continent, damaging ecosystems and killing wildlife with their toxins, or outright eating the animals.

The toads were originally released in Queensland in an attempt to control the cane beetle, but instead of doing its job, the toad spread to the south and to the west and may potentially reach western Australia, on the opposite side of the continent. Many unique and endangered species are threatened by the cane toad's invasion.

That's where Nifty comes in. She has been trained to locate live cane toads, dead cane toads, and cane toad skins in all sorts of environments including buildings, cars, trucks, bushland, and other open areas.

"The dog has to be 'scent associated' to the target odor of cane toad, and as such, a requirement of the dog is that it must be active, agile, and have a strong prey [chase] drive towards toys and other items," said Mark McGowan, minister for the environment at the time of Nifty's training.

If Nifty proves herself to be a success, other dogs will be trained to help prevent the spread of the cane toad to western Australia, a project that already has $2.5 million allocated to it. Unfortunately, cane toads are also poisonous to dogs if licked or eaten—death can result within minutes—and account for sending many dogs to emergency clinics each year.

Grandmother's golden mix and a rescue rookie save the day

Some humans openly confess that they can't live without their dogs. For Pauline Muggleton, that statement couldn't ring truer. Her golden retriever mix, Goldie, stayed by her side all night in near-freezing temperatures until Charlie, a border collie search dog, eventually found the two the next day.

Muggleton had been walking Goldie in Ferndown Common in Dorset County, England, when she suddenly fell and was unable to get up. When she didn't return home that evening, her husband went searching for her. When he couldn't find her, he immediately called the police, who sent a helicopter and a rescue team to look for her.

Faithful Goldie had stayed by Muggleton's side the entire time, keeping her warm even though she was unable to get up.

The next morning Charlie found the pair trying to stay warm and led the search team to them. A few more hours in the cold and Muggleton would not have survived. A helicopter and its heat-detecting equipment couldn't locate her because she was so cold, and paramedics struggled to determine whether Muggleton was alive when they reached her.

For Charlie, Muggleton was his first find as a rescue dog,

and his owner is very happy with his success and the happy endings all around.

Australians have no beef with norm

Australia exports large quantities of beef to many countries around the world and is well known for its "clean green" image when it comes to beef production. To maintain that image, a lot of careful monitoring ensures the meat is as free as possible from contaminants.

Norm, a golden retriever Labrador mix, and his owner, Greg Horrocks, work hard to maintain that reputation by carefully monitoring export meat for drug residues. Norm is highly trained and highly motivated. When inspecting a property for drug contamination, he will follow the smell to its strongest point and frantically scratch at that area. Horrocks can then collect a sample for analysis and give Norm his reward: lots and lots of playtime.

The chemicals that Norm avidly searches for include organochlorides, which in the past were used to control insects that parasitized cattle. They have not been used for many years since high levels in meat caused a temporary ban in Australia on exporting beef to some countries, but because the chemicals last such a long time in the environment, they still cause problems today. Cattle pick up low levels of the drug when they graze on contaminated grass, and the chemicals accumulate to high levels in their body over time.

Norm has been extremely successful in his work, with an accuracy rate of 98 percent and the ability to locate the biggest source of contamination. He has also enjoyed a long working life—having been detecting drugs for five years—and is expected to continue to work for another four or five. He gets weekends off, and with a working day filled with games, that's a pretty good life, doggone it!

Dog finds drugs hidden in hedges

It was an otherwise ordinary day in Bournemouth, in Dorset County, England, when a woman walking her dog came across what was believed to be a drug dealer's dropoff point: Almost $8,000 worth of cocaine was pulled out of the hedge by the dog. The surprised woman quickly phoned the police, who came to seize the shopping bag full of drugs.

"It's hard to speculate why it was there, but perhaps someone was expecting to pick it up later, or perhaps someone dealing on the street was using it. This was an unexpected seizure and we are obviously grateful to the dog walker," said the spokesman for the Dorset police.

Dog rattles planks and saves children

Some time in the early 1900s, a group of young children were playing hide-and-seek in Brooklyn, New York, before the sub-way had been completed. Edward Rowan and Paul Black decided that a hole in the planks covering the tunnel would be the perfect hiding spot, and so they crawled in. Several other children watched.

At the end of the game, Edward and Paul had not reap-peared. The children who had seen the two boys crawl into the tunnel called to them but got no reply. Immediately they sought help from the men working on the subway, who quickly realized that the two kids were in danger. The construction site was hazardous, with poor lighting, dripping sewer pipes, and drying concrete. In a short time one hundred men were search-ing for the boys. Three hours passed, and the fathers of the lost boys arrived to help with the search, with twenty firemen behind them.

It was a long and tiresome search, but a passing detective noticed a big, black stray dog—known as "Bones" by the chil-dren who played with him—scratching at pieces of wood farther along the subway construction. He alerted the other searchers, who pulled up the heavy boards, revealing the two boys, who were unconscious. They were rushed to the hospital.

It was believed that the boys had sought an exit from their hiding place and climbed up a chute that was used to drop supplies to the workers, a plan that wasn't so clever in hind-sight. When they reached the top, they could not get past the wooden planks and probably passed out from the sewer fumes wafting past them. It was very fortunate for them that Bones had been there to sniff them out. Without him, they certainly would not have been found in time.

Dog retrieves real reason to run away

It was a foggy morning when Stefan Bojanowski took his two gundogs for a walk and decided to keep to the road rather than take their usual path. He let them off the leash for a few minutes to play around, when one of them, Jake, ran down a track and out of sight.

Jake returned a few moments later with something in his mouth. Stefan was not worried at first—Jake usually retrieved little treasures he found in the bushes like tin cans and dead birds—but this "treasure" caused him to do a double take and back away.

"I was absolutely terrified. I took a while to convince him to drop it, and then rushed off back up the track to my house," said Stefan, a resident of Plumstead in Norfolk County, England.

It was a rusty hand grenade, and Stefan carefully convinced Jake, a fifteen-year-old Labrador that is blind in one eye, somewhat deaf, and tends to walk unsteadily, to drop his find and come away. Stefan quickly called the police, who called the bomb disposal squad, which destroyed the grenade in a controlled explosion.

Stefan guessed that the grenade was from World War II,

when a practice range had been in the village. Stefan and his dogs still go for walks in the village, but Jake is insured now, thanks to his nose for danger.

Bug-busting dog gives exterminators a run for their money

Dogs are often trained to sniff out drugs, explosives, and lost people, but some dogs have been trained to sniff out termites and other insect pests.

Cody, a plucky little sheltie, is one of them. He sniffs out live termites for his owner, Josh Jones, in return for a game with his favorite Kong toy. Cody is one of fifty termite detection dogs working in the United States, but most of the others are Labradors or beagles.

The faculty of entomology at the University of Florida has conducted research that shows that insect-tracking dogs have an accuracy rate of at least 90 percent, and can be as high as 96 percent—which is a great result. Josh can also be sure that Cody is sniffing out active infestations, because the termites he tracks are live, so he won't accidentally locate wood that has been previously affected by termites if there is no active infestation.

Termite dogs like Cody are expensive to maintain because they need constant training, and many people still don't believe in their phenomenal sense of smell. The public tends to think that the dog is more of an advertising gimmick than a useful tool for the job. That doesn't matter much to Cody, though. For him, his work is just one long play day, starting with termite hide-and-seek followed by playing with his Kong.

Family dog finds unique treasure in garden

There was a flurry of activity in Derby, England, when a family dog walked into its owners' house—carrying a human hand. The hand was unearthed from a backyard and was estimated to have been there for several months. Police found the rest of the male body in another part of the yard and were treating the find as suspicious but did not suspect murder because there was no sign of trauma.

The man was thought to have had no fixed address and spent his time alternating between friends' houses, which may have been the reason nobody had reported him missing. It may not be a happy ending, but without an inquisitive dog, who knows how long the body would have been there waiting to be found?

Rocco sniffs out world-record truffle

Traditionally, dogs and pigs have been used to detect truffles growing underground so that humans can easily dig them up. Pigs are often preferred because they seem to be naturally attracted to the fungus, but it was a dog that found the biggest truffle on record.

Rocco and his owners were searching for truffles near Pisa, Italy, when Rocco knew he was on to something good. The truffle-sniffing dog began sniffing vigorously at a particular patch of dirt and started to dig with great enthusiasm. His owners, Christiano and Luciano Savini, tied him to a tree to prevent him from digging further and damaging the truffle, and they carefully extracted a massive white truffle.

They went to the local police station to have it officially weighed. It was 3.3 pounds, distinctly bigger than the previous champion in *Guinness World Records,* listed at 2.86 pounds. This gigantic truffle was auctioned for $330,000.

One would think that a find this valuable would keep the truffle hunters and Rocco living comfortably for a while, but the money raised at the auction was donated to three charities: one that helps people afflicted with genetic diseases, an organization that helps London street children, and Catholic charities in Macau.

Canine Calamities

*He listens to his trainer real good. He just doesn't
listen to me. I still can't get him to do nothing.*
—Evander Holyfield

The dog. A human's very best of friends. A dog will make us smile, often cry—and sometimes just flat out try to kill us. Whether dogs mean it or not, there are times when their legendary penchant for reckless abandon will cross over from their lives to ours. Sometimes, like us, dogs can have bad days, reminding us all that they are the product of their upbringing and environment. Failure to train a dog can sometimes lead to disaster and tragedy, and at times, their innate desire to get themselves into scrapes and engage in shenanigans leaves a trail of pure mayhem in their merry wake. Only a dog can manage to burn down a house, shoot a man with a shotgun, or generally cause unadulterated chaos, yet retain its popularity and circle of friends. Only a dog!

Live by the gun, die by the gun

During a hunting trip in Lagrangeville, New York, an East Fishkill resident managed to shoot himself in the stomach. After being airlifted to Westchester Medical Center, the hunter succumbed to his extensive injuries. Fortunately for his two hunting companions, he managed to survive long enough to tell law enforcement officers how he got his serious gunshot wound.

After the incident, one of his hunting companions told the media what happened. He said that the wounded man had noticed that his faithful dog had what he believed to be a deer's leg in its mouth. He attempted to take it from the hound's mouth, but the dog was having none of it. In his frustration the hunter used his loaded shotgun as a club, and after swinging wildly and missing the dog, he eventually hit something. Unfortunately, the hard, packed ground he hit caused the shotgun-cum-club to discharge a shot, which hit him in the abdomen, and proved to be fatal.

Mad dog scene creates quite a stir

In July 1922, Joseph Bird raced to his local police precinct, the Gates Avenue Station, in Brooklyn, New York, to inform officers that he thought his dog had gone completely mad. Patrolman Jacob Schreiner captured the dog by the collar and lowered it into a barrel Bird had managed to obtain.

Things could only go downhill from there. The patrolman drew his pistol, aimed at the barrel, and discharged the weapon. The bullet entered the barrel, grazed the dog before exiting the barrel, continued on across the road and, after ricocheting off the curb, hit a twelve-year-old child in the chest. Fortunately for the boy, it was a minor wound, and the officer made sure the boy was fine.

A crowd soon gathered as Patrolman Schreiner returned to the dog in the barrel. His second shot was slightly better; this one entered the barrel, hit the dog's leg, and bounced back—hitting the officer in the foot. Finally, a third shot, at point-blank range, managed to take the sick dog out.

Poor dog fetches arrow—in her side

A golden retriever was taken to a Dayton, Ohio, veterinarian's office after it returned home with an arrow from a hunter's bow. Unlike most retrievers that carry their finds in their mouths, this unfortunate dog carried an arrow that penetrated her side, went under her spine, and protruded from the opposite side of her body.

Because of the dog's coloring, a hunter may have mistaken her for a deer and taken a shot before identifying her. Remarkably, the dog survived what should have been a fatal wound, and managed to make it home before being taken to a veterinarian. Even though this accident had a happy ending, it does underscore the danger dogs face during hunting season. A simple misidentification can have very unhappy results.

Gun dog accidentally guns down owner

Perry Alvin Price III was goose hunting near Stowell, Texas, roughly sixty miles east of Houston. After making a successful shot and downing a goose, he returned to his vehicle to release his gundog. He placed his shotgun in the bed of his pickup truck to free his hands to allow him to open the tailgate and release the hound, but what happened next is anybody's guess. The dog may have stood on the trigger mechanism, causing the gun to discharge. The blast hit the victim in the femoral artery, in his thigh, and he later died from extreme blood loss.

According to Sheriff Joe LaRive, Price's chocolate Labrador, Arthur, left muddy paw prints on the shotgun. "It's the strangest case that I've seen," he said. "We couldn't talk to [the man Price was hunting with] because he was at the front of the truck when he heard the shotgun blast and didn't see what happened."

Dog comes back from the dead!

Cats are renowned for having nine lives. However, a stray female dog named Dosha appears to be blessed with the same attribute!

A car had accidentally hit Dosha, and to save the poor animal from the pain of her extensive injuries, the attending Clearlake, California, police officer decided it would be best to put her out of her misery. The officer shot Dosha in the head and then took her to a local animal control center, where the dog was put in a freezer to await disposal.

Several hours later, animal control interim director Denise Johnson was informed of the incident. But when she went to the freezer she couldn't believe her eyes. "I went to the freezer and found that she was alive and cold," said Johnson. "She had hypothermia and a gunshot wound, but no broken bones from the car accident."

Several animal humane groups are raising funds to pay for her care.

The one time you don't want your dog to fetch

An unconfirmed story dating from July 2002—but reported and talked about around the world soon after—involves a forty-year-old Ukrainian, his dog, and a hand grenade.

The deputy was reported to have taken his working dog out for a walk when he crossed paths with a police academy cadet walking two women home. The cadet pointed out to the deputy that he should not be walking the dog without a leash or muzzle on a public street. The two men began to argue until suddenly the deputy pulled out a hand grenade and threw it at the cadet's feet.

Dogs will be dogs, and the deputy's dog retrieved the grenade and loyally returned it to his master. Needless to say, the owner and his canine companion did not survive the blast.

The princess, the bull terrier, and a right royal ruckus

Princess Anne, of the British royal family, found herself fined and with a criminal record after her dog Dotty bit two children. She appeared in court in November 2002 and was ordered to pay $292 in court costs. District Judge Penelope Hewitt also ordered that Dotty be kept on a leash in public places and that she undergo training.

Dotty injured the children, aged seven and twelve, as they rode their bikes in the park on April 1. The princess and her husband were charged with having a dog that was dangerously out of control in a public place and injured the children.

The court heard from dog psychologist Roger Mugford that the three-year-old dog should not be put down, claiming Dotty was "an utterly placid, playful dog." However, the incident was not the last time the princess would find herself in hot water as a result of a dog attack. One of the queen's own corgis was put to sleep after being savaged by an English bull terrier owned by Princess Anne.

Titch in a stitch after rabbit-chasing romp goes bad

Fire crews in Gloucestershire in southwest England spent six hours attempting to free an energetic little Jack Russell terrier named Titch from a twenty-foot-deep rabbit burrow. In fact, ten men and an industrial digger were needed to help free the dog after he disappeared while chasing rabbits.

"He just dashed off and disappeared. I knew that he couldn't get out, as he's usually quite chicken and wouldn't want to explore on his own," Titch's owner, Penny Parry, explained to officials. "He was whimpering and I could tell that he was stuck . . . so I went home and phoned the fire brigade."

Titch might have been left to his own devices if it turned out that he had gotten trapped in a badger's home. Badgers and their dwellings are protected in the United Kingdom. But, thankfully, luck was on Titch's side.

Disgusting doggy habits are forgiven

Sharing a home with a canine companion is a fulfilling and congenial way of life for most dog owners, but a 2005 survey in the United Kingdom carried out by pet publishing firm K9 Media Ltd. on behalf of a leading pet insurance company revealed there are the odd occasions when Fido's animal instincts can test the tolerance levels of even the most thick-skinned pet lovers.

Of the one thousand owners questioned, 100 percent admitted that their dogs had done something at least once that had shocked, embarrassed, or disgusted them. More than 30 percent of couples claimed to have been interrupted during intimate moments with their partners, or had a romantic mood completely destroyed by their pooch.

Over 96 percent of those surveyed admitted to being quicker to forgive their dogs than a friend or family member for causing them embarrassment.

THE TOP FIVE MOST DISGUSTING DOG HABITS

1. Sniffing or eating dog poop leading to parasitic infestations such as worms. This was deemed the most disgusting dog habit. Eighty-nine percent of owners said they wouldn't be able to tolerate sharing their home if they knew their dog had worms.

2. Chewing underwear. Fifty-five percent of owners claimed to have had to stop their dog from chewing or picking up dirty underwear.

3. The dog-breath belch. Forty-three percent of owners admitted that their dog was capable of producing a particularly pungent burp, normally straight after eating.

4. Indoor urinating. A habit befalling male dogs and apparently affecting 28 percent of all male dog owners, who claim to have discovered a urine stain down the side of a potted plant or a household object at least once.

5. Self-service food—doggy style. This trick tends to be performed by sick dogs, usually preceded by loud series of heaving noises, and then followed by quickly eating the regurgitated food before owners have time to clean up the mess.

Cake-loving canine sets home on fire

Peggy, a rottweiler mix living in Burnley, Lancashire, accidentally turned on an electric stove while reaching for a mouthful of a birthday cake left temptingly on the stovetop in a newly renovated home.

The six-month-old canine made the calamitous cake move that ended up setting the cake box on fire and causing a conflagration that totally gutted the owners' kitchen. The scared puppy fled to the bathroom, where firefighters found her almost dead. Owners Tony and Lorraine Shaw, along with their two children, were not in the house at the time.

According to Tony, rescue workers spent forty-five minutes on the dog as they attempted to revive her. One of the neighbors went over to Peggy to say good-bye, but that's when he felt a slight movement. The dog survived the freak accident.

Doughnut-loving dog burns down house

A doughnut-loving dog spent some serious time in the dog-house after being blamed for starting a house blaze near Vancouver, Canada.

Investigators believe the dog caused the fire after jumping up in an attempt to get to a box of doughnuts on a counter and accidentally switching the stove on in the process. Nobody, including the hapless dog, was injured in the fire, but the fire department said there was about $75,000 worth of damage.

Distracted dog crashes while learning to drive

A woman in Hohhot, the capital of north China's inner Mongolia region, crashed her vehicle after attempting to give her dog a driving lesson.

The woman said her dog enjoyed crouching on the steering wheel and she had noticed that the dog often watched her while she drove around town, so she thought it would be acceptable if she let the dog "have a try."

As the dog's owner operated the accelerator and brake, the dog was encouraged to take care of the very important task of steering the wheel driving. Sadly (and perhaps thankfully), they didn't make it very far before crashing into an oncoming vehicle.

Television host's bulldog becomes part of Maserati mishap

Proving that dogs crashing cars doesn't only happen once, Harvey, a bulldog belonging to British television host Johnny Vaughan, got his head stuck under the glove compartment of the star's Maserati sports car on a trip to the veterinarian's office. Panicked, Vaughan pulled the car over to help his stricken, wrinkly-headed pal.

"As I freed him he jumped onto the accelerator pedal. The car lurched forward and accelerated with me in the passenger seat and Harvey in charge," Vaughan told London newspaper *The Times*. "I remember shouting, 'Stop, Harvey!' It was like a scene from a comedy film. We plowed into a builder's bulk refuse container and were both shaken up."

While no one got hurt, he added that the funniest thing was telling his insurance company that his dog had crashed his sports car. The representative asked him to repeat the story because it seemed so unbelievable. "After all that, they said that I couldn't make a claim, as Harvey wasn't a named driver," Vaughan said.

Queen injured after being bitten by her own dog

Getting stuck between two riled-up royal rovers seems to be something that Her Majesty Queen Elizabeth II is no stranger to. The queen suffered a hand injury following a bite from one of her own beloved corgis. She was spotted wearing a cast on her right hand (one of her much-needed waving hands).

The visible cast stirred up a flurry of speculation that Her Majesty may have been placed on an IV or had recently given blood. She revealed all to guests at a private birthday bash at London's exclusive Ritz Hotel.

"Her Majesty is in robust health," confirmed a Buckingham Palace official.

Why People Need Pet Insurance

A Canadian psychologist is selling a video that
teaches you how to test your dog's IQ. Here's how it
works: If you spend $12.99 for the video, your dog
is smarter than you.—Jay Leno

B ulldogs crashing cars might not entitle owners to an insurance payout, but fortunately for dogs (and for us!) there are now pet insurance services designed specifically to protect everyone from catastrophe. To older generations, the idea of paying a monthly premium to insure the life and health of their pets—and indeed the life and health of the people who encounter their pets—may have seemed like a far-fetched flight of fancy that only the rich, or crazy, would ever latch on to. But as time goes on and our dogs' attraction to random acts of naughtiness shows no sign of abating, we learn more and more that a dog's love of the rock-and-roll lifestyle can sometimes cause unmitigated damage and disaster.

Here are 101 *real* pet insurance claims, as reported from the United Kingdom.

1. Luke, a four-year-old Doberman from the West Midlands, ran up a bill of more than $400 after a thirty-eight-inch leather belt had to be removed from his stomach.

2. Rusty, a bull terrier from Kent, astonished vets after managing to consume a pair of bicycle handlebars.

3. A. Mills of Motherwell, Scotland, whose border collie, Mandy, was not insured, attempted to file a claim on his homeowners insurance after he accidentally peppered poor Mandy with air rifle pellets.

4. Following an attack from a pet Burmese python, Rudy, a German shepherd mix, suffered injuries that cost his owners the princely sum of $4,747 in veterinary fees, plus the loss of the snake.

5. Bayley, a five-year-old dachshund from Hinckley in Leicestershire, required urgent attention after snacking on two of his owner's golf balls.

6. Sian, a three-year-old mongrel from Swansea, broke her leg after falling off a riding lawnmower. This cost Huw Pickering, a retired insurance broker, $3,955 in vet bills.

7. Lee Sidney was left in tears after falling on top of his West Highland terrier, Jake, and fracturing two of the dog's ribs during a barbecue at his rugby club.

8. Lincolnshire couple Ruth and Marco LaBrie were charged $427 by the vet to remove assorted nuts and bolts from the stomach of Nelson, their basset hound.

9. Gemma, a miniature schnauzer from Reading, flirted with danger after swallowing a tube of Super Glue. A second operation was necessary when the stitches came loose.

10. Gentle giant Mal, a Saint Bernard, needed surgery after destroying his gums by trying to clean the remaining bits of potato from a potato peeler at his home in St. Helen's.

11. Thirsty German shepherd Lucy got a nasty gash on the back of her head after a toilet lid slammed down on her.

12. Melanie Silcox had to rush Duke, her six-month-old rottweiler, to the vet after her three-year-old son fed him the contents of an ashtray with his dinner.

13. A dalmatian puppy named Jordan caused trouble for himself in Portsmouth after licking the wet paint from the side of his kennel. Luckily, he only suffered a mild case of poisoning.

14. Charlie, a Yorkshire terrier from North Wales, managed to damage his left eye severely after pulling a cuckoo clock from a wall and onto his face. The cost of his treatment was more than $2,000.

15. "Sam has always been a naughty dog, but he has done nothing like this before," said a woman rendered homeless by her dog's actions. Sam chewed through an empty aerosol can in front of an open fire, igniting a fireball that shot through the property, completely destroying it. No dogs were hurt, but two cats were injured.

16. Firemen in Blackpool spent two hours trying to release Danny, a two-year-old springer spaniel, from underground pipes in a children's park near his home. He got stuck in the same place two weeks later.

17. Leo, a five-year-old Labrador from Harrow in Middlesex, ended up underneath his owner's motorcycle after chewing through the kickstand. Leo didn't regain full mobility for five weeks.

18. Embarrassment was overcome by fear for one dog owner in Devon. He had to drive his Manchester terrier, Alfie, to the vet after the dog ate his wig.

19. Junior, a mixed breed from Warrington, scared the wits out of his owner, Lindsey South. While out walking, Junior ran off to fetch a stick that Lindsey had thrown for him. The dog returned with an unused firework hanging from his mouth.

20. Berry, a ten-month-old collie, suffered in the name of soccer. The family's eight-year-old son had put his Manchester City soccer team's jersey on the dog, inadvertently restricting her walking ability. It was only a matter of time before poor Berry went flying down the stairs, severely hurting her front leg. The cost of her treatment was more than $2,000.

21. Robin Wylde and his dog, Sally, were out walking in a local park when a toy remote-controlled airplane,

which seemingly came out of nowhere, slammed into the side of the dog's head. Sally needed six stitches in her ear.

22. Bad breath was the least of Irish setter Shane's worries. He was treated by vets in Swindon after eating an entire leather shoe.

23. Sky, an eighteen-month-old German shepherd, shocked his owner after chewing through a can of shaving gel and then eating the entire contents. Although he was rushed to the local vet, Sky showed no ill effects.

24. Inquisitive mongrel Stanley, from Whitehaven in Cumbria, needed rescuing after getting his head firmly lodged between two steel railings near a local school. Stanley had escaped and may have been trying to visit the ducks that the school kept as pets.

25. More than $270 was the total cost of treatment required for Ghandi, a Saint Bernard that ate his owner's hair curlers.

26. Unlucky basset hound Willy had two near misses in one day. First he was taken to the vet's after consuming half a container of shoe polish; then later in the day he returned for surgery after swallowing a battery from a television remote control.

27. Because of the time it took his owner to notice they

were missing, Yorkshire terrier Barney had to wait three days before thirty-three jigsaw puzzle pieces were retrieved from his stomach. The X-rays alone cost his owners more than $350.

28. A dalmatian puppy named Lincoln got himself into a dicey situation in his hometown of Leeds. He chewed the head of a Barbie doll and then swallowed it, causing himself a severe stomachache.

29. Sheba, a two-year-old German shepherd from Scarborough, caused havoc recently, when she nearly burned down her house. She stood up on her hind legs to inspect the contents of what turned out to be an empty saucepan. The owner claimed that Sheba must have slid the stove's dial to a high setting, and the woman didn't notice it until it was too late. Nobody was hurt, but the house had the unwanted smell of a burned saucepan for a while.

30. Sue Greenway was shocked to return to an empty parking space after popping into a shop for some flowers. She had left Sooty, her three-year-old black Labrador, in the car. During her absence Sooty somehow managed to release the hand brake, causing the car to roll backward into a recycling bin. Police officers insisted that the hand brake was not fully engaged, while Sue maintains that it must have been Sooty's doing. Sooty suffered a minor leg injury.

31. Vets in north London were astonished to discover more than $1,100 worth of jewelry, including a platinum-plated brooch, inside the stomach of Luther, a four-year-old bull mastiff, after he became lethargic and lost his appetite. Equally astonished were Luther's owners, who did not recognize any of the pieces!

32. Charlie, a thirteen-week-old poodle from Nottingham, amazed his owners and a local vet after being run over by the family's vehicle. "Charlie just sprang up and ran into the garage. I thought we would be scraping him off the drive," said next-door neighbor Jason Webber.

33. Two-year-old poodle Abbey from Leicester did not make the best impression at a street barbecue in 1999. She polished off an entire bowl of punch containing half a bottle of vodka. The vet had to make a house call as no one was sober enough to drive Abbey to the emergency clinic.

34. Legal action was taken against Ross Shepard after it was alleged that his Labrador, Lloyd, had urinated on a six-month-old baby in a stroller. The case never got to court because the child's father could not prove it was Lloyd who committed this most heinous of deeds.

35. Lucy Moore, a sixteen-year-old dog walker from Bristol, thought she had seen the last of Bradley, a German shepherd belonging to her next-door neighbor,

after throwing a stick for him near a local quarry. The traveling stick proved too tempting for Bradley, and he promptly followed it to the bottom of the quarry. The fire brigade had to be called out to help. Unfortunately, the overzealous dog broke a leg for his retrieval efforts.

36. Christmas was ruined for eight-year-old Jason Bellamy from Preston. Jason's twelve months of impeccable behavior earned him, quite rightly, a brand-new video games system. However, family dachshund Glen demonstrated his disgust at receiving an inferior gift (unconfirmed reports suggest it was a squeaky Santa dog toy) by relieving himself on Jason's new present, subsequently invalidating the warranty. This cost Jason's stepfather the better part of $400.

37. Chubby Jack Russell Bobby from West Sussex was showing off his hunting prowess when he managed to get himself firmly lodged in a rabbit hole. He had to be pulled out by his owner.

38. Ralph, a Yorkshire terrier puppy from Mablethorpe, cost owner Aaron Johnson—a self-employed painter and decorator—about $1,380 after he ate the contents of Aaron's wallet.

39. Dog owner Geoff Millburn had to be restrained after his dog was nearly run over by one of the city council's steamrollers.

40. Being late for work seemed rather irrelevant to Ian Russell from Telford after he discovered that his missing car keys had been eaten by his border collie, Ramsey. The vet's invoice came to more than $1,150.

41. Motorist Darren Talbot was $230 poorer after his dog, Lucy, completely ruined his gearshift by chewing it.

42. Old English sheepdog Blake needed urgent attention, not from a vet but from a groomer, after he managed to cover himself with industrial waste.

43. Bedford vets marveled at the lack of damage suffered by Belle, a cocker spaniel that set her tail on fire in her owner's kitchen when she accidentally wagged it through the grill of a gas-powered fire.

44. Chelsea, a fun-loving West Highland terrier, enjoyed a relaxing afternoon in the backyard after consuming the contents of an unattended platter next to the barbecue grill.

45. Gordon, a wirehaired pointer, suffered daffodil poisoning. His treatment cost about $1,000.

46. Slug pellets consumed by a dalmatian on the Isle of Man meant veterinary bills of about $1,350 for the dog's owners.

47. Unlucky Labrador Eddie was hit in the face by a cricket ball. Surgery and treatment cost more than $1,500.

48. Three operations were needed for Yorkshire terrier Manu to rectify stomach problems caused by his vast consumption of seaweed.

49. A short-sighted Doberman from Shropshire needed more than $1,500 worth of treatment after he smashed his way through a patio door window.

50. Treatment for severely lacerated legs caused by a glass-top table that came crashing down on their poor dog cost the owners of Sumo, a Staffordshire bull terrier, more than $2,700.

51. A springer spaniel named Danny suffered severe electrical burns in his mouth after chewing through electrical wiring at his home in Devon. Treatment cost almost $400.

52. Ricky, a Shetland sheepdog from London, suffered painful cuts in his mouth and on his tongue after snacking on his owner's mobile phone.

53. Black Labrador Shadow was completely oblivious to any commotion after wolfing down half a bottle of sleeping pills that had fallen from a shelf in the bathroom. His treatment cost his owner just over $500.

54. Urgent surgery was required for Benji, a bull terrier from Cardiff, after he swallowed a hearing aid. His owner couldn't believe what he was hearing when he was told the cost of surgery would be almost $500.

55. Josh Westly from High Wycombe had to shell out nearly $800 after his dog, Silver, ate a plastic trash-can liner, almost choking herself to death.

56. Cross-breed Andy from Dorset suffered cuts to his mouth after chewing on a very rotten piece of wood.

57. Inquisitive mongrel Ruben was on the wrong end of a horse's hoof at a farm in Northamptonshire, fracturing his jawbone in five places. The cost of resetting his jaw was more than $1,700.

58. A basset hound named Kim was left in severe pain after disturbing a wasp nest in her yard.

59. One-year-old Anakin the akita was poisoned after swallowing an eye solution left on a table. This cost $652 in vet's fees.

60. Too many chocolate coin candies proved costly for the owners of Rosie, a seven-year-old poodle. They had to spend $257 on the day after Christmas to treat the dog for obromine poisoning.

61. After killing and eating a rat—that had eaten rat poison—Freddie, a seventeen-month-old West Highland terrier, was lucky not to have suffered more than he did. Treatment cost just under $200.

62. After falling in his neighbors' vehicle inspection pit, used for examining the underside of cars, elderly terrier Hamish was trapped for three days until the

neighbors returned from a vacation. The poor guy suffered from hypothermia and lung congestion and had damaged his claws trying to scramble out.

63. Poisoned by ingesting the anticoagulant drug warfarin, a farm dog called Casper required a blood transfusion. This cost his owners well over $3,300.

64. Kara, a six-year-old pointer, locked her jaw when bringing in the mail for her owner. She was referred to a specialist, which cost her owners about $1,500.

65. A six-year-old dalmatian from South Shields on Tyneside required surgery costing $2,000 after she pulled a shovel from a hook on the garage wall and it landed on her back.

66. Rupert, a four-year-old greyhound from Sheffield, needed eye surgery after he bit into a guitar string. The string snapped and whipped his face, causing severe lacerations to his cornea.

67. Tess, a four-year-old rough collie, needed close to $1,500 worth of treatment after the gate to her kennel blew shut, hitting her in her face.

68. Jackie Reece's two English springers cost her approximately $767 when they destroyed a neighbor's water feature.

69. It cost just under $1,200 for the owners of Stella, a four-year-old Weimaraner from Basingstoke, to treat

the dog's left eye following a fence collapse in their garden.

70. Kelley, a six-year-old crossbreed from Denby in North Wales, incurred veterinary bills of almost $4,000 to repair her front legs when she knocked over a ladder and toolbox.

71. Delia, a Yorkshire terrier from Liverpool, needed urgent attention after drinking from a freshly bleached toilet. She suffered severe blistering in and around her mouth.

72. When nine-month-old Doberman Ray attempted to chew a broom, lots of bristles got stuck in his gums and throat causing the poor dog to undergo extensive treatment at the vet's and a course of antibiotics to treat the infection.

73. Yorkshire terrier Tiny found himself on the wrong end of a playful bite from a rottweiler. It cost his owner about $1,100 to have Tiny's broken ribs repaired.

74. Border collie Amba has always had an intense fascination with stones. This has cost her owners more than $5,300 to have them removed.

75. Mick, an English springer from Nottinghamshire, had to have pins in his shoulder after he was accidentally hit by a bicycler.

76. A fourteen-month-old cocker spaniel in Lincolnshire managed to completely burn down his owner's house after bringing in a smoldering stick from an unguarded fire outside.

77. Hansel, a nervous German shepherd, was being cared for by family friends when he was taken in for a routine veterinary appointment. Unfortunately, Hansel made a break from his temporary custodians in the vet's parking lot, ran out into the road, and caused a car crash resulting in a medical claim of more than $148,000.

78. When Seeker, a young rottweiler from North Carolina, took herself on a stateside tour of America, her owners ended up paying more than $5,000 in advertising to recover the wandering canine. They collected her from a rescue center in Michigan.

79. Rocking rover Ronnie disappeared from his home in Suffolk and managed to hike his way to Leeds, an amazing canine journey of some two hundred miles.

80. Strange but true: A mixed-breed dog from South Africa had to have a complete, full-sized rugby ball removed from his stomach.

81. Tanika, a crossbreed owned by Danielle and Gavin Reece from Newport in Wales, cost her owners more

than $2,000 when she had to have her leg repaired following a run-in with a large, unseen stone.

82. Sparky, a largely overweight cocker spaniel, had to have treatment for arthritis in his hips. This cost his owner more than $7,000.

83. Benji has a penchant for a little-known culinary delight called coal. His love for the fossil fuel prompts him to collect several pieces and eat them in his bed along with raw potatoes, small stones, and tennis rackets.

84. A Romanian woman named Natasha Bitca was left feeling sore after she was shot in the arm by a mystery gunman. In reality, she had been shot by a dog that accidentally knocked over a hunting rifle.

85. Horst Bachmann's pet dog, Hajo, thought it would be fun to play fetch—with a live World War II hand grenade he had discovered under a bush!

86. Peter Swailes found his puppy, Dino, making mincemeat out of all of the clothes Peter received at Christmas. Total cost of damage: $269. Total value of Peter's not having to wear the sweaters his aunt gave him: priceless.

87. Elsa is a Labrador with an interesting hobby. She enjoys jumping into the trunks of cars, whether or not the trunk in question belongs to her owner or a complete stranger. Elsa doesn't even mind if the trunk is open or not—she'll jump anyway.

88. Shakey, a Great Pyrenees, severely cut his nose after getting too close to the cooler fan on an overhauled refrigerator.

89. Showoff spaniel Tim from Norfolk broke his leg after falling off an unsteady table.

90. Lance, the elderly poodle, wondered why he had to have his feet in bandages. He'd walked through a pile of burning trash and wood, and burned his paws.

91. Welsh couple Lee and Danielle Cort discovered their rottweiler puppy, Fraser, with his head stuck in a cat door. They had to replace the whole door.

92. Debby Wiseman rushed her dog, Paddy, to the vet's in Eastbourne after he began to choke on an acorn.

93. Cassidy wasn't feeling too well after he stepped on a piece of wood with a rusty nail through it. He required stitching and antibiotics.

94. A rottweiler named Bud was subjected to a horrific ordeal after being shot in the head at close range with a shotgun by a gang of unruly street thugs. Amazingly, the lionhearted dog came through the surgery, having had 150 pellets removed from his head. The vet's fee was more than $24,000.

95. Lady, a six-year-old dalmatian, astonished her owners by consuming ten golf balls. She had to have surgery to have them removed and is now muzzled whenever she's taken for a walk on the golf course.

96. Crossbreed Ricki was lucky that he only suffered from shock and a few cuts and bruises, after being thrown from a truck traveling at sixty miles an hour.

97. Monty, an excitable boxer, lived up to his breed's name when he accidentally knocked out a couple of his owner's teeth when jumping up on him.

98. A Labrador–German shepherd mix named Eagle broke his leg after falling from a balcony. He was lucky he wasn't injured more seriously, according to the vet who treated him.

99. Plucky Blue, an Australian cattle dog, suffered puncture wounds after saving his eighty-four-year-old owner from an alligator attack in Florida. What a brave dog!

100. A bull terrier from Sweden proved that dogs quite literally eat into your finances, when he swallowed his owner's bank notes.

101. And finally, one poor dog got struck on the head by a box of Japanese car parts. Yes, he really did think it was raining "Datsun Cogs." Seriously, that probably hurt like hell.

Man's Best Friend

If you can look at a dog and not feel vicarious
excitement and affection, you must be a cat.
—Anonymous

The world is positively rife with tales and news stories about the legendary loyalty of dogs, and the faithfulness of our canine companions is the stuff of myth and legend the world over. From the dog Argos in Homer's *Odyssey,* who waited twenty years for his master's return, though most thought him dead, to the tale of Gelert, who devotedly fought off a wolf to save his master's baby's life—only to be slain mistakenly on his master's return—stories abound of the true devotion of dogs to their human companions and how this devotion can sometimes go wrong or be misread. So how far will our favorite four-legged friends really go to show us their love, and what will they do if they don't think we love them back quite enough?

Faith from the Far East

One of the most endearing tales of dog loyalty comes from Japan. Hachiko, an akita belonging to a Professor Ueno of the University of Tokyo, liked to follow his beloved master everywhere, including to Tokyo's Shibuya railway station in the morning on the professor's way to work. Hachiko would faithfully wait for his master's train every afternoon, ready to join him on the walk home. When Hachiko was less than two years old, Ueno suffered a fatal stroke at work, so he didn't get off the train to meet his faithful friend that day, or ever again.

Day after day, year after year, at the time his master's train was due, Hachiko dutifully waited at the station to meet him, and the stationmaster eventually befriended the dog and even found him a place where he could sleep during the day while he waited. Nine years later, in 1932, as the daily ritual continued, the story was reported in a major Tokyo newspaper after one of Ueno's students became interested in the dog's behavior. Hachiko became a national hero in Japan and an icon of duty and loyalty still remembered to this day.

Hachiko was present at the unveiling of a bronze statue of himself two years later, which was replaced after being melted down during World War II. This new statue still stands at the entrance to the station where the faithful dog used to wait, now named the Hachiko Exit, and his preserved remains are on display at Tokyo's National Science Museum.

The fame of Hachiko continues not only in Japan, where a movie was made of his life in 1987, but throughout the world. *Hachiko: A Dog's Story*, starring Richard Gere, telling the story once again of the dog so unswervingly loyal that he waited in vain for his dead master for eleven years, right up until his own death, is scheduled to begin production in late 2008.

Dog remains loyal to the death

'Til death us do part may be fine for married couples, but for some loyal companions it obviously isn't enough. When loner John "Jake" Devine went walking in his local park in Glasgow, Scotland, one evening with Chico, his four-year-old fawn-colored Staffordshire bull terrier cross, it would be their last walk together. While on their walk Jake was attacked and fatally wounded, his body left lying hidden among the trees.

Loyal Chico stayed with his master faithfully for an estimated four or five days, guarding the entrance to the wooded area where Jake lay and scaring off passersby before eventually returning home and being looked after by a neighbor. Chico's long presence at this particular spot in the park finally alerted some curious onlookers who wondered what had been keeping his attention for so long, thinking that perhaps a litter of puppies may have been under his protection.

They went to investigate after Chico left, finding his master's body. As well as comforting his owner's family, Chico became central to the police appeals for witnesses and later returned with them to the park in an attempt to stir the memories of those who had passed by during his vigil. Despite his breed's reputation for aggression, Chico showed his loyalty and protective instincts toward his owner, staying by his side even after death, and frightening off other people who might have been trying to harm him. Although he couldn't save his master's life, he showed just why Staffordshire bull terriers make such wonderful and loyal family companions and guardians.

Pups stay put with master despite circumstances

Retired U.S. Air Force commander Col. Gary Lorenz disappeared from his Colorado ranch while out with his two golden retrievers, Merry and Pippin. Lorenz, a fighter pilot in Vietnam who had gone through survival training during his time in the air force, was suffering from the early stages of Alzheimer's disease when he disappeared. Although the crashed remains of his all-terrain vehicle were discovered, there was no trace of him or his dogs for a number of days, and an extensive search was launched by local rescue services.

Unfortunately, after the searchers had scaled down their efforts, his body was discovered just a few miles from home nearly a month after he had last been seen. What was remarkable was that the two loyal companions he had taken out with him were still at his side, despite being desperately hungry and dehydrated, having stuck with him as he succumbed to the elements and for a considerable time after. They may have been trying to alert the Lorenz family and rescuers to their location by barking, but the noise was assumed to be coming from a neighbor's property and was not investigated. What is certain is that they stayed with their poor master even when he could no longer call for them, rather than trying to find their way to food and shelter for themselves.

A tale of bravery at the Twin Towers

It isn't just in death that owners can count on their dogs' displays of loyalty, as Omar Eduardo Rivera, a blind computer technician, found out firsthand in the World Trade Center in September 2001. Rivera, like many people who suffer from blindness or other disabilities, had a service dog to assist him, a four-year-old Labrador retriever named Dorado.

So many people have reason to be grateful to their dogs for helping them through life, but on that fateful day Rivera found out just what loyalty really means. Working on the seventy-first floor with his Dorado at his feet when disaster struck, surrounded by the panic and chaos, Rivera resigned himself to his inevitable fate as a blind man unable to negotiate the obstacles and escape from harm.

Out of love and devotion to Dorado, he released his companion as the shattering glass fell around them, and ordered him to go, hoping that he would flee in fear and get out of the damaged tower safely. A few moments later, however, his faithful friend returned to his side to guide him toward the exit, overcoming his own fear in order to help his master. As they worked their way through the confusion and into the stairwell filled with panicking coworkers, the faithful dog and owner paused to help one another. The hero dog spent an hour leading the blind man slowly down the emergency stairwell and out to safety. The escape that had seemed so unlikely back at his desk became a reality, thanks to the devotion of his dog companion. Soon after, the building collapsed.

"I knew then that he loved me as much as I love him," Rivera said.

Alligator attack not enough to kill dog's spirit

Dogs seem willing to risk their lives to protect their owners from many dangers. But when eighty-five-year-old Ruth Gay went for her evening walk outside the home she shared with her daughter and son-in-law in Florida, she had no idea what risks the family's dog, Blue, would take to protect her. Blue was an Australian cattle dog, a strong and hardy breed of keen intelligence, created to endure harsh conditions while fearlessly keeping cattle herds on the move, and often used for guarding duties.

Taking the dog out while her family was out of the house for the evening, she slipped and fell on the wet grass and injured herself. Blue was lying against her as she lay where she fell on the ground, calling out, a mere fifty feet from the banks of a rain-swollen canal where earlier that day three alligators, up to twelve feet in length, had been seen.

Suddenly Blue growled and leaped off into the dark, while his owner could only listen helplessly to the sounds of a confrontation, and the pained yelps of poor Blue. After a while these sounds stopped, and she feared the worst for her loyal friend. When the rest of the family arrived home an hour later, they were greeted by an agitated and soaking-wet Blue, who led them straight to their injured family member who was suffering from a dislocated shoulder and a broken nose. After she had been taken to hospital, medical attention was sought for Blue. He suffered thirty puncture wounds, including one in his stomach that needed to be stapled. If it weren't for the bravery in combat of that faithful family companion, it could have been so much worse for both of them.

Faith in face of sheer horror

Sometimes all we need from a faithful companion is just for them to stay by our side when we are shocked and hurt, keeping us company until help arrives. The importance of this was discovered by James Clock after a horrible car crash on a Connecticut highway that left three people dead and three more injured—including Clock.

He was driving a tractor trailer along Interstate 95—Tiny, his little pit bull terrier, sitting next to him—when a tanker truck carrying diesel fuel lost control and broke through the center barriers, crashing head-on into his vehicle and four other cars. As Clock struggled to free himself and his little companion, the dog refused to leave his side. Tiny ignored the calls of worried onlookers who were trying to get him to jump to safety, away from the smoldering wreckage.

It wasn't until Vincent Gagliari went to the damaged vehicle and managed to get the stressed but friendly Tiny attached to a leash that he would leave. While Tiny seemed to be wanting to find his owner, Gagliari spent the next couple of hours walking around the area to keep the worried dog occupied as rescuers freed Clock and took him to a nearby hospital.

After Gagliari received word that Tiny's worried owner at the hospital was looking for his beloved animal, the two friends were reunited. Tiny was even allowed to stay at the hospital until a friend could come and collect him, and his owner was extremely grateful to Gagliari for the care he had given his furry friend.

Cisco's system for saving his owner's girlfriend

Another pit bull whose worthy efforts to do his duty were much appreciated by his owner was four-year-old Cisco from Wisconsin. When he was taken out to the backyard one night by his owner's girlfriend, Martha Sorrells, who was home alone with him at the time, nothing more than his usual business of relieving himself was expected.

The performance he gave when Sorrells slipped and broke her foot on a patch of ice was a great deal more notable than that, though. As she lay in pain and the cold began to seep through her unseasonably light attire, it dawned on her that nobody would be able to hear her if she called for help from the yard—and that her boyfriend may not be returning for hours. Cisco had no plans to desert her in the cold and answered her pleas for him to help get her back to the house. He pulled hard on his leash and began to drag his unfortunate companion slowly along the ground, not stopping until he had managed to get her all the way to the steps of the house. She was then able to get herself inside to summon assistance, grateful for Cisco's "heroic effort."

English setter drags master to safety

Faithful hunting companion Sadie, an English setter, dragged thirty-six-year-old Michael Miller home to safety from the woods in Newport, Kentucky, when he suffered a heart attack while out searching for quarry.

It was precisely this purpose that Sadie was engaged in—looking for quail on the other side of a wooded hill close to Miller's home—when the crushing pain of heart failure overcame the hunter, who whistled as he fell to the ground to alert the searching Sadie. Unable to walk or maintain a constant level of consciousness, Miller managed to hold on to his loyal companion's collar while she dragged him through difficult terrain. She struggled all the way back to their home despite the fact that her weight was only one-quarter of her owner's, and once they had reached the door, Sadie stayed at his side, calling his wife to her unconscious husband.

After major heart surgery and his subsequent recovery, Miller said, "I certainly would have died in those woods if Sadie had not been with me."

September 11th brings out the best in canine heroes

In the wake of the terrorist attacks on the World Trade Center, some 250 search-and-rescue dogs were sent in. Of those, the earliest to arrive on the scene was a golden retriever named Bear who got there with his handler just thirty-eight minutes after the second plane hit and continued to work the west side of the site alone for the first six or seven hours.

During eighteen-hour shifts at the site immediately following the attack, Bear was lowered into pockets of debris, among glass and rubble, in the search for the living and the dead. He was the only rescue dog to find a survivor in the wreckage, and he had the dubious honor of finding the remains of New York City Fire Department Chief Peter Canci.

Unfortunately, Bear lost his own life as a result of time spent at ground zero—a wound he suffered on the first night eventually became cancerous. He passed away on September 23, 2003, and was honored with a fireman's funeral.

Instinctive loyalty aids escape

Linda McDermott has two faithful rottweilers, but their loyalty proved to be an unexpected problem when she got hopelessly stuck in a muddy peat bog while out on a walk with them at Waldridge Fell, a park in Chester-le-Street, County Durham, England. Her companions stayed with her as she waited for help.

When members of the local fire brigade arrived, they were unable to get to the poor woman. Her trusty dogs, true to their instinct to look after and protect their owner, made it clear with their growls that they were not going to allow these strangers to "attack" their mistress as she struggled, ignoring her pleas to let her rescuers past. "We just couldn't get anywhere near her," fire station manager Peter Hewitson said.

Luckily, more help arrived, this time in the form of the trapped woman's friend—a face the dogs knew—who was armed with a package of cookies! The dogs were coaxed across a nearby stream, where a park warden helped her to lead them away so their owner could be freed.

No beauty sleep in this household

Noel Hanley, a retiree from Cork in Ireland, is certainly ecstatic that his dog jumps on beds. His four-year-old King Charles spaniel, Beauty, suddenly jumped onto his bed in the middle of the night while he was fast asleep and began licking him and tearing at his pajamas, causing such a fuss that the little dog's out-of-character antics alerted Hanley's wife, Rita, who came to see what was going on.

Unable to rouse her husband from his slumber, she immediately called for help. The lucky dog owner was suffering from a dangerously low blood-sugar level, although he was not a known diabetic, and had slipped into a deep coma in his sleep.

Dr. Mortimer O'Connor, who treated Hanley, said this was the first time a dog was known to have detected this problem in an owner with no history of diabetes. It is not yet fully understood exactly how a dog—even a King Charles spaniel that is bred to be a close, loving, and intelligent human companion—could be aware of such problems.

Beauty proved that such things are possible, and her frantic actions, at odds with her normally placid nature, certainly saved her master's life. Today, Noel Hanley is still glad to be looked after by Beauty, who continues to act strangely whenever she senses he could be in danger.

Speedy thinking on dog's part saves owner

Sometimes things happen so quickly and with such dramatic results that change the immediate future of all participants, we can't know for certain whether a dog commits an act of selfless honor and loyalty or whether a dog's instinct to protect its own was so strong that it sacrifices itself. Such has been the case with many people around the world, including a young man in Wake Forest, North Carolina, who had reason to be grateful to his faithful Labrador retriever, even though she was not a specially trained assistance dog.

As fifteen-year-old George Compeaux Jr. started to cross a road not far from where he lived, his female black Labrador may well have noticed what George did not: the truck that was rumbling toward him. Whether her actions were a deliberate and willful assertion of her true, unswerving faithfulness will never be known for sure, but what is certain is that she chose that exact moment to jump up at George, knocking him out of the path of the oncoming vehicle. Unfortunately, that put her directly into the truck's path and she was killed instantly, but she was hailed a hero by her family for making the ultimate sacrifice to save her best friend.

Burgers, barking, and a burned-out kitchen

Saving silly humans from the results of their own moments of unobservant foolishness is something that our loyal four-legged family members seem to excel at. When nineteen-year-old Carl McMahon made the probably less-than-wise decision to cook himself some burgers at 2:30 a.m. after a night out drinking with his friends, it was only the devotion of his rottweiler companion, Lennox, that saved him from his own stupidity.

McMahon was staying at his sister Kathy's house in Accrington in northern England at the time, while he and his girlfriend cooled off after an argument. Upstairs, his sisters and their children were alerted to danger by the sound of the smoke alarm and the sudden loss of electricity. They were able to escape through thick black smoke that was generated by a fire in the kitchen. Carl himself had seen the smoke coming from the room and had gone to investigate just as the oven's glass door exploded in his face, knocking him unconscious.

A friend, who was also in the house, tried to get Carl out but wasn't able to find him in the fume-filled darkness. When the firemen arrived they took over the search wearing special breathing apparatus, but it didn't take them long. Lennox had stayed with his master throughout his ordeal, and his yelps and cries led the firefighters straight to where McMahon lay, enabling them to quickly get him out of the choking atmosphere and to the medical attention he so urgently needed. Once again, a faithful pet rottweiler followed his instincts to look after his master in a situation he could so easily have escaped from to protect himself, and in doing so he allowed such a quick rescue it probably saved his master's life.

Although the fire damaged the kitchen quite badly, McMahon's sister's house survived the experience. "I definitely won't be able to do any cooking here again," McMahon said. "I *know* that!"

Dalmatian alerts family to fire

Sometimes canines' sensitivity to danger and the instinct to protect their "pack" of humans rather than to seek escape to save themselves can save our own lives. A dalmatian named Kiwi ultimately paid the price for her devotion to her caretakers, the Stanfills, when fire engulfed their home in Tennessee.

Acting on instinct, Kiwi ran over to her owners' bed to wake them as the fire and thick black smoke rapidly filled the house. They escaped unharmed with Kiwi and their other dog, but unfortunately poor Kiwi had breathed in so much of the choking fumes in the time she had spent making sure that her family was safe that she did not survive. She disappeared after the family got out of the house, and her body was found about an hour later. When her family needed her help and sense of devotion the most, she came through for them, and without a doubt saved all of their lives.

A dog "nose" when danger is present

Not as easy to identify as a ferocious house fire, carbon monoxide—hidden, silent, and odorless—was putting the Walderbach family in danger at their home in Iowa. When Janet Walderbach tried to comfort the children after they awoke feeling mysteriously ill, she too began to suffer the effects of the invisible gas, falling unconscious.

Thankfully, her daughter's faithful German shepherd, Shelby, was there to help. The attentive Shelby managed to wake Janet up again and then proceeded to wake Janet's husband, John. They mistook her obvious stress and nervousness as a request to be allowed to go out, but her continuing odd behavior made them realize something was wrong, allowing them to escape the fumes, which had by then built up to a very dangerous level.

If Shelby had not been so persistent and conscientious, the building levels of the gas would have certainly been life threatening. For her loyal service to the family, she was given a Dog Hero of the Year award by a pet food manufacturer. After hospital treatment, all of the occupants of the house made a full recovery.

Hero dog left homeless

Sadly, not all canine loyalty and heroism through dangerous situations ends up being rewarded with a happy ending of continued companionship with those they have dutifully saved. Poor B. J., a pit bull cross, was left somewhat out in the cold after he alerted his owner, Kimberly Frye, and her boyfriend that there was a fire in their house in Fulton, Columbia.

The human occupants had been foolish enough to neglect their responsibility to themselves and their dog by failing to make sure their smoke alarms were working. It was left to B. J. to take on the role of a fire-warning system. Hearing his noisy bark-siren the couple escaped the inferno just in time.

Unfortunately, despite B. J.'s best efforts, Frye and her boyfriend suffered serious burns and, therefore, could no longer care for their dog. B. J. was placed in an animal rescue shelter.

"He saved his family and now, due to circumstances out of his control, he's become a homeless dog," animal control officer Laura Schroer said. "We need to find him a home."

Pop princess discovers dogs really are man's best friend

Sometimes our dog's devotion can turn from loyalty to jealousy when we decide to change the routine of our living situation by bringing another person into the home. Australian pop icon Kylie Minogue experienced this bitter streak when she encountered her former partner Olivier Martinez's Rhodesian ridgeback dog, named Sheba.

The ridgeback is a large and powerful hunting breed that originated in South Africa and is still often used for tracking game. It also has a reputation for being unfriendly with new people. Not only did she show her breed's instinctive aloofness with her owner's new friend, but Sheba wasn't pleased when the singer moved into Martinez's Paris apartment. It was *her* space and she had no intention of sharing her owner's affection.

Sheba would get even by stealing shoes from Minogue's wardrobe and eating them. It took a while for Sheba to warm up to Minogue, but eventually she did. And when Minogue was diagnosed with breast cancer, Sheba supported her with warmth and cuddles when she was at her lowest. The bond between the two became a very important comfort when it was most needed, and after Minogue's recovery and subsequent split from Martinez, it was Sheba that Minogue referred to as "the love of my life."

Dog shows no respect for King's teddy

It isn't just new family members that can cause our dogs to have jealous pangs, as security guard Greg West recently discovered when he was on duty at an exhibition of toys at Wookey Hole Caves in Wells, England. At the insistence of the insurance company, experienced guard dog Barney accompanied West as he stayed close to the rare and valuable collection.

Barney was a Doberman pinscher, a breed originating in Germany in the nineteenth century. Bred to be the perfect personal protection dogs, Dobermans have been used around the world as reliable dogs for all kinds of security work. Barney, however, proved not to be quite such a dependable sentinel when he took exception to his coworker's stroking the head of one particularly rare Steiff teddy bear named Mabel.

Like Barney's ancestors, Mabel had also originated in Germany, in 1909, and was said to have previously belonged to global icon Elvis Presley. She was a unique piece of Elvis memorabilia—and worth an estimated $75,000—but that didn't stop Barney from a berserk and frenzied attack on the poor, unfortunate, elderly teddy, ripping off her head and pulling out her stuffing.

This began a teddy killing spree involving about one hundred members of the collection, some of which had what were referred to as "quite devastating injuries." Understandably, after this night of jealous teddy terror, Barney was not invited back to continue his role in charge of security of the toy collection.

Blind racer makes history with help of dogs

Some people rely heavily on their canine companions not only for company but to keep them safe in dangerous circumstances, and none more so than those who choose to spend time being pulled around trails covered with ice and snow at high speeds by teams of sled dogs. Mushers depend entirely on their companions' instincts to detect problems and potential threats, such as hidden streams beneath the snow, long before they know about them. The trust and loyalty these teams of dogs have toward their handler has to be complete and unquestioning to enable humans and dogs to travel effectively together and arrive safely at their destination.

This is especially true in the case of Rachael Scdoris, the youngest person ever to complete a five-hundred-mile sled race. Rachael, who celebrated her sixteenth birthday during that race, has little eyesight and is considered legally blind. She has been relying on the special bond of devotion with her dogs to help her throughout most of her life, and in 2005, thanks to her own spirit and determination, along with the devotion of her trustworthy team of dogs, she completed the grueling one-thousand-mile Iditarod Trail Sled Dog Race in Alaska, the first legally blind person to do so. She has managed to compete with her dogs at the highest level in the sport, tasting adventure that most people with full sight will never be able to experience.

Dog in wolf's clothing becomes hero

An elderly couple in New York state were rescued by their dog during a snowstorm that felled a tree in front of the Enchanted Forest Wildlife Sanctuary—which the couple own and operate—trapping them outside in the cold.

On that fateful night Norman and Eve Fertig had gone out to check on the animals in their care when the snowstorm struck. Not clothed or equipped for the conditions or the situation at hand, they struggled to find a way back into the sanctuary and their house but were unable to climb over the great obstacle, and ultimately decided to huddle together for warmth. But Shana, the couple's seven-year-old German shepherd and timber wolf mix, took matters into her own paws, and began to dig a tunnel under the tree. When her emergency escape route was complete, she pulled, carried, and dragged her grateful owners through the tunnel to the house.

Once inside the house, which lacked electricity because of the storm, Shana lay with her owners and kept them warm and alive until help came from the local fire department. Her owners were determined to return her devotion and refused to leave and head for safe shelter with the firefighters when they said that Shana would have to be left behind. They stayed in the house without power for three days—while trees were cleared from outside and food and water were brought to them—until the shelter at the firehouse was emptied of enough people that they could all go there together.

Dog becomes prisoner of war

A stray bulldog terrier crossbreed called Soochow proved that you really don't need to be pure of blood and born into a noble family or a wealthy home to be a faithful and supportive companion to humans.

The little stray became a marine company's mascot during World War II after following one of the company's privates around while on duty in Shanghai, adopting his chosen human to such an impressive degree that the private broke the rules and smuggled him into the barracks. Sticking with his new owner and his comrades through their terrible combat experiences, Soochow was captured by the Japanese along with his marine buddies and spent nearly three years cooped up in prisoner-of-war camps at their side.

For his devotion to his comrades in arms, Soochow was awarded several medals and ribbons, and in October 1946 a birthday parade was held in his honor at his retirement home in San Diego, the Marine Corps Recruit Depot. The Marines' slogan Semper Fi (Always Faithful) sums up the character of this particular little soldier, despite his humble, rough beginning on the streets of Shanghai.

Dogs of war display bravery of soldiers

Even in wartime most stories of loyalty and devotion are the day-to-day tales of the companionship that enriches the lives of people the world over who chose to share their homes and working lives with dogs. In 1989 a memorial service was held for another stray canine crossbreed that ended up a companion to servicemen on active duty.

Sinbad was a notorious drinker and hell-raiser who spent the best seventy-seven dog years of his life aboard the U.S. Coast Guard cutter *Campbell*. He traveled the world with his crewmates and accompanied them through their toils of war and their inevitable onboard drinking sessions. He kept their spirits up with his devoted companionship, even appearing with his life jacket at roll call to answer his name with a bark, and his shipmates felt safe and protected by his presence.

He had his faults, and like many sailors, he knew how to enjoy his time between duties—being found drunk or hung over on a number of occasions—but the memory of such a wonderful friend moved some of his former comrades-in-arms to tears at the belated ceremony held in his honor, nearly forty years after he passed away.

Honey finds help for her owner

The loyalty of dogs is the stuff of legend, and canines like Honey that epitomize this trait occasionally step forward. The bond they share with their owners goes to the next level in times of need.

Michael Bosch had brought Honey, a cocker spaniel, into his life two weeks previously from the Marin Humane Society in Novato, California, by formally adopting her. She had been surrendered by an owner who couldn't care for her, and when Michael saw her for the first time, he knew she would change his life, but he didn't expect her to actually save it.

It was a sunny morning when Michael was backing his SUV out of his driveway in the remote woods of Marin County, so sunny that the sun blinded him. He backed his SUV just a little too far, and it crashed down a thirty-foot ravine, flipping over, crushing his leg and trapping him.

Things looked bad, but fortunately for Michael, Honey was in her crate in the back of the car, unharmed. They were stuck like that for seven hours before Michael managed to free Honey from the crate. Nobody had seen the car go down, so nobody knew they were in trouble.

Honey roamed the woods for almost half a mile before reaching a neighbor's house and getting his attention. She led him back to the edge of the ravine, where the car could be seen below. The neighbor called fire crews, who arrived just in time—if he had been stuck there much longer, Michael would probably have lost his leg.

Chihuahua tackles rattlesnake to protect baby

A tiny Chihuahua named Zoey was hailed a hero after battling a venomous rattlesnake in an effort to protect her owner's infant grandchild. The little dog leaped in front of the child and took the full force of the attack herself after the serpent struck out at the baby boy.

The youngster had been splashing his hands in a birdbath at his grandparents' Colorado home when the snake attacked. "She [Zoey] got in between Booker [the grandchild] and the snake, and that's when I heard her yipe," said Monty Long, the child's grandfather.

Zoey required extensive veterinary treatment and the prognosis was not promising, but the brave dog made a full recovery, battling and overcoming the ill effects of the deadly toxin.

5

Pup-pourri

If you think dogs can't count, try putting three dog
biscuits in your pocket and then giving Fido only
two of them. —Phil Pastoret

When dogs first came to the attention of mankind thousands of years ago, who could have dreamed of the impact they'd make on our lives and society in general.

They share so much with us, and in many ways their lifestyles and habits can reflect our own. This means that dogs are as capable as we are of getting into the sort of situations that make them second only to man in the newsworthy stakes.

Whether they are heroic dogs, funny dogs, tragic dogs, or amazing dogs, they all share one thing in common; we'll never tire of hearing and reading about their incredible antics. Here we examine just some of the reasons why dogs have a habit for hitting the headlines.

Viagra saves dog's life

A three-year-old border collie has an improved life thanks to the erectile dysfunction drug Viagra. The dog, named Talisker, suffered from an enlarged heart and a lung infection. According to owner Lesley Strong, of Northhamptonshire, England, he would lose consciousness when he became excited, because his body could not pump blood fast enough. Without treatment, she was told he could die.

However, Strong's vet recommended that Talisker undergo treatment with a drug similar in properties to Viagra, which could improve blood flow to the heart.

"I was shocked when the vet recommended Viagra, and it raised a few eyebrows when I first collected the prescription—but it's given Talisker a new lease on life," said Strong.

German police dogs wear shoes

German Police K9s are outfitted with their own protective footwear to protect their paws from injury during the course of their work. Officials of the city of Düsseldorf have taken the decision to protect the paws of the canines, a team of twenty Belgian shepherds that are constantly exposed to the risk of damaging their pads on broken bottles and other dangerous debris as they go about their police work.

The dogs are being trained to get used to wearing the shoes as they work, and they will be expected to wear the shoes while out with the force on normal patrols, which involve protection work and narcotics detection.

"There are many people and sometimes in the late evening or during the night we have drunken people and they throw their bottles or glasses away," Gunter Herring, a police spokesman told the BBC News. "Now we are conditioning the dogs to wearing their shoes to protect them in these areas from the glass."

Socialite Paris Hilton intends to resurrect dead dogs

Paris Hilton revealed in 2007 that she intends to have her two dogs cryogenically frozen upon their deaths in order to resurrect them later on in life. The hotel heiress and party girl said that it would be "cool" to meet up with her dogs in the future. She is also planning to be cryogenically frozen herself, to be brought back to life when the technology becomes available, and it has been reported that she has invested a large sum of money in the world's biggest suspended animation cemetery, Cryonics Institute.

Company gives dogs a leg up by manufacturing artificial canine limbs

A British scientist set up a business in 2005 manufacturing artificial limbs for dogs, a venture designed to enhance the lives of family pets that have suffered the loss of a leg.

University of Salford's Glyn Heath set up the unique service by designing, manufacturing, and fitting prosthetic body parts. The ex-zoologist successfully fitted limbs on fifteen amputee dogs as part of an initial research project and even solved a paraplegic rat's mobility problems by building a wheeled chariot for it to push itself along in.

"What we're able to do is a feat of engineering and completely unique in Britain," he said. "Helping disabled animals to walk and move about again has the potential to improve the lives of pets, preserve gene pools, and support breeding programs."

Britney Spears wants to be buried with her dog

If Paris intends to be brought back to live alongside her permafrozen dogs, her pop contemporary Britney Spears revealed she has no such plans to be resurrected, and instead wishes to be buried with her dog, Lucky. She claimed to love her dog so much that she wants a burial like the ancient Egyptians had, in which pet dogs are buried with their masters.

"You know how the Pharaohs used to get buried with things they loved? I want to do that with Lucky. She should be laid to rest with me when the time comes," Spears reportedly said. Britney neglected to mention what she plans to do with the Chihuahua should they not die at exactly the same time, which given the fact that Chihuahuas live approximately sixty years less than humans, is quite likely.

TV toilet paper icon inducted into world-famous wax museum

It's an honor usually granted to only the most famous faces

in show business, and a sure sign that someone has really made it. But by public demand, an advertising icon moved in to Madame Tussauds in London, sharing a home with the likes of Kylie Minogue, Brad Pitt, and even Madonna.

The Andrex puppy is a Labrador used to promote toilet paper in the United Kingdom, and the fictional, eternally eight-week-old puppy attended his own induction ceremony, coming nose to nose with his waxwork lookalike. The Andrex puppy emerged the winner in a poll to name the United Kingdom's favorite fictional TV character, subsequently securing his place in the illustrious Madame Tussauds wax museum.

Iranian officials build dog prison to stop "un-Islamic behavior"

In 2007 Iranian police created a dog "prison" in the nation's capital, Tehran. As part of a crackdown on so-called un-Islamic behavior, city officials were said to be removing dogs from the care of their owners and placing them in holding pens. The crackdown initially targeted young men and women who were said to be dressed inappropriately, but dog owners were also targeted.

Dog ownership is widely debated in Islam, with many Muslims citing it as dirty and insulting to the values of the religion. Some clerics have denounced dog ownership as "morally depraved," although other Muslims have said it is only the "wet" areas of a dog, such as its nose or tongue, that could be considered anti-Islamic.

Despite harassment and fines from officials, dog ownership has grown in popularity in Iran, particularly among young
people. One young person whose dog was removed was
twenty-three-year-old Banafshe, who claims she was walking
her puppy when Iranian police snatched the dog and put it into
the makeshift jail. Her "crime" was walking the dog in public.

"They said, 'We want to get rid of Western culture.' They said,
'You live in an Islamic country; it's not right to have dogs. Are you
not Islamic? Why does your family allow you to own a dog?' They
insulted me. They even told me that they hope my dog will die,"
she told Radio Farda, an American government–funded station
that broadcasts to Central Asia and the Middle East.

Electronics giant donates suicide bomb detection dog to work in Iraq

A Labrador retriever called Pyeonghwa, which means peace
in Korean, was donated to work as a suicide bomb detector in
war-torn Iraq in 2005. The Labrador, trained in Korea by specialized police officers from the United Kingdom, was donated by
electronics giant Samsung to aid allied forces in their attempts
to instill order in the country.

She was the first dog in history to be trained for the specific purpose of preventing would-be suicide bombers from
detonating their devices. She was specially taught to detect the
explosive substances in self-detonating bombs used by suicide
bombers.

While most bomb-detecting dogs are trained to find concealed explosives, Pyeonghwa was trained to spot combination of human body language and explosives located on a person's body. She was trained to pick up facial signals and body language and then covertly investigate any suspicious people, giving a passive signal to her handler, who would then tackle the potential bomber.

Famous artist fond of dogs

For Pablo Picasso, a walk along the Seine River in Paris was made justifiable by the presence of his first dog, an Afghan hound called Kazbek, with whom Picasso had gone through the war. Picasso would tell friends he needed to take in the beauty of the city, and he owed a debt of gratitude to Kazbek for giving him the motivation to do so. Picasso owned many more dogs after Kazbek, including an incontinent dalmatian that appeared in some of his later works.

Canines need to be cautious of identity theft

A champion poodle became the unlikely victim of the growing crime of identity theft all around the world. Crucial pedigree information about the poor victim, named Blue, was stolen from a Web site by an unscrupulous dog owner who went on to use the impressive stats and figures on his own dogs to hike up their price.

The con man was caught when he tried to claim that the pedigreed poodle Blue, whose registered name is Afonwen Welch Fusilier, had had a litter of puppies. The thief made one fundamental error: Afonwen Welch Fusilier is a male.

Blue's genuine puppies can have a value of up to $2,000, but the ones being passed off by the fraud were not guaranteed to be from good, healthy stock. The con man, who also used the address of a Glasgow graveyard to avoid detection, was caught when a vigilant dog buyer sensed something was wrong.

A west London woman became suspicious after telephoning the trickster and being told she'd need to pay cash up front. She Googled the name of the dog and managed to locate the real owner of Afonwen Welch Fusilier.

Real owner Lynne Day told *The Mirror* newspaper in England, "Anybody buying a dog on the Internet needs to be aware of this. Some will send cash up front. The thing that upsets me most is that a crime was committed in my name."

Smoking ban gives collie wobbles

A nicotine-loving canine with a cigarette habit was said to be suffering withdrawal symptoms following the United Kingdom's ban on smoking in public houses. Sarah and John Taylor, who are both smokers themselves, say they have been taking their dog, Archie, to the local drinking establishments since he was a pup.

"He couldn't get enough of looking at people smoking and if one stubbed out, he switched his attention to another," said Sarah. "He loved to sniff it and just watch it [the smoke] drift through the air. It's a bit bizarre, I know, but he seems to be well and truly hooked."

She added that the locals had started joking that the couple would have to invest in some nicotine patches for the addicted dog, but she suggested that a nicotine-flavored dog biscuit might work better.

Forget therapists, dogs are better listeners

A study carried out among 6,800 pet owners revealed that 95 percent of people preferred to confide in their pets instead of family or friends. Results showed that 58 percent of pet owners would talk to their pets about their day, and while the adage about never talking to friends and family about politics may be true, some even admitted to revealing their political views to their pets.

Confirming that there is a special bond between pet and pet owners, 75 percent of those surveyed said they wished they could understand what their pets are trying to tell them.

So integral is the relationship between pet and owner that

dogs and cats were found to follow the owners' routines, with over 62 percent of pets preferring to follow "mom's" routine over that of the rest of the family. The survey, conducted by a pet food company, also found that 29 percent of pets chose to wake up at the same time as their owners, and, amusingly, some owners chose to follow their *pets'* routines instead—they cook dinner for themselves when their dogs are hungry!

Woman stuck inside dog for an hour

Horrified and surprised, a woman found her arm trapped inside the mouth of her pet boxer for over an hour. Vicky Morl, of Maidenhead, England, was attempting to remove a fishhook from her dog's mouth but managed to also become entangled and trapped herself until the emergency services arrived to help.

The dog had gotten the fishhook stuck in his throat after rummaging around in a bin in the yard. When the pregnant mom realized what had happened, she instinctively decided to carefully attempt to maneuver the hook out of his mouth, but found that she was unable to wriggle free! What first seemed like a relatively easy task turned into an emergency that resulted in a skin graft for the unlucky owner.

"Every time someone got near the dog, it moved. And every time the dog moved, Vicky had to move with it. It was a difficult job—and it was certainly very different," said an emergency-services spokesman.

Dog makes headlines by "giving birth" to a kitten

The Chinese village Huayang celebrated an apparent miracle after it was claimed that a mixed-breed dog gave birth to a kitten there. According to local veterinarians, the catlike creature was a genetically mutated dog. The vets told Chinese press that the animal was the third "puppy" born in the litter.

"The first two puppies the dog produced were both normal but when the third baby came the whole family was very surprised to see a catlike creature," one of the attending vets said. "It is a cat, not a dog at all."

Needless to say, with such tales of canines producing felines, local villagers flocked to the house to lay eyes upon this catlike canine creation, which actually "yapped" like a puppy.

Dog "jailed" for life after attack on child

A seven-year-old German shepherd that attacked a child was spared by a judge in New Jersey who opted instead to sentence the dog to life imprisonment. Ozzy, the dog in question, was due to be put down but will now live out the rest of his life in solitary confinement.

After accepting the appeal from Ozzy's owner, Kelly Allard, the municipal judge agreed that Allard's proposal for the dog to patrol a perimeter fence at a local prison was "the right alternative."

Allard protested the original decision to have the dog put down and proposed that the dog could be of use at the George W. Hill correctional facility. Superior Court Judge John T. McNeill, III, agreed. "He [Ozzy] will be here until he dies. He won't be adopted by another family. He won't be released to the public," he decided.

Woof! Je ne parle pas Anglais . . .

Canine rescuers had to speak French to a Jack Russell terrier that was trapped down a drain, because the little Franco-Fido seemed to be having trouble understanding English.

After vanishing on a walk in Hampshire in southeast England, Milo was discovered by a neighbor, who alerted emergency services to his predicament. It was only when his owner arrived on the scene that she was able to explain to firemen that the dog had belonged to a French family and he didn't understand any English words.

The lucky dog escaped unhurt after spending a day and half stuck in the hole.

Animal rescue specialist saves trapped German shepherd

Angel, a young German shepherd, found herself in a tight spot after getting her head trapped in a concrete wall in Hampshire, England. The dog's owner found her so completely stuck in the openwork design of the garden wall that she had to call the fire and rescue service for assistance.

Rural Safety Officer Anton Phillips responded, giving the owner advice on keeping the dog calm until his arrival. Once on the scene, he was able to safely extricate the inquisitive four-month-old pup using a lump hammer and bolster to chisel off the area of wall where her head was trapped.

Anton praised the owner for controlling the dog before and during this challenging rescue. "This was quite an unusual call and the owner did a great job in keeping her pet as calm as possible before I got there," he said. "Without the owner's patience and ability to keep the dog quiet, this could have resulted in a much worse scenario for Angel."

Sheepdog brings piglets back from the dead

A Romanian farmer told news agencies how he was left reeling in shock after discovering that his sheepdog had nursed two apparently dead piglets back to life.

Vasile Borza said that he had disposed of the bodies of two piglets that were apparently stillborn, but was intrigued by an unusual sound coming from the kennel of his sheepdog, named Lola.

Lola, who was nursing her own pups, had rescued the young piglets and allowed them to suckle her along with the puppies. The two piglets made a full recovery.

Mother dog nurses three . . . tiger cubs

Visitors to China's Paomaling Wild Animal World were amazed to see a dog nursing three tiger cubs that were abandoned by their mother. The dog, a mixed breed named Huani, took to the cubs immediately. Staff at the zoo said that the four are "getting along fine."

Not baaaaad for a new mother

Molly, an eleven-month-old rottweiler belonging to Maria Forster, a farmer in Wales, decided to take it upon herself and "adopt" two young lambs—and she's taking rather good care of the delicate little creatures! The lambs needed special attention after they were born because they were suffering from circulation problems.

Forster placed the lambs near an oven to keep them warm and it was then that Molly took an instinctive, nurturing approach to caring for them by gently licking them as their mother would have. Forster explained that she also has a protective desire to sleep with them and keep them away from harm in general.

"The cat came into the kitchen the other day and walked over to the bucket where the lambs were sleeping, but Molly pushed her away as if to say, 'They are mine,'" Forster said. "She will let the sheepdog have a look, but only for so long before she pushes him away as well." Forster added that the two lambs cannot be returned to their mother because they would be rejected by her after being apart for so long.

NASA employs top dog

One of NASA's newest workers is a top dog . . . literally. A golden retriever puppy named Aries goes to work every day at NASA's Langley Research Center in Hampton, Virginia, as part of the Leader Dogs for the Blind program. Her mentor is structural engineer Evan J. Horowitz, who raises service dogs.

As a child, Horowitz had seen a movie character raising a guide dog and it made a huge impression. "I've always wanted to give like most people do," said Horowitz. "Lots of people give money to charity, but I wanted to do something a little more, something more hands on, more from my heart."

Horowitz works on the rocket and capsule project that will take astronauts back to the moon but he used to be in charge of structural engineering for a research aircraft known as ARIES, short for Airborne Research Integrated Experiments System. That's how he came up with a name for his canine student.

The goal of Aries' training at NASA is not to turn her into a rocket scientist, but into a well-socialized dog with knowledge of basic commands. Horowitz says he's supposed to walk around and work with the puppy as if she weren't there, but that's not easy to do considering the attention the golden retriever attracts. "She's a lot of fun," said Horowitz. "She gets me to meet a lot of people . . . because she's just a magnet for socializing."

Superwealthy advised to get dogs to beat taxman

The superwealthy in Britain were given high-level advice to get a pet to relieve their tax burdens. British millionaires attempting to claim residence in another country for tax reasons were advised that owning a pet in another country will help convince the authorities in Britain that their claim of nonresidence in the United Kingdom is true.

One large bank offered the advice to wealthy Brits at a seminar in a swanky London hotel. For years, wealthy individuals have sought ways and means of paying the least amount of tax they can legally get away with, but never before has a financial institution issued such pet-related advice.

Essentially, the guidance was offered to those having trouble convincing HM Revenue and Customs (Britain's version of the Internal Revenue Service) that their overseas residence was legitimate. It was proposed that keeping a pet would help convince any skeptical investigators that the individual was definitely a nonresident Britain.

The laws governing residency were described at the seminar as being "a bit floaty." According to a report in the Sunday

Times newspaper, a lawyer said, "It's a very good thing if you've got pets there [abroad]. The Revenue gets the [right] impression."

Movie pirates issue Mafia-style hit on two drug-sniffing dogs

Crooked movie importers placed two black Labradors on a gangster-style hit list after the keen-nosed dogs uncovered a cache of illicit CDs and DVDs, costing the criminals almost $3 million in lost loot. Six people were arrested after the airport dogs led handlers to some of the stolen goods.

The dogs, named Lucky and Flo, had to be moved to a secret, safe location.

The discovery made by the dogs, which were trained in Northern Ireland, lead to six arrests, prompting threats of revenge from the criminal underworld that want the dogs out of the way so that they can carry on their illegal trade.

Officials in Malaysia said the dogs made enemies as soon as they started their job and began to get results. Enforcement director Firdaus Zakaria told a British newspaper, "They are a problem for the pirated disc syndicates so they want them out of the way."

Delinquent Korean teens brought to heel with dogs

A dog-training program for young offenders in South Korea has been designed to bring troubled or criminal youngsters in line using the power of the canine/human relationship. The rehabilitation scheme brings together simple tasks such as basic dog training, grooming, exercise, diet, cleaning up after the dog, and general health care. The program is the first of its kind in the country.

The Cheonan Male Juvenile Correction Center offers young offenders the chance to interact with carefully selected dogs over a one-year period to develop positive social interaction skills. Inspired by the POOCH (Positive Opportunities Obvious Change with Hounds) Project in the United States that provides a youth/shelter dog therapy program in correction centers, the Cheonan project is home to around four hundred men ranging in age from eighteen to twenty-four who have committed offenses from homicide and rape to assault.

The center is the only juvenile correction facility in Korea and it falls under the jurisdiction of the Korean Ministry of Justice. T. Y. Moon, one of the center's representatives, said, "Anecdotal results from staff to recipients include greater motivation and confidence, and a real sense of purpose and ambition, which they [the juveniles] so severely lacked. The project is carefully supervised by staff to look after the welfare of both dogs and participants to ensure the highest care is given."

Mamma mia! World-record-breaking dog litter

When Suzanne Whittingham traveled three thousand miles to find a hot-blooded Italian mate for her beloved six-year-old

Spinone female, Mia, she didn't realize their union would be quite so . . . productive.

Just two months later, Mia gave birth to a brood of *seventeen* cute and cuddly pups, setting a world record for her breed and more than doubling the size of the average litter! Even though Mia—a dog more than used to setting records, as she is the only Spinone to have won Best of Breed at the Crufts international dog show in Birmingham, England, three times—had given birth to big broods before, the size of her litter stunned staff at the Prince Bishop Veterinary Hospital in Leadgate, England.

According to practice owner Jacqui Molyneux, "We knew that she was probably expecting a few more pups than average but when they kept coming, we couldn't believe it. We had to get most of our staff—including our receptionist, and even a couple of builders who were working at the practice—in to help."

She added, "This is the by far the biggest litter we've had over more than twenty years at the practice, and is not too far behind the world record of twenty-three pups by a Great Dane, which is a much bigger breed."

Whittingham plans to keep at least one of the puppies, and says that despite their ordeal mother and pups are thriving. "Mia is shattered but doing really well, as are the pups, who are just brilliant. They are more than a handful, but my family [have] been total heroes helping out. My mother does the day shift when I'm at work, then my brother and I take over at night."

"World's strangest inventions" mostly
go to the dogs

A study conducted by an aggregator Web site revealed that among the wacky and ingenious inventions from past and present, 30 percent of the top ten were intended for dogs. Proving that dog owners are either exceptionally innovative and ingenious people or that they are actually a little bit nuts, the Bow-Lingual, a dog-to-human translator device, came in sixth place—one spot above antiflatulence underwear and one place behind an alarm clock that runs away and hides. Neuticles—testicular implants for castrated dogs—took fourth place, one place behind a self-perfuming business suit.

The highest-placed dog-related invention, however, was the Lavakan, a washing machine for cats and dogs. According to compilers of the list, "The co-inventors of the Lavakan, Eduardo Segura and Andrés Diaz, decided in 1998 that their dogs deserved the same treatment that humans get from a shower massage. The side-loading automatic pet washing machine is safer and less stressful for the animals than washing them by hand. It soaps, rinses, and dries dogs and cats in less than half an hour."

They claim it has a series of conical nozzles that wash and massage animals all over, while dirt and soap are filtered through a hose at the bottom of the contraption. Operators are able to use the Lavakan's touch panel to choose the best wash cycle for their pets' size and dermatological needs.

Protests in China as Beijing bans dogs

Chinese capital Beijing was the scene of protest in November 2006 as more than two hundred dog lovers voiced their opposition to restrictions on pet dog ownership. The demonstrators clung to stuffed animal toys and claimed new laws that limited families in the capital to owning just one small dog were inhumane.

The protestors were concerned that a ban on larger breeds will lead to dogs being confiscated and routinely destroyed. Earlier in the year a mass culling of dogs sparked outrage from animal lovers in the southwest part of the country. The "one dog" policy was said to have been introduced as part of the Chinese government's efforts to combat rabies.

One protester reportedly said that proposed legislation was unfair. "We hope the world will support us in stopping the meaningless hurting and killing of dogs," she said. "The height of a dog doesn't make them guilty or fierce!"

The growth of the Chinese economy—resulting in greater pay for Chinese workers in general—has led to a boom in dog ownership, which is viewed as a sign of affluence in the country.

Dogs will (literally) eat up all your money

A rottweiler mix named Otis that was put up for adoption by his owners has quite a following at the kennel in Glasgow, Scotland, where he's staying. Why? Because every time the staff goes to clean out his kennel, they find money!

"Otis is a real character and we couldn't believe it when we started finding money in his kennel when we came to clear it out. Needless to say there has been plenty of staff offering to clean his kennel now!" said one employee. Apparently he has a thing for eating loose change and later "depositing" it in his kennel.

"On a more serious note Otis is looking for a new loving home with owners who are experienced with such energetic breeds and also one where money and other valuables aren't left lying around," the employee added.

It is often estimated that a dog will cost an owner in the region of $20,000 to care for over the course of its life. With a dog like Otis, it may be worth budgeting a few dollars more!

Head-butting police dogs trained to protect human rights

Politically correct police chiefs working for the North Wales police department were so afraid of human rights complaints if the service dogs in the K9 corps bit anyone, they ordered the dogs to be trained to head-butt suspected criminals instead.

The policy was said to be employed as a response to the growing number of compensation claims from suspects apprehended by police dogs. Officers suggested that toothless "attack" tactics provide a more injury-free way to take down uncooperative suspected offenders, and they envision dog squads across the entire United Kingdom adopting the method if it proves to be a success.

Critics were quick to jump on the issue, deriding it as yet another example of politically correct policing, placing the rights of criminals ahead of proper protection of the public. Rather than laying teeth into the suspects, the K9s were instead taught to leap at their targets and deliver a flying head butt.

"Instead of biting, the dog is muzzled and launches itself like a missile at the midriff of the target," said Clive Wolfendale, deputy chief constable of North Wales.

Added Sgt. Ian Massie, "We believe it is a safer option for an offender to be head-butted."

Dog receives series of blood transfusions, owner sets up blood donation center for others

Diana Cruttwell's golden retriever, Abi, was seriously ill and needed a blood transfusion to treat her autoimmune hemolytic anemia. She was referred to veterinary internal medicine specialist Dr. Clive Elwood at Davies Veterinary Specialists in Hertfordshire, England, for urgent treatment. Luckily, Cruttwell's three other golden retrievers all had the same blood type and were each able to donate a pint of blood to Abi. After three transfusions and specialized medical care, Abi pulled through what is often a fatal condition. Today she is in excellent health.

"I asked Clive what would have happened if my own dogs couldn't have been donors for Abi. He told me they have great difficulty finding blood donors and that normally only one trans-fusion can be given—in which case Abi would almost certainly have died," said Cruttwell. Immediately she came up with the idea to create an online blood donor center with her vet: Dog BloodDonors.com.

Registered donors are contacted by a local vet whenever an emergency may require blood donations from dogs that have suitable blood-type matches to the dog in need. The revo-lutionary service is expected to save the lives of thousands of dogs now and in the future. "I think it's important that people know their animals can be donors," said Cruttwell.

Patrolman uses dog to start car

A dog that ate a car's immobilizer chip was used to get the driver's vehicle up and running in a bizarre breakdown incident. A patrolman was called to the rescue of the stranded female driver, whose dog had eaten the car's immobilizer chip.

Thirty-nine-year-old Juliette Piesley had changed the bat-tery in her electronic car key ring but then realized she was unable to start the engine. Patrolman Kevin Gorman arrived at the scene to discover the car key's immobilizer chip was not present.

All eyes turned to George, Piesley's curious dog, who prob-ably ate the chip! Gorman decided to try an experiment. He ordered George to get in the front seat of the vehicle in order to activate the immobilizer, and subsequently started the car with the key. It worked.

"I was glad to get the car started," Gorman said. "It is the first time that I have had to get a dog to help me to start a car."

But, he added, "They will now have to take George with them in the car until things take their natural course."

Mummified dogs discovered in South America

In 2006 archaeologists in Peru discovered the mummified remains of some forty dogs buried with blankets and food, and, interestingly, they were found alongside the remains of their human masters.

The canines were uncovered during an excavation of two members of the ancient Chiribaya people, believed to have lived in Peru between 900 and 1350 A.D. Finding the dogs buried with their masters prompted some experts to claim the Chiribaya believed their animals could enjoy an afterlife—a belief previously thought to be exclusive to ancient Egypt.

Prior to the European conquest of South America, the Chiribaya civilization valued dogs so highly they would always ensure they were buried with their human companions when they passed away. The dogs were identified as Chiribaya shepherds for their llama-herding abilities and were never sacrificed, unlike dogs in other ancient cultures. They resembled a smaller version of the golden retriever.

Biologists began working with the Peruvian Kennel Club to try to establish if the dogs represented a new indigenous South American breed. The only other indigenous Peruvian breed is the hairless dog, which is over two thousand years old and was only recognized as a unique breed twenty years ago.

Soccer star lands himself in hot water over death of dog

Belgian soccer player Gilles De Bilde found himself in trouble with his club, Willebroek, after he missed a game to mourn the death of his dog. De Bilde is famous in the soccer community for his passion for animal rights.

It is not the first time the pet-loving player has courted controversy because of his affection for dogs. In 1999 after he arrived to play for the Sheffield Wednesday soccer club in England, he was exposed by a tabloid for smuggling his two Dobermans through the United Kingdom's tough quarantine system. While denying the offense, the outspoken soccer star said, "Quarantine laws are shit laws because they affect dogs' health. That's not a good thing."

Paul Jewell, a former coach who managed De Bilde when he played for Sheffield, spoke about the player and his passion for his dogs. "I fixed him up with three months on loan at Aston Villa [soccer club] but when I called him in to tell him, he said, 'I've got a problem. I've got nobody to look after my dogs if I go there.'"

For the Love of Dog

Talking to dogs is one of the few acts of faith still
made nowadays. —Paul Jennings

I't's no surprise that dogs will sometimes risk their own lives in situations of extreme danger rather than leave their owners' side. Or they will make astonishing journeys to be reunited with the owners who thought their cherished dogs were lost forever. Then of course we have the humans who are *so* devoted to their dogs that they'll organize and hold lavish celebrations in their honor, and then even go so far as to shower them with exuberant gifts in their wills—sometimes leaving their furry family members more than they leave their human family members! There is no doubt that our dogs are capable of loving us every bit as much as we love them, and the following stories definitely demonstrate this.

"Queen of Mean" had a heart for hounds

She lives in a luxurious penthouse apartment, eats only the finest food cooked by a gourmet chef, and has an entire staff on hand twenty-four hours a day to cater to her every whim. Her personal fortune stands at over $12 million. With her expensive, silky coiffure and her gorgeous dark eyes, she certainly turns heads as she sashays down the street, but she isn't a pop star, actress, supermodel, or the most recent It Girl. She is a nine-year-old Maltese named Trouble—and she is one of the richest dogs in the world.

Trouble was adored by her late owner, the New York hotelier Leona Helmsley, and after her death in August 2007, Helmsley's will became a talking point the world over. She had disinherited two grandchildren but left a trust fund of around $12 million from her estimated $4 billion fortune to her dog! In fact, Trouble was the second largest beneficiary of the will, receiving more than several of Helmsley's family members.

Leona Helmsley was notorious for her harsh treatment of employees, and even relatives, and her tyrannical behavior earned her the nickname "Queen of Mean," but there can be no doubt at all that she was devoted to her beloved pet.

She left strict instructions about how and by whom Trouble was to be cared for, and Helmsley stipulated that when the pampered pooch dies, she is to be buried alongside her mistress in an ornate mausoleum with stained-glass windows, granite columns, and an annual $3 million maintenance allowance. Trouble's final resting place itself is still in dispute, however, as the staff at Sleepy Hollow Cemetery, the site of the mausoleum, has said that state law forbids them from burying animal remains in a human graveyard.

The lawyer in charge of overseeing Trouble's trust fund estimates that the cost of keeping her in the style she is accustomed to should be around $300,000 per year, which includes groomers, vet bills, specially cooked meals, and an around-the-clock security team.

Life isn't all plain sailing for Trouble, though, and her vast wealth has brought its fair share of problems. She received about two dozen death threats in the months following Leona Helmsley's death and had to be moved to a secure and secret location. Her personal security team was increased, and when she travels (by private jet of course), she does so under an assumed name in an attempt to throw any would-be dognappers off the scent. It has also been reported that a former member of Helmsley's household staff is planning to take legal action against Trouble to secure some of the $12 million as compensation for bites the Maltese allegedly inflicted on her while she was in Helmsley's employ.

President worries over safety of dog

Former President Franklin D. Roosevelt, upon joining the Allied Forces after the Japanese attack on Pearl Harbor, was so concerned for the safety of his Scottish terrier, Fala, that he had a horoscope drawn up for his dog by a local astrologer.

In 1941 this was not viewed as a normal thing for an American president to be doing. Fala outlived his master, and a statue of the dog was erected at the Franklin Delano Roosevelt Memorial in Washington, DC.

A hoax or a hound with a home to die for?

Perhaps the most notorious story about excessive canine wealth is that of German shepherd Gunther IV. He supposedly inherited a fortune of about $200 million and lives a true jet-set lifestyle, more than living up to his nickname, "the Material Dog." Many people cast doubt upon the credibility of the Gunther story; however, it seemed authentic enough to fool the *Guinness Book of Records,* which in 1998 listed Gunther IV as the richest dog in the world.

The story goes that in 1992, a German countess named Charlotte Liebenstein died and left her entire estate—including over $80 million—to a dog named Gunther III. He was allegedly part of a German disco act called The Gunther Group, which used the dog's barks and howls on its recordings. The countess was said to have admired the group's work so much, she had her will altered in favor of the dog. Gunther III had savvy advisors who invested his money wisely and increased his portfolio until it had an estimated value of over $150 million. Upon the death of Gunther III, this money was inherited by his son, the imaginatively named Gunther IV.

Gunther IV appears to be guided and cared for by a group of five people calling themselves the Burgundians (according to medieval legend, Gunther was a Burgundian king). They accompany Gunther on his public appearances and show up on his Web site, guntherdog.com, where they are described as "young, euphoric people" whose sole purpose is to improve Gunther's mood and alertness.

A true tail of rags to riches

An early part of Jasper's life was spent in a Battersea Dogs' Home kennel, in London, where he eventually caught the eye of a potential adopter. The lady who gave the Doberman-Labrador cross a home was none other than Diana Myburgh, heiress to England's Ramsden brewery. Not long after Jasper moved to his new home, Myburgh died at the age of seventy-four and bequeathed almost $50,000 each to Jasper and her other dog, Jason. Jason died soon after, leaving Jasper the new possessor of an approximated $100,000.

Appointed as Jasper's caregiver was Myburgh's son-in-law, Sir Benjamin Slade. Thanks to his wise investments on behalf of Jasper, the $100,000 soon became $160,000—more than enough to fund Jasper's lavish lifestyle. A far cry from his former life in Britain's best-known dogs' home, Jasper now lives on a vast Somerset estate, and has his own chauffeur-driven car to ferry him around. He eats sirloin steak, Dover sole, mussels, and tripe prepared by a chef.

You may sniff the bride

Some people love their dogs so much they are always included at special occasions—even weddings. When Dianne Johnston, of Cumbria in England, married her husband, Andrew, in 2005, she decided that her six beloved pugs would be an integral part of the day, and began planning a ceremony that would include them.

The dogs accompanied their owner to the wedding ceremony at city hall and were dressed in tailored wedding outfits— silk dresses for the females (Becky, Buttons, Lottie, and Mabel) and top hat and tails for the males (Elf and Sherman).

"Top of my list were my dogs. They've always been there for me and have never let me down. When I went down the aisle everybody gasped and just couldn't believe it," said Johnston. She also said that city hall staff had commented that the dogs were better behaved during the ceremony than many of the children who attend weddings.

Though their manners were impeccable throughout the wedding itself, by the time the reception began, the pugs were apparently so tired they all slept through it.

A marriage made in doggie heaven

When Sonia Wilde was given Lucy Brown, a young collie cross, the two became best friends in no time. Lucy accompanied

Sonia whenever possible, and curled up on her bed at night. As Wilde and her fiancé, Steve Begley, were planning their wedding in 2005, Wilde realized that she wanted Lucy to be a big part of the day. After some thought, they wondered if Lucy would be able to take part in the actual ceremony, as Wilde's maid of honor. What started out as a joke quickly became a serious proposition, and the couple decided to mention it to the vicar who would conduct the wedding.

Brian Statham, the vicar of St. Matthew's Church in Stockport, England, was initially taken aback at the suggestion, but after considering the issue he decided to allow Lucy to be part of the big day.

"It is quite bizarre really, the most unusual request I had heard in twenty-six years as a vicar. Then reason and logic kicked in and I thought, 'Well, I've had dogs at funerals because they have been the lifelong partners of people, so why not at a wedding?'" said Statham.

The couple confesses that some of their friends and family were less than certain about the inclusion of Lucy Brown in the wedding party, and indeed some said they were crazy for even considering it.

"I'm not crazy and I'm not eccentric. I just love my dog to bits; she's like a daughter. I cannot think of anybody else I would rather have as chief bridesmaid," said the new Mrs. Begley.

Something old (English sheepdog), something new . . .

When Julie Brammer, a dog handler with the Staffordshire Police Department in England, married Paul Hargreaves, a fellow police officer, Julie knew she needed a very special someone to stand in for her father, Geoffrey, who had passed away two years before. She hit upon the idea of having Thom—her treasured Old English sheepdog—walk her down the aisle and give her away.

Brammer and Thom had been inseparable for thirteen years, and it seemed only right that he should do the honors at her wedding. "My dad died two-and-a-half years ago and nobody could ever replace Dad, so Thom was the obvious choice, and besides, he's been in the family so long he needed to be there," Brammer said.

Thom behaved wonderfully and more than lived up to his role as honorary father of the bride during the wedding. His collar was adorned with Dutch roses to match those in Brammer's bouquet, and he even made a special visit to a grooming parlor before the big day so he was assured of looking his best.

He also displayed some impeccable comic timing during the ceremony itself. "When the registrar asked the congregation if there was anyone present who had any objections to the marriage, Thom sneezed really loudly. It really broke the ice though. He couldn't have timed it better!" Brammer said.

Thom was spared the ordeal of having to make a speech at the reception, as the bride did it for him. He did accompany her and Paul on their wedding night, however, staying with them at a bed-and-breakfast, before joining the guests in waving the happy couple off on their honeymoon to Spain the next day. The honeymoon was the one occasion Thom was definitely *not* invited to.

Wag a tail for the happy canine couple

If your treasured pooch meets the dog of its dreams in the local park, you can now make things official with a full doggy wedding ceremony in Harrods, the London department store. After a chance meeting in the Harrods pet department, and the ensuing friendship, Muffin, a shih tzu, married her dashing groom (a bichon frisé named Timmy) in a lavish ceremony that took place at the store in 2006. Muffin wore a traditional white dress and veil and arrived in a horse-drawn carriage. Timmy awaited her dressed in a tuxedo and bow tie.

The owners of the pooches, Rachel Little and Dominique Day, said that after their first meeting in Harrods, they kept in touch because their dogs seemed to get on so well. After someone said what a lovely couple the canines made, the idea of the wedding came about, and the owners seemed delighted with the ceremony. For this first Harrods dog wedding, the store did not charge the owners, but anyone wishing to use the store to have their dogs united in holy matrimony in the future will need to cough up $5,000 for a luxury wedding, or $7,000 for a "Premium Package."

A world record for mutt marriages

In 2007 a new world record for mass dog weddings was set in Littleton, Colorado. Almost fifty canine "couples" were married at the Aspen Grove Lifestyle Center, easily beating the previous record of twenty-six couples in the Netherlands. The event, titled Bow Wow Vows, took place on May 19, and the $50 donation made by each participant went to a Denver animal welfare organization.

In the weeks before the ceremony, the center even provided a speed dating service so that dogs planning to take part could find their perfect matches before pledging their troth. The brides wore gowns and veils, while the grooms were smartly attired in tuxedo jackets and unique bow ties. A reception for dogs and owners took place afterward, and a spectacular tiered wedding cake was specially created for the event. The cake was adorned with iced bones, hearts, and paw prints, and topped by a replica canine couple in full wedding regalia. Many owners acted as maid of honor or best man for their pet, and each received a special commemorative dog tag to mark the occasion.

Celebrities go barking mad for dog marriages

Of course, when it comes to doggie weddings, none are more elaborate or high profile than those given by celebrities for their beloved pets. When former *Baywatch* star Pamela Anderson hosted a commitment ceremony for her two dogs, she doubt-lessly envisaged a moving and beautiful occasion that would touch the hearts of all who witnessed it. Instead, it turned into a comedic farce when the wedding was crashed by *Ali G* star Sacha Baron Cohen—as his Kazakhstani television reporter character, Borat.

Anderson had arranged for the wedding to take place on a Malibu beach on August 17, 2005. The dogs getting hitched were Luca, her Chihuahua, and Star, a golden retriever. The actress had invited her closest friends and family members to witness the joyous event. Midway through, however, there was a disturbance slightly offshore in the water, and Cohen appeared on the back of an inflatable turtle. Dressed in shorts and a leather cap and jacket, he made his way to the beach where he ran toward Anderson and knocked her to the ground. As her bodyguards seized the intruder and hustled him away, Anderson got to her feet, brushed the sand from her dress and asked that the ceremony continue. Happily, the canine companions were united in matrimony with no further interruptions.

Bobbie the "Wonder Dog" astonishes all

In 1923, Frank and Elizabeth Brazier left their home in Silverton, Oregon, to take a road trip. Accompanying them was their dog, Bobbie, a collie-shepherd mix. When they stopped to refuel their car in Wolcott, Indiana, Bobbie was suddenly chased by a pack of stray dogs and he disappeared. The Braziers searched for weeks on end, asking locals to look out for Bobbie and taking out a long-running advertisement in the local newspaper to publicize his disappearance. Despite their best efforts, they were unable to find him and eventually they returned to Oregon, devastated by the loss of their beloved pet.

Exactly six months later, the Braziers' youngest daughter saw a thin, bedraggled-looking dog on a street in Silverton. As she got nearer, she was astonished to see that it was Bobbie! On closer inspection, his paws were bleeding and his nails were worn down to the quick—he had walked 2,500 miles home by himself! The dog hurled himself at her and clearly recognized all the members of his family. If there had been any doubt at all that it was the same dog, this one possessed the same scars Bobbie had as a result of some puppyhood injuries.

Bobbie recovered from his ordeal and became very well known, receiving letters from thousands of well-wishers, some of whom claimed to have fed him as he passed by on his journey. He was presented with a silver collar and was the subject of books and movies. He was nicknamed "the Wonder Dog," and after his death in 1927 he was honored and buried in the pet cemetery at the local humane society. Each year in Silverton, a ceremony including a pet parade commemorates Bobbie and his incredible display of strength and determination.

Three lucky dogs are set for life

Three lucky Maryland dogs were the recipients of a large inheritance late in 2007 when their owner, Ken Kemper, passed away. Buckshot, Katie, and Obu-jet inherited $400,000 and the Hagerstown house in which they now live with a caretaker—totaling an $800,000 inheritance.

They are content with their life in the yard, and with their weekly special spaghetti, meatballs, and garlic dinners that their caretaker makes for them. The dogs will remain at the house for the remainder of their lifetimes, and once they pass away the rest of the estate is likely to be donated to an animal charity by the executor.

Dogs That Found Fame

And then there's the personal question so many
of Lassie's fans want to ask: Is he allowed on the
furniture? Of course he is—but, then, he's the one
who paid for it. —Julia Glass

Through bravery, loyalty, unusual behavior, or the things their human companions sometimes do, some of our four-legged friends just cannot avoid fame. Some dogs have the ability to make us laugh or smile while others bring us to tears with tales of their touching acts.

Quite simply the dog is a winner. A winning animal with more talent than humans have been able to fully explore and harness even to this very day. Dogs are adaptable, famously friendly, they understand us—or we certainly like to think they do—and live our lives with us, enhancing and enriching our very existence. But a dog is even more than just a good friend and entertainer. A dog is a life saver, a forecaster, an unparalleled genius, and one hell of an athlete.

All the dogs in this chapter have definitely earned their fifteen minutes of fame—even if sometimes only in the eyes and hearts of their personal caretakers. Either way, these stories take a look at some of the craziest canines that managed to jump into the public spotlight. *And . . . action!*

Singer all smiles after being reunited with lost dog

Pop singer Lily Allen was quite relieved at being reunited with her English bull terrier, Maggie May, who was stolen from the back of a van in east London on December 28, 2006. The singer said she received information from a man claiming to have her dog, so Allen's friends met with him to see if it was hers.

She was, in fact, the real dog, and Allen forked over cash to get her back. She expressed her concern that Maggie May was thin, riddled with fleas, and looked as if she had been mistreated. Allen, the daughter of actor and musician Keith Allen, also said her friends were offered additional puppies by the same person who "returned" her dog.

"These people were obviously in the business of moving dogs. Now I feel guilty for having given these people money and contributing to their cruel business but I love that dog and felt I had no choice," Allen told Britain's BBC television network.

Clinton's Buddy stays loyal

After the Monica Lewinsky scandal broke across the United States, Bill Clinton's wife, Hillary, commented in her memoir, *Living History,* that Buddy, their chocolate Labrador, was the only member of the family willing to keep the president company.

In 1997 Buddy was adopted by the Clinton family and spent his puppyhood in the White House. Clinton received more than five thousand suggestions on names for the pup, but he eventually settled on naming him after an uncle who had passed away earlier in the year. Buddy was at Clinton's side when he ordered the bombing of Iraq, when he was unfaithful to the First Lady, and even when he stepped down as president.

The devoted dog lost his life on January 2, 2002, in Chappaqua, New York, when he was accidentally hit by a car. "We are deeply saddened by Buddy's death. He was a loyal companion and brought us much joy. He will truly be missed," the Clintons said in an official statement.

Psychoanalysis founder values canine companion

"Affection without ambivalence" is what the father of psychoanalysis, Sigmund Freud, said he got from his loyal chow, Jo Fi. Freud valued his chow's "one man dog" attitude and his unfailing loyalty.

Jo Fi became synonymous with Freud and even used to sit in on his therapy sessions, as Freud thought Jo Fi helped with assessing his patients' mental state. He also believed his dog had the ability to calm distressed patients.

Two sled dogs swoop in to save the day

In 1925, Nome, an Alaskan gold rush town of about fifteen hundred people, recorded a case of diphtheria. The lone doctor's supply of antitoxin for the disease had expired the summer before, and his new supply had not arrived as he had requested before the port closed for the winter. Icebound for the next six months, the doctor panicked and sent a message to the U.S. Public Health Service in Washington DC stating that an epidemic was almost inevitable and that one million units of diphtheria antitoxin were needed. Access to the outside world was only available via the Iditarod trail by dog sled. It was decided that the drug would be transported by dog sled—and two dogs in particular rose to fame.

Togo led the dog team for musher Leonhard Seppala. Though the lesser-celebrated of the two heroes of what became known as the Great Race of Mercy to deliver the serum to Nome, Togo's team ran farther than any other team in the relay, taking the antitoxin from just outside Shaktoolik and running ninety-one miles to Golovin, which was thirty-eight miles more than any other team. His leg of the serum relay was the most dangerous of all, crossing Norton Sound at temperatures of minus thirty degrees Fahrenheit and with a wind chill of minus eighty-five degrees Fahrenheit.

Balto and his musher, Gunnar Kaasen, took the final leg of the relay, traveling through blizzards so severe that Kaasen couldn't see the dogs, and they missed their hand-off because of the poor visibility. Balto led them safely on, until the high winds caused the sled to roll over, dropping the cylinder of anti-toxin. Kaasen had to dig for it in the snow, giving him a severe case of frostbite.

The antitoxin was successfully delivered and although Balto was initially celebrated as the dog that delivered the serum (causing much sadness for Seppala), history has seen to it that Togo's deeds and his bravery were remembered also. To this day the Great Race of Mercy is commemorated by the Iditarod Trail Sled Dog Race.

Spice Girl causes controversy and treadmill trauma at gym

Some people find their dogs so amazing that they like to take them everywhere they go. Spice Girl and celebrity dog owner Geri Halliwell, better known as Ginger Spice, was asked to leave the gym where she works out after she tethered her dog to the treadmill she was using.

It was reported that the dog was agitated and frightened by the loud noise of the treadmill and the hustle and bustle of a busy gym in the first week of January. Halliwell was told by the gym manager that dogs were not allowed in—for obvious health and safety reasons, as well as for animal welfare reasons. He then asked her to leave. The furious former pop star is alleged to have said that if her dog was not welcome she would not be coming back. She has not been seen at the gym since.

First fire rescue dog finds a home

A former emergency response dog that was trained to react when a fire alarm sounded has made retiree Betty Williams, from Eastham in Merseyside, one very happy woman. Ern is the very first emergency response dog in the United Kingdom to find a home as part of an innovative project organized by Britain's Fire Support Network charity.

Should wheelchair-bound Williams's smoke alarm sound, Ern is trained to shut the two of them in the room, push a cloth against the bottom of the door to stop smoke from entering, and then alert Britain's equivalent of the 911 emergency service. Once help arrives, the dog is trained to bark excessively so he and his owner can easily be located. Little Ern was one of three emergency response dogs placed in the community in an attempt to protect some of its most vulnerable residents.

Williams read about the initiative in her local paper and thought she would be a suitable applicant, having had both legs amputated a couple of years before. Linda Mitchell, manager of the Fire Support Network, said, "I knew immediately that Betty would be an ideal person to benefit from our emergency response dogs. She had limited mobility and was socially isolated."

She added, "Ern will do so much more than just help with fire safety, he will give Betty a friend. And with the network of volunteers who are involved in the project, she will get regular visitors and support. . . . Everyone will benefit."

Vladimir Putin to the press:
"Don't feed my dog"

On the eve of the 2003 Russian parliamentary elections, Vladimir Putin had more on his mind than some might think. Not only was Putin hoping to keep his position as president of the Federation of Russia, but his dog, Koni, had just given birth to eight puppies. President Putin was forced to issue a statement to all members of the press: "Please don't feed my dog."

He went on to qualify his rather unusual presidential request. "Sometimes, Koni leaves a room full of journalists with a very pleased expression on her face and biscuit crumbs around her mouth." It is not the first time the president had asked them not to feed his dog, but because some members of the press were seemingly unable to resist the charms of the president's black Labrador, Putin felt compelled to reiterate the request on his Web site.

Koni is well known in Russia, as she has been known to sit on the president's lap during meetings. She also crashed an official Kremlin party by escaping from her quarters to join the president on stage while he addressed a congregation of press, politicians, and members of the public.

In the wrong place at the wrong time

Otis was destroyed in 1996 for being left without a muzzle in the back of his owner's car. Owner Harry Bates said he believed that private property rules applied in his own vehicle. He also figured Britain's Dangerous Dogs Act didn't apply to him because Otis wasn't an American pit bull terrier, one of the breeds targeted by the law that are required to be muzzled in public—but police officers and the courts disagreed.

Bates spent a total of $100,000 trying to save his dog but all appeals failed. Ultimately, the appeal to the highest court—the European Court of Human Rights—also failed because it was not lodged within the required time, just fourteen days after the dog had been taken.

Taro and Jiro—*Eight Below*

Taro and Jiro were Sakhalin husky littermates—the only survivors of a dog sled team that was abandoned by their handlers. In 1958 a Japanese survey team in the Antarctic was waiting for a second team to relieve them.

Unfortunately, the arrival of the second team of scientists was prevented by severe weather conditions. The men in the first team were transported out by plane, but there was no room aboard for the fifteen dogs.

The dogs were tethered to the base to keep them from wandering off and getting lost. Sufficient food for a week was left, as the handlers expected to be able to return within that time to resume the survey and tend to the dogs. The huskies could only survive the conditions they would be exposed to for a month.

The planned rescue attempt was canceled because of severe storms and fuel limitations; it became apparent that any rescue would have to wait till spring. Only eight of the eleven dogs were able to escape their chains and hunt for food.

The handlers returned a year later, expecting to bury all of the dogs. Instead, they were greeted by two survivors—Taro and Jiro. How they survived no one will ever know. Seven of the dead dogs were still tethered to the base, and yet Taro and Jiro did not turn into cannibals. Also, the food the survey team had left for them at the base was still there.

Two movies were made about Taro and Jiro and the situation they were left to face. The first was completed in 1983 and released as *Nankyoku Monogatari* in Japan and titled *Antarctica* in the United States. The second, *Eight Below,* was released in 2006 by Walt Disney Pictures.

Girls Aloud concert delayed by dog

If one Spice Girl taking her dog to the gym isn't proof enough of how amazingly popular and demanding dogs can be, how about having an entire concert delayed because of doggie demands? British pop group Girls Aloud was an hour late for one show after singer Cheryl Cole's Chihuahua "refused" to let her leave her London home.

According to Cole's bandmate, Nadine Coyle, the dog was so determined to be with his owner he kept following her out of the house. In the end Cole decided it would be easier to bring him along to the show after the pint-sized pooch made his way into the band's tour bus and decided he didn't want to get out.

"It was the first time he'd seen me live," Cole told *The Sun.* "It was like having my number one fan with me."

Pickles wins World Cup for England

On March 20, 1966, four months before the FIFA World Cup in soccer was held in England, the Jules Rimet Trophy that was to be awarded to the winning team was stolen. It had been on display in London's Methodist Central Hall in Westminster before the tournament began.

Fortunately, the solid gold trophy was found seven days later when Pickles the dog uncovered it while out for a walk. It was wrapped in newspaper, lying under a hedge at the edge of his owner's yard. David Corbett, Pickles' owner, said, "I feel like a lucky man because it's not been a very lucky cup."

Pickles was renowned as the dog that found the trophy, and it was particularly important because that was the year that England had its big win—a win that wouldn't be repeated for several decades. Sadly, Pickles died in 1973 after catching his collar in the process of chasing a cat and choking to death. This, it has been noted, was a continuation of the infamous curse of the cup.

The cup was again stolen in 1983 in Rio de Janeiro, Brazil, and was never recovered. It is believed to have been melted down.

Dogs make history in outer space

Before progressing to manned space flights, the Soviet Union sent dogs into space to see if it was possible for an animal (and ultimately a human) to survive in space. They also tested spacesuit designs at this time. Dogs were chosen for the program because of their perceived ability to cope with the small space as well as the stress involved with being sent into orbit or suborbit.

A suborbital flight at around sixty-two miles above the earth carried dogs Dezik and Tsygan for the first time on July 22, 1951. They were released by ejector seat and returned to Earth safely, both unharmed. Dezik made a second suborbital flight with another dog named Lisa in September 1951. Unfortunately, they became the first of five dogs to lose their lives in the Soviet canine program.

Though there were others that went before her in suborbital flights, Laika—a Siberian husky crossbreed—is most commonly acknowledged as being the first (Earthborn) living creature in space. She traveled in *Sputnik 2,* on November 3, 1957, and survived about five to seven hours in orbit before she died of stress and overheating, which was not made publicly known for another forty-six years. The Soviets led the world to believe that she lived for two or three days in orbit before a failure in the capsule led to her death. She was three years old at the time of the flight and was nicknamed Muttnick by the American press.

Belka and Strelka were the first dogs to enter orbit and return safely to Earth again after a day spent in the capsule on August, 19, 1960. They traveled in *Sputnik 5* with other animals and plants. Strelka later got pregnant and had healthy puppies, one of which was actually presented to American presidential daughter Caroline Kennedy.

Laika and other canine astronauts have since appeared on postal stamps in honor of their contributions to the advancement of science and to Neil Armstrong's being able to walk on the moon on July 20, 1969.

World's first cloned dog makes headlines

Snuppy became the first successfully cloned puppy when he was born in 2005. The Seoul National University (SNU) puppy—as his name stands for—was created from DNA taken from the ear of a three-year-old Afghan hound that was implanted in a genetically empty egg and stimulated so that it would begin to divide as a normally fertilized egg would. A yellow Labrador carried the egg for sixty days before the puppy was delivered by caesarean section.

Snuppy was one of one thousand implantations into 123 surrogates, but only three pregnancies took, and of those only two pregnancies were carried to term. One puppy died shortly after delivery, leaving only Snuppy. Other animals have been successfully cloned far more easily than dogs.

It remains to be seen whether Snuppy will develop health issues similar to Dolly the sheep, which died in 2003 of cancer and also developed arthritis at an early age. Some time after the initial publicity surrounding Snuppy, it was revealed that his "creator" had been less than truthful about his innovation: Scientist Woo Suk Hwang did not create the cloned stem cells to create Snuppy, as he had originally claimed. The dog, however, is still synonymous with canine cloning because of the huge publicity surrounding his birth.

Dogs prove their intellectual abilities

When rescue dog Donnie, a Doberman pinscher, was rehomed, he was nervous and unwilling to interact with his new owner—flinching at any physical contact. While this is normal for a dog in a new home, he began showing another type of behavior that was not, at least not for a dog.

Whenever he was let outside, Donnie began laying out his many stuffed toys in particular geometrical arrangements in the yard, sometimes grouping them according to type. His owner contacted Barbara Smuts of the University of Michigan, a professor of psychology, who did not believe her until she viewed his behavior with hidden cameras. Smuts is now looking for other dogs with similar cognitive abilities.

In another incident, a ten-month-old border collie named Rico needed indoor entertainment after he became sick. His owners attempted to teach him the names of his toys. Soon enough, he was fetching all of his toys by name. His impressive vocabulary grew to about 250 words, and he finally came to the attention of scientists at the Max Plank Institute for Evolutionary Anthropology in Leipzig, Germany, when he was seen competing on a television show.

Julia Fischer led the research in which Rico successfully retrieved thirty-seven out of forty toys, but in addition, he was able to fetch never-before-seen toys when told their never-before-heard names. This, of course, demonstrated reasoning on his behalf and memory when he showed that he remembered those new words a month later.

His fast mapping ability—with which he can learn a new name with a single exposure and respond to that name a month later—was comparable to that of a three-year-old child, and is an ability that even chimpanzees do not have.

Seizure-detecting dog can smell trouble

A four-year-old rottweiler named Faith in the state of Washington has been trained to use her sensitive nose to detect when owner Leana Beasley is about to have a seizure because of changes to her body chemistry. As an assistance dog, Faith then alerts the owner so that she can make sure she's in a safe situation before the seizure begins.

But Faith is also trained to render assistance if her owner gets hurt, and she performed her job in an exemplary manner when Beasley became ill after her liver had a strange reaction to her medication and she fell out of her wheelchair. Faith knocked the phone handset off the cradle and pushed a quick dial button with her nose, repeatedly barking into the phone. The dispatcher knew from the persistent barking that something was wrong and immediately sent help.

Dog proves to be golden lifesaver

Toby, a two-year-old golden retriever, saved his owner's life when she began choking on a piece of an apple. The woman, in Calvert, Maryland, attempted to dislodge the apple herself by banging on her chest but failed to clear the obstruction. This drew Toby's attention, and likely also gave him the idea of what he had to do to help her: He stood on his hind legs and knocked her to the floor.

Once she was lying down on the floor he jumped on her chest, and continued jumping on her chest until the piece of apple became dislodged. Essentially he had performed his own modified version of the Heimlich maneuver, and he followed it up by licking her face to keep her from passing out. The woman was left a little hoarse by the experience, but her doctor believes that without Toby, she would not have survived.

Two-legged dog walks tall

Faith, a chow crossbreed that was born with only three legs needed one of her legs amputated because it was severely deformed. With no front legs, and no carts or devices available to aid dogs in that situation, the vet suggested that owner Jude Stringfellow, in Oklahoma, should put Faith to sleep.

But Stringfellow didn't think that giving up was acceptable and so she began training the puppy with spoonfuls of peanut butter, encouraging her to learn to sit up to reach it. Soon the puppy figured out how to hop to get around. Whenever she hopped she would be rewarded with more peanut butter, and lots of love.

The final motivation for Faith's learning to walk upright came when another dog in the household ran away with her bone. Faith would have none of it. She started running after the dog on her two legs to get it back! Since then she has refined her walking technique and has appeared on TV, on shows such as Montel Williams and Oprah Winfrey, to show off her skills. Today, despite only having two legs, Faith is otherwise a very healthy dog and is expected to have a normal life span.

Wrongly accused dog put on death row for four and a half years

Kizzie, a mongrel, was wrongly held for four and a half years under the United Kingdom's Dangerous Dogs Act. She was picked up one night while being walked by a neighbor of the family in 1992. The initial prosecution failed and the dog was to be released, but when owner Jeannette Cragg went to get Kizzie, she was told by police that they were proceeding with charges under another section of the act.

The magistrate who heard the new case decided that Kizzie was a pit bull and that, as such, under the unbending Dangerous Dogs Act, she must be destroyed. Cragg appealed the decision, and the court ordered the release of Kizzie.

But the police refused to release her once again, stating that it would be unlawful. The case went back to the court, which secured the animal's release—all at taxpayers' expense. Total cost: more than $140,000 and four and a half years on death row for an innocent dog that British Kennel Club veterinarians had stated was *not* a pit bull. But their expert opinion was ignored while the police fought to find another way to obtain destruction orders.

What is worse in this case is that the police have informed Cragg's lawyer that they may seize the dog again and launch fresh proceedings. Kizzie is free, for now, but some death row dogs, no matter how wrongly accused, don't always end up so lucky.

A plethora of puppies proves to be a handful

A yellow Labrador named Tawnie made headlines in Utah and surprised owners Dallan and Susie Alldridge when she delivered her first litter of puppies on September 29, 1999. At first the Alldridges thought there were ten puppies—and then they saw fifteen.

But when they were able to get a closer look the next day, they counted a total of *eighteen* new puppies! They were immediately concerned about Tawnie's ability to feed so many pups, given that the average litter size for a Labrador is just *eight.* Following the vet's advice they began supplementing the puppies throughout the day to be sure they received sufficient nutrients. Needless to say they were kept rather busy!

The mother herself was soon on a new diet, too—one high in fat and more normally suited to puppies themselves in order to supply her with enough dietary calories to meet the nursing needs of so many. Despite the large litter, Tawnie coped well and doted on them all. She was later named mother of the year for one major pet brand.

Pug becomes professor's pet project

A pug named Oscar was forced into fame because his owner, a university professor at Virginia Commonwealth University, gave his advertising class the assignment of making the little dog famous. Normal techniques were employed by most students—flyers and the like—but one student got a little bit more creative.

Using the hugely popular online community MySpace, the anonymous student threatened to kill the pug. This caused outrage among animal activist groups worldwide. Through that outrage—and from the subsequent investigation—the six-year-old pug really *did* gain fame, but the assignment backfired when it appeared that Oscar might really be in danger.

The threats were traced to a particular student who could not be named for legal reasons but who failed to come forward when given the opportunity. It is believed that it was only an advertising ploy and that the dog was never in any danger, but the student was left facing expulsion.

Other students used methods such as online viral marketing to get Oscar's name out, and one even convinced an Internet celebrity to write a song about Oscar, which was posted on YouTube. Oscar's fame will be continued by the university with its plans to use him as an example of what not to do for future classes.

No laughing matter for one little pup

Snickers the puppy is a lucky little fellow, considering what he's been through. At just a month old, the catamaran his owners were sailing on developed sail problems and began drifting. For three months they drifted before running aground on Fanning

Island, a small, inhabited coral atoll in the Pacific, in the Republic of Kiribati, 1,000 miles south of Hawaii.

The owners swam safely to shore with Snickers—and a pet parrot too!—but they were unable to take them both with them when they were rescued. Thinking they were doing the best for the animals, they signed over their ownership temporarily to islanders until the Hawaiian Humane Society could arrange for their return.

However, the society never got in touch with the original owners, and the islanders who took the animals had very different ideas about pet care. Snickers, just four months old upon arrival, ended up spending the next four months fending for himself on the atoll. Eventually news spread that both of the animals were to be destroyed as unwanted property of the Kiribati government.

At this point a rescue was arranged, with Norwegian Cruise Lines taking Snickers from Fanning and transporting him to Oahu Island, Hawaii, before his being taken on to Los Angeles for his ultimate rehoming.

Dog causes controversy after skydiving with owner

Miniature dachshund Brutus didn't want to be left behind when his owner took off in an airplane—destined for a skydiving adventure—and attempted to chase the aircraft. His owner, Ron Sirull, decided at that point to take him up. Even more, he decided to strap the dog onto his chest and let him make a dual jump (wearing custom-made goggles, of course).

Although the dive caused a stir among animal activists, condemned as exploitive and cruel, it was cleared as safe by Brutus's vet and the Arizona Humane Society, and Brutus has now completed over one hundred jumps. The only thing he dislikes is the sound of takeoff, during which Sirull covers his dog's ears. Protesters claim that jumping cannot be fun for the dog, but Sirull insists that Brutus gets extremely excited when he sees the jumping gear being prepared.

Brutus has become famous for his free-falling antics, clocking up television and magazine appearances around the world. In 1997 he set the world record for the "highest skydiving dog" (for a nonmilitary dog), for a fifteen-thousand-foot jump over Lake Elsinore. The record had previously been held by Kate, a Jack Russell terrier, for a twelve-thousand-foot jump.

Bruising encounter for dog that fell off cliff

The aptly named Bruiser fell two hundred feet off a cliff near England's Lulworth Cove and miraculously only suffered minor cuts and bruises. His owner, knowing Bruiser's curious nature and the danger it posed to him as they were walking alongside the cliffs, approached him to clip his leash back on—just in time to see the poor dog fall over the edge.

He watched in shock as Bruiser bounced off some rocks

before finally tumbling to the ground below. Horrified, he quickly climbed down toward the dog, expecting to find him dead. Amazingly, Bruiser was alive, and even more amazingly, the veterinarian gave him a clean bill of health, finding only a cut on one paw and some bruising.

Diva's dog stakes own claim to fame

Jack Jr., or JJ for short, the beloved pooch of Mariah Carey, is probably the most well-known of the celebrity-owned pooches. Jack Jr. is definitely used to living in the same style as Carey herself.

Early in his life when Carey had to travel, she took Jack Jr. with her in his own first-class seat aboard airplanes. That was until the airlines decided that the dog was too large and not famous enough for his own seat and would no longer be permitted to travel with her in first class. From then on he became accustomed to flying in a private jet—that she paid for. Otherwise, he is driven around by a chauffeur to wherever Carey wants him to be. He has even been known to be driven the *entire* distance between her Los Angeles and New York homes because she doesn't want him to have to fly economy, next to a stranger who might feed him.

But when they arrive at a hotel, life really starts getting cushy for little Jack Jr. At home and when they are away, they both bathe only in expensive French mineral water, and Carey openly admits that Jack Jr. will frequently bathe with her—just jumping in whenever he wants to, to play with the water jets in the tub.

Of the two of them, she claims her dog has the bigger ego. She says he's the most demanding, growling at a flight attendant as he was carried off a flight when Carey once incorrectly filled out his papers. In fact, when Jack Jr. made the cover of the UK publication *K9 Magazine*, Carey was so proud of her beloved pet's first cover that she mentioned it in most of her interviews, helping to raise Jack Jr.'s star status even higher.

Pop princess receives award—for worst celebrity dog owner

While pop princess Britney Spears is known for being in the spotlight around the clock, she found herself really being scrutinized when the Society for the Prevention of Cruelty to Animals (SPCA) was called in to investigate after her $3,000 Yorkshire terrier, London, suffered a broken leg. Ultimately, the SPCA decided that the pup's injury was simply an accident that happened when he was stepped on.

A year later Spears and London were in the news again when she strangely allowed the little dog to soil a $6,700 gown by designer Zac Posen. Worse, she previously gave away a pet Chihuahua because the dog did not like her boyfriend, Kevin Federline, whom she ended up divorcing soon after giving the dogs away. Lucky was given to an assistant, and two other Chihuahuas were rehomed in a similar manner around the same time. She was voted worst celebrity dog owner in 2006 by online readers of *Hollywood Dog* and *New York Dog* magazines.

Dempsey defies death row

Dempsey, an American pit bull terrier, became one of the most infamous dogs sent to death row in the United Kingdom under the Dangerous Dogs Act that requires pit bulls to be muzzled at all times while in public. It didn't matter that she was registered, tattooed, microchipped, insured, *and* spayed in accordance with UK requirements.

In April 1992, family friend Mark Cichon was taking Dempsey for a walk when she started to gag. Immediately, Cichon removed the muzzle to allow Dempsey to vomit rather than choke. Unfortunately, two police officers pulled up in a patrol car and told Cichon he was breaking the law. The officers weren't interested in the fact that it was a temporary unmuzzling because the dog was sick.

Cichon was summoned to appear in court on charges under the Dangerous Dogs Act, but he never told Dempsey's owner, Diane Fanneran, and so he appeared alone and pleaded guilty. He figured he would just receive a fine and then it would all be over; instead he was found guilty of breaking the law and Dempsey was sentenced to death.

And so began three years of legal battles that saw the case tried in three courts, ending up at the House of Lords. In April 1995 the police told Fanneran that Dempsey would be destroyed within the week, and a moratorium was only granted when the family lawyer threatened to sue if the dog was destroyed without Fanneran's permission—a message that was sent to every vet in the United Kingdom via fax. For the vet performing the lethal injection to be protected, the High Court had to issue a final ruling on the case.

Juliette Glass, an anti-Dangerous Dogs Act campaigner, came to the rescue just two days before the case was to be heard, by finding legal precedence. An earlier case had been dismissed because the owners had not been summoned, only the person who was with the dog at the time. The argument was that had Fanneran been in court at the beginning, the original case may have had a different outcome. Dempsey was released into Fanneran's care the following day under the court ruling that a breach of justice had occurred in not informing Fanneran of the case.

During the high-profile case, French actress and animal rights activist Brigitte Bardot had attempted to intervene on Dempsey's behalf, offering the dog refuge in her French animal sanctuary, covering the costs herself. The British government refused to allow it—in fact the whole issue seemed to be to make an example of Dempsey.

Dempsey, at one time a canine household name in the United Kingdom, passed away in 2003 at seventeen years of age.

Dogs making it big on the big screen for years

It would be unfair to showcase famous dogs without mentioning some of the phenomenal four-legged friends that found fame and fortune on the big screen. Jean the Vitagraph Dog, of Vitagraph Studios in Hollywood, was one of the first canines to really succeed. Beginning in 1908 she became a regular on the silent movie scene.

This opened the way for other movie dogs, such as Ace the Wonder Dog, featured in numerous movies in the 1930s and 1940s. Rin Tin Tin was actually played by several German shepherds and starred in many Warner Brothers films and television shows. Shows such as *Lassie,* featuring a rough collie, lasted for decades and even inspired movies, books, and radio shows. *Wishbone,* airing from 1995 to 2001 on public television, showcased a Jack Russell terrier. Movies such as *Turner & Hooch*—featuring Tom Hanks and the rare Dogue de Bordeaux named Beasley, but called Hooch in the film—and *The Little Rascals* with Pete the Pup, an American pit bull terrier, have given screen time to all of these beloved canines. Our love of dogs ensures that they will continue to play memorable roles on the big screen and in our homes.

Traveling Tails: Lost and Found

Husband and dog missing . . . 25 cents
reward for dog. —Anonymous

Numerous books and movies tell us about dogs that got lost from their caretakers on camping trips, at the airport, or while on vacation—dogs that miraculously traveled hundreds and sometimes thousands of miles to be reunited with their owners once again. But when these stories actually happen, when they make international headlines, we often stop and think, *wow*. These are the stories we never forget, and we only hope that if our beloved Fidos ever get lost they'll know how to find their way back home too. These are the stories that make us check, and double-check, to be sure that our dogs are sitting happily in the backseat—with their tongue hanging and their tail wagging—waiting for the next great family adventure.

A different kind of lost baby

A New York couple found out the hard way that during family trips they should check to be sure all passengers are aboard after stopping. Jeffrey and Nicole Stefanek took their four daughters and two-year-old Pomeranian, Baby, to visit Jeffrey's mother in Shelby, North Carolina.

On the way home the Stefaneks stopped at a shopping mall to pick up some toy sunglasses for the young girls. Even though Nicole stayed in the car with her children while her husband went inside the Dollar Tree, somehow Baby got out. By the time they got to Virginia and stopped for a break on their seven-hundred-mile journey they realized Baby was no longer in their van and they panicked. They immediately backtracked forty miles to where they had last stopped for gas. Not finding Baby there, they had no choice but to continue on home and pray someone would find the dog.

The day after Baby was lost, Jeffrey's mother, Joan Spencer, opened the newspaper to see a story about a dog that had been found and that matched Baby's description. A couple from Shelby had turned him over to the humane society after finding him at the mall. Joan picked Baby up and he stayed with her while the rest of the family made plans to go back to pick him up during Memorial Day weekend.

Ugly Betty star avoids ugly predicament

Ugly Betty television star Vanessa Williams had just returned from a Memorial Day parade with her son in New York when she discovered that her Yorkshire terrier, Enzo, was taken from her apartment. She had left her home as usual, never thinking she would have to worry about someone stealing her dog instead of her other valuables.

She called the police and immediately went to work posting flyers all over the city offering a reward for poor Enzo. Officers suggested that perhaps a hawk or other predator took off with him, but Williams recalled seeing a suspicious car around the time he was taken. She knew this was no accident.

Williams began giving interviews and begged for the return of her beloved dog, no charges would be pressed, no questions asked. She also mentioned he was microchipped, so he could be found by routine scanning at a vet's. Enzo was found in Connecticut eight days later. As promised, Williams did not press charges, but based on other reports of missing dogs in the area, a dognapping ring was suspected.

Williams is glad she had Enzo microchipped. Although microchips are about the size of a grain of rice, they are one of the most useful tools in recovering lost animals. They are implanted under the skin and can be scanned by many vet and rescue facilities to find an owner's information. While Enzo was slightly the worse for wear, he probably fared better than Williams and her family members, who were worried the whole time while looking for the lost dog, going door to door, and searching the Internet.

Through fire and forest

The owners of Mills Wilderness Adventures of Montana, Tucker and Amy Mills, can thank their lucky stars that their half border collie, half Australian collie, Bandit, miraculously made his way through a huge forest fire after they had accidentally left him behind.

The Millses were leading a group of hikers from New York and Florida into the Bob Marshall Wilderness when a dangerous wildfire unexpectedly came to life, cutting them off from their return route. The group took an alternate, much longer route to safely get home. Exhausted after their journey, everyone helped load twenty-six horses, along with all their other equipment, onto various trailers and headed home. Unfortunately, Bandit wasn't among the things they loaded up for the ride back.

Amy isn't sure if Bandit got confused about where he should have been, lay down to take a nap out of the way in the shade, or what. What she does know is he was left behind in the confusion and they really thought he was gone forever. When they got home they called the ranger station to check if someone had seen him.

The next day the Millses received a telephone call that Bandit had been spotted running past the station, thirty-two miles from Holland Lake where they had left him. Bandit seemed to be trying to get back to them, but there was a bigger problem: The blazing fire that had caused the Millses' group to change direction was directly between Bandit and his way home.

Tucker and Amy worried about Bandit's trying to get through the fire and being injured or worse, but there was nothing they could do. However, the next day when they opened the door, Bandit came charging in. He was a bit sore from covering ninety-six miles in two days, but he fully recovered. The Millses say they will definitely keep a closer eye on him from here on out.

Missing dog scare has sweet ending

Fifteen-year-old deaf-and-blind Fulton, a husky mix, is one very lucky dog. If it weren't for the other dogs in his family, he could still be wandering the woods without a chance to get back home.

Owner Bill Hurley was out walking with Fulton when the dog decided to wander off. Hurley used to walk Fulton in the woods of Rye, Maine, until his physical impairments made it too difficult and he started bumping into stumps and other obstacles. Hurley continued to take the dog to a nearby field—in the middle of 190 acres of woodlands—as it allowed him to wander about a bit without problems. While Bill turned his head to see about his other dog, Gigi, Fulton wandered into the woods.

Hurley, his wife, and their daughter immediately began searching for Fulton. They put up flyers all over town, asking for help from residents and other dog owners in the area. They stayed out well past midnight the first night looking for Fulton, but it's hard to search for a dog when you can't call for him because he can't hear you. While Fulton has a tag that says he is deaf and blind, the Hurleys were still concerned for his safety.

They searched endlessly trying to find Fulton before something happened to him.

Finally another of the Hurley's dogs—a one-year-old Collie mix named Zamboni—sniffed out Fulton while he was lying down in a section of the forest that was mostly swamp. Both dogs received vanilla ice cream from a local scoop shop before returning home to bed after the ordeal.

Leaving *La Vida* of Las Vegas

Tamara Beckett never thought she'd see her beloved shih tzu, Bailey, again. The dog had disappeared and eventually Beckett gave up on finding her. But she thought of her dog often and her heartbreak was endless without the closure of knowing what happened. Little did she know the surprises in store for her.

A year after the shih tzu disappeared, the Animal Foundation of Las Vegas contacted Beckett telling her they had found her dog. A routine microchip scan of a shih tzu revealed Tamara's contact information. Amazingly, the shelter that had Bailey was in Las Vegas; Beckett lives in Tulsa, Oklahoma—more than twelve hundred miles away. No one knows what went on during the year she was missing or how she got to Las Vegas, but Beckett is very glad her dog was found.

Beckett had kept all of Bailey's toys and her bed, so she was excited to start making arrangements to bring her back home. Best Friends, another animal rescue organization, helped financially to fly Bailey to Tulsa where she belonged. Beckett commented that Bailey looked fabulous with her sparkle collar and bows when she arrived home from Las Vegas. She had never completely given up hope of finding Bailey because the microchip had up-to-date information. Apparently, what happens in Vegas doesn't always stay in Vegas.

Catch of the day is catch of a lifetime

Ross Deschenes, of Tarpon Springs, Florida, took his family's German shorthaired pointer, Mitzi, and his two sons out in their twenty-three-foot boat one early Saturday morning. When they got about twelve miles out in rather rough seas, they realized Mitzi was no longer in the boat. Zigzagging the entire way back to shore, they failed to find the lost dog.

Fifteen miles off the coast, Orlando Gonzalez was spending the day fishing in the Gulf of Mexico when he saw something fuzzy swimming on the horizon. Upon closer inspection with binoculars he realized it was a dog and went to the rescue. Once he got the dog on board he offered her part of his evening meal and some water—he had definitely caught something more than he expected! He noticed the dog's collar said "Mitzi" and had a telephone number on it. Gonzalez called the number without success. Turns out, the number wasn't Deschenes'—it was his mother's—and she wasn't home to receive the numerous calls.

When he got home he continued to call the number for another couple of hours before finally calling the Coast Guard, worried the dog may have been on a boat that capsized and the owners could be in trouble as well. The Coast Guard checked with local agencies before launching a massive hunt and found a report by Deschenes about his missing pet that he filed with Florida Marine Patrol.

The Descheneses were overjoyed to hear that someone had found their dog. The odds against finding something as little as a dog in the big sea were overwhelming. They drove out to Gonzalez's home to pick up Mitzi later that evening. Mitzi was very lucky Gonzalez was out fishing, even if he caught more than he expected.

Our best friend in low places

When Pat Rondeau set out to do some gardening in her yard she could have never predicted how it would end up. Rondeau was watering plants at her Wisconsin home while her two-year-old West Highland white terrier, Reggie, was poking his nose around a culvert nearby. He was there one minute, and gone the next—leash and all.

Rondeau frantically began searching the surrounding area on foot and by bike but could not find Reggie. Her twelve-year-old son printed flyers and helped post them all over the town, and they also reported Reggie's disappearance to the sheriff's department, as well as to the town constable.

A couple of days later, a pair of preschoolers—Dominic and his sister, Stephanie Xiong—were dropping rocks through a manhole cover a few miles away from Rondeau's house when they heard a dog barking. They told their father, Kou, who after some convincing decided to go check it out. Sure enough there was Reggie running around at the bottom of the six-foot sewer line. Xiong got his fishing rod and used it to catch Reggie by the collar and haul him out.

It is suspected Reggie survived by catching rodents and drinking stormwater while in the sewers. Rondeau rewarded the Xiongs for their help in getting Reggie safely back home.

Have you seen Heidi?

Despite being deaf, Heidi the beagle's hearing deficiency was never an issue until her family began their move cross-country from California to Maine. Heidi was shipped out ahead of the family.

Everything seemed to be moving along just fine until Heidi got to the Portland Jetport in Maine, where she somehow managed to slip out of her collar and bolt. She was hit by a car and rolled over three times before running off, according to the startled driver. At this point the hunt for Heidi was on. One of her owners went to Portland to try to locate her but she proved to be a hard dog to find.

There were only a few Heidi sightings in the next two weeks. Lots of people looked for her without much success in the woods surrounding the jetport. Her owner eventually had to return to California to finish some personal business before the final move to the east. Once he left, Heidi vanished and there were no more sightings of her. It was almost as if she knew he was no longer around.

Back on the West Coast, Heidi's family was heartbroken. They didn't want her to think they had abandoned her. They never lost hope, though, and continued preparations for their big move. They were eager to start their new life—preferably with their beloved dog.

When her owner returned to Portland, Heidi was spotted at the jetport that same day. She hadn't been seen in some time but miraculously turned up the same day her owner flew in. He decided to camp in the woods that night near where she had been spotted, hoping she would find him, but had no luck. A couple of days later he was back camping at the jetport, as Heidi seemed to know that she shouldn't go far from where she got loose, kind of like a lost child who has been taught to stay in one place and not leave it.

Early the next morning Heidi finally came to him. Although she had lost some weight and was covered in ticks and smelled rather rank, she was otherwise unharmed. After almost two weeks of being lost in the Maine woods, she was finally back with her family where she belonged.

You can't keep a cowboy still

Cowboy, a terrier mix, disappeared after jumping out of the window of his owners' truck one day. While Larry and Peggy Hinson of Montross, Virginia, quickly set out to search for their dog, they were unable to find any clues on his whereabouts.

Larry would often take Cowboy to work with him at the Dahlgren naval base. However, on this particular day test firing was taking place. The loud noises most likely startled the dog and made him run off for cover.

Some time later that afternoon, a guard at the gate told Larry a dog matching Cowboy's description had been seen fleeing through the gate, but after spending the entire night looking Larry still couldn't find his dog. He felt defeated going home.

Larry refused to give up. He used the local radio station to spread the word and put up flyers in a forty-mile radius hoping to increase his chances of finding Cowboy. A week later, someone finally called with a sighting of Cowboy. Larry got excited, but his hopes were dashed when he still wasn't able to locate his dog, even after receiving the tip.

Another call came in from someone almost twenty miles from the Dahlgren naval base. Larry was skeptical that the dog sighted was Cowboy, but after the caller described his one black ear and other unique markings, Larry was sure it was Cowboy. He had to have passed some very busy roads and dense forest to get where he was. A new flurry of searching by Larry and friends turned up nothing yet again.

A few days later someone else called to say that Cowboy was right in the person's backyard. But even a tasty steak wasn't enough to tempt Cowboy into staying still long enough to be caught. Larry took the day off from work to search for Cowboy but to no avail.

He decided to try one last thing. He left the truck sitting at the last place Cowboy had been seen. He took the next day off from work again to continue searching, convinced it was only a matter of time now to find Cowboy and convince him to come home. He stopped by the truck before heading out to search and was delighted to see a somewhat thinner Cowboy sleeping on the front seat, safe and sound as if he'd never left the truck.

Doggie paddles for miles and miles

A golden retriever mix that was believed to have drowned turned up alive a few days later after falling into the current of the James River in Newport News, Virginia. The owners of the dog, who had been fishing along the river, said the dog jumped off the pier. A security guard called 911, then made a second call to cancel the first after no sign of the dog was found. The dog was believed to have drowned.

Two days later the missing dog was found stuck in a culvert along the shore, and although people were trying to reach it, they weren't able to. When the tide came in, the dog was washed out of the culvert and caught.

At some point the dog suffered a dislocated hip, but it popped back in and the dog recovered at a shelter and was later rehomed. The dog's survival is amazing because it would have had to tread water or swim for three days to avoid drowning before it was finally found.

A long road home for dog hit by car

When Mona, a rottweiler, was finally found on the side of the road thirteen miles from where she had been hit by a car and after spending a month in the cold wilderness, it was a miracle she was still alive.

Misti White was driving along Highway 89 near McArthur, Nevada, when she saw a scraggly looking rottweiler eating out of a plastic bag on the side of the road. The dog was malnourished and hungry, but when Misti approached it with a handful of Chex Mix, Mona came straight for her, dropping the bag. She went willingly into the car as well, although she required some assistance.

Back at home, where Misti regularly fosters dogs, she spent several days making sure the dog got enough to eat at regular intervals, even if it meant getting up in the wee hours of the morning. With its sweet nature, it was obvious the dog had been someone's beloved pet and Misti set about finding the owners.

Finally, she heard about a rottweiler that went missing after a car wreck a month and a half earlier. The description of the dog Misti found matched the description of Mona, the dog belonging to Eduardo Cortez, who had hit a patch of black ice and flipped his truck. Although Eduardo only hurt his shoulder, Mona was lost in the resulting confusion while emergency workers cleared the scene. Eduardo worked in Reno and made the long trip between his job and his home in Medford, Oregon, twice a month.

The day of the wreck, the Cortez family looked for Mona with no luck. They searched again a couple of weeks later, also with no sign of Mona. They were starting to adjust to not having Mona when the call came that she may have been found. They were overjoyed to find out the dog really was Mona, as they had just about accepted the fact that she could not have survived in the wilderness for so long.

Dachshund runs away when owner dies

A dachshund named Sam rarely left his master's side, but when Teddy Crockerall lost his battle with cancer, Sam suddenly disappeared—even while wearing an electric fence collar. Crockerall's wife, Marcene, said she believed the dog must have sensed something was up.

A couple of days later, after plenty of searching for Sam, Marcene and the rest of the family showed up at the church for Crockerall's funeral. They saw Sam sitting on the doorstep of the church, just shivering. As soon as they called him, he ran right over, obviously delighted to see them.

Although there is no way to determine why Sam decided to run away from home, or how he ended up on the doorstep of the right church—a church he had never been to before—it seems rather difficult to say it was just a coincidence. The church is over six miles from where the Crockeralls lived. Marcene's son-in-law said he thought that Sam was looking for his owner and didn't stop until he found him, unfortunately, at the church.

Puppy dodges fate, reunited with family

When the Safrans got into a car accident in Florida while returning home to Ohio, the only thing worse than their injuries—which weren't bad, considering their SUV flipped twice—was the fact that their six-month-old puppy, Diesel, was missing.

The windows were smashed completely, the puppy's cage door had popped open, and Diesel was thrown from the vehicle. While the family stayed a couple of days in a hotel to recuperate before going back home, they hoped they would also find their beloved puppy, but they had no luck. The Safrans had also just lost their ten-year-old German shepherd, so the pain of losing two dogs was almost unbearable.

However, they decided to put a picture of Diesel in the local newspaper, and shortly after they returned home, a man called with good news: He had their puppy. The Safrans were overjoyed to be reunited with the lost pup, which they had adopted only three months earlier.

Cujo comes home after six years

Cujo, a golden retriever, is finally back where he belongs with the Barczewski family—after a six-year journey and a couple other homes. Although he's a bit older, a little thinner, and starting to turn gray, he's undoubtedly the same dog that ran away back in 2000.

When he was seven he sneaked out of the yard of the Barczewski's home in St. Louis, Missouri. Somehow he ended up over one hundred miles away at an elderly woman's home. When she entered a nursing facility, he was taken to a humane society in Columbia, Ohio. His ears were so infected he could barely hear, his coat was matted, and he had cysts that needed removing. He was truly a sad sight, but far from giving up his travels.

Bob Tillay, the president of Dirk's Fund (a golden retriever rescue group that has helped place hundreds of goldens in the past decade), arranged to have him brought to St. Louis and cleaned up before he was then placed in a different nursing home as a pet for the residents. Unfortunately, the anxious dog wasn't ready for retirement living just yet and it was decided to try and find him somewhere he could run off-leash. Ultimately he was placed on the Dirk's Fund Web site for adoption.

This is where fate took over. Michael Barczewski, Noreen Barczewski's brother-in-law, had visited the site at random, looking for a dog to adopt. He immediately recognized Cujo by the heart-shaped marking on his head and his white feet— Michael and his wife had bred Cujo themselves. Within days Cujo was reunited with the family that never did forget him.

Kayla Barczewski was only four when Cujo ran away but insisted upon hanging his stocking every year at the holidays. She said that a piece of her heart knew he was alive and fine and that he would come home some day. Cujo, at thirteen years old, finally did just that. Maybe this time around he'll be content to just stay in the yard.

The random path of a moon

Doug Dashiell took his three dogs on a weekend camping trip in Nevada when Moon, a Siberian husky, somehow came unhooked from her collar and wandered off. She managed to make the over seventy-mile trek back home in about a week, across terrain that included a desert, a mountain, and a river, as well as forests and a lake.

Moon, who was just a few months shy of two years old, had run off before but always came home without fail. So when Dashiell couldn't find her after searching for a couple of hours, he simply headed home. He knew that Moon had headed northwest toward the Duckwater Shoshone Reservation, so he called the tribal police to inquire if they had seen her and asked to be contacted if someone did. No one had seen her at that point.

Dashiell had practically given up when he was contacted by his veterinarian. Moon had walked into town, where she was found by Alvin Molea, who took her home for the night and gave her a meal and a place somewhere warmer than outside to sleep. He called the vet's office in the morning because Moon was wearing an identification tag.

The only trauma Moon seemed to have gone through was being skunked when she most likely chased one of the creatures on her way back home. Dashiell had a bath waiting for her and hoped to get her back to normal before long. It's definitely much less than he might have had to deal with after such an ordeal.

Tibetan terrier goes on two-year trek

Arnie, an eleven-year-old Tibetan terrier named after Arnold Schwarzenegger, finally found his way home after being missing for almost two years. He disappeared from his yard in County Cork, Ireland, twenty-one months before being found. His owner, Gillian Singleton, believed he was taken to be used for breeding.

Singleton's children were deeply affected and they searched long and hard for the dog but found nothing to point them in any direction. As the months wore on, the family took in another stray named Lucky. But just when they thought Arnie was gone for good, he turned back up.

While the family was away on vacation, they got reports of a dog matching Arnie's description running around their yard and in the general area. When the family got home, they were able to positively identify Arnie, even though he was now a much skinnier pup.

Whether Arnie suffered at the hands of whomever took him or on his journey back home, his owners are simply glad he's back. He and the family's other dog get along like two peas in a pod, with a little scuffling over who is top dog to keep life interesting, but that is the least of the Singletons' worries.

Down-under dognapper takes pup for a ride

Rusty, an eight-year-old Maltese poodle cross, is back home after turning up more than twenty-two hundred miles from where he disappeared in Woy Woy, Australia. The dog, owned by Shirley and Dennis Lowry, simply vanished when Shirley took him with her to get the daily paper and a loaf of bread.

She admits she left his leash tied to a pole as she did every day but swears he was gone in a matter of seconds, not minutes. When she went out to try to find him, a woman nearby asked her if she was looking for a small dog. When Shirley anxiously answered yes, the helpful woman said a man on a bicycle had ridden off pulling the dog along on its leash. By the time Shirley went running after him, he was nowhere to be seen.

While putting up posters for Rusty, she saw other posters for more little dogs that were also missing—all in the same week. She went on the radio pleading for help and called the Royal Society for the Prevention of Cruelty to Animals Australia looking for the dog. At one point someone from the local animal pound called and said Rusty was there, but it turned out to be a different dog.

Almost three months after Rusty disappeared, the real Rusty was found. Luckily, he was microchipped, and when the dog was scanned, the Lowry's contact information showed up on the computer screen.

The Lowerys weren't told where the dog was found, just that a ranger had found him somewhere. Rusty was covered in fleas and ticks and brown dust, and someone had even dyed his hair pink. Shirley said she was working on cleaning him up, as she still had all of his things—including his bed, brushes, and flea shampoo. Rusty had barely left her side since he was a puppy, and if he has anything to say about it, he's not likely to again!

Special psychic service dog gets lost

When Deleyna White got into a car wreck in Houston, Texas, and her dog, Gabe, disappeared, she was not only heartbroken—she was concerned that she had lost her independence. Gabe isn't your ordinary canine; he's a service dog trained to help White know when she is about to have a panic attack as a result of her post-traumatic stress disorder.

Luckily, the Landry family in Beaumont found Gabe about a week after the accident. They found him alongside the road and were amazed when Gabe seemed to know when their son Tyler, who suffers from epilepsy, was having a seizure. Gabe would lean into the boy while he was having a seizure, and they knew he must be a special sort of dog.

With a bit of media attention, they were able to find where Gabe belonged. While Tyler's family was sad to see Gabe go, they are looking into getting their own service dog, and White is just happy to have her wonder dog back.

Dog burglar forgets to take all of his loot

A stolen van of dogs was returned after it was taken from the Arizona Humane Society, but with only six of its seven passengers. Luckily for Sweet-ums, a cocker spaniel mix, he ended up under the stairwell of a concerned citizen's apartment complex.

Ben O'Grady of Phoenix had opened his door to check out the rainstorm outside when he found Sweet-ums huddled under the stairwell of his apartment building. His dad later called to say he thought the dog was featured on the news as missing. Ben was given a reward for returning the dog, which he has said he will use for rent.

At the humane society the workers were very excited. Sweetums, a two-year-old dog, was to be put up for adoption, and the staff anticipated fielding a lot of inquiries for him because of the extra media attention.

The man who stole the van and dogs was arrested and will be charged.

At first the humane society staff thought the thief intended to sell the dogs and had already sold Sweet-ums, but they now believe he probably escaped through an open window or door. From the time the police sent out bulletins to the local media, it took only a matter of hours for the van to be spotted. It was left running with the keys inside with the air conditioning left on for the dogs. At least the dogs didn't suffer much.

All Dogs Go to Heaven

If there are no dogs in Heaven, then when I die
I want to go where they went. —Unknown

Do dogs come back after death to warn, protect, and comfort their human guardians? According to reports from around the world, the answer is a resounding yes!

In life, dogs have been humans' closest animal companions while they hunted and farmed. So it is also natural for dogs to be our closest companions in death and the afterlife. Unfortunately, dogs' shorter life spans mean that they will often precede their human guardians in death, but that is not the end of the story. Those who study ghost dogs say these four-legged spirits can reach out in many ways. Sometimes ghost dogs caress their living families with breezes or speak to them in audible barks and whimpers or try to get human attention by scratching on doors. Other times, families will hear the tapping of nails on floors, smell their canine visitors, or feel spirit dogs as they press against them or climb up on beds and other furniture. Let's take a walk with ghost dogs that continue to love, guide, and protect their human and animal families.

Dream visit removes guardian guilt

Springer spaniel/border collie mix Sam was seventeen years old when his owner made the decision to help him go to the Rainbow Bridge. Sam was suffering with a brain tumor that caused him to have strokes. He had trouble standing, walking, and was just plain tired. He had lost an eye to glaucoma.

Sam's owner made the decision to put him out of his constant pain and discomfort, but she felt pangs of guilt. She thought that maybe she had made the wrong decision. Like many people who must make that final decision, she was worried that maybe there was more she could have done for Sam.

But Sam had a way to let his human know she had made the right decision for him. He removed her guilt by coming to her in a dream two weeks after he passed away.

I was standing in our kitchen and I could hear the tap, tap, tap of his toenails on the hardwood floor. I peeked around the corner and standing there was Sam. He was all woolly (God, I hated his hair), panting (he never stopped panting in the 11 years I owned him), had both eyes (he had glaucoma and we had to surgically remove one eye approximately 4 months previously) and he was wagging his tail. I looked at him and said, "Buddy, what are you doing?" He looked at me and of course he didn't talk but I could just understand that he was telling me he was okay. I got the feeling of him saying I did the right thing, that he wasn't mad, and he was ok. He then turned and walked over to his spot on the couch and jumped right up. He laid down with his head on the armrest like he always did and wagged his tail and slept.

I woke up in tears. It's like he knew, wherever he was now, that I needed to hear that. I spent day after day just beating myself up over the decision and he let me know I needed to stop.

Sam's dream visit relieved his owner's guilt. But Sam didn't stop there; he also helped bring the next dog into their lives. A few weeks after the dream, Sam's owner was on the Internet looking for a shelter dog to adopt. She came across a large dog that reminded her of Sam with his big, sad eyes and black-and-white coat.

She went to the shelter to see this Sam lookalike only to find that he was not a good fit for her family. But Sam had a plan. His owner was depressed that the dog she had seen wouldn't work into her family so she strolled down the line at the shelter and found the dog Sam had wanted her to see. Sitting at the end of the line on a dirty pad was a little pug girl who needed a lot of help and love.

Winnie the pug was so much like Sam that his owner wondered if Sam hadn't been reincarnated as this patient, sad little girl. Like Sam, Winnie was older, had an eye condition, and was housebroken. She also needed an expensive hip operation. Besides, Sam's owner had always wanted a pug. When the shelter staff tried to talk her out of adopting Winnie because Winnie needed so much help, she brushed off the warnings and has been happy ever since about the decision to adopt the little pug. She believes that Sam sent her to Winnie to save her life. As Sam's owner says, "She is the perfect dog and I love her. I thank Sam everyday for sending us to her. I also thank him for being my best friend for 11 years and I only wish I had 11 more."

Toys show presence of spirit dogs

Sometimes a dog toy is more than a dog toy, to paraphrase Sigmund Freud. Sometimes a dog toy is a gift from beyond the grave from a loving dog spirit.

Matilda, a collie that had lived her life with a family in Australia, died in her sleep. Matilda wanted to reach her family, but her owner wasn't ready for Matilda's nighttime visits.

Matilda would whimper at the door at night. Her owner reported that Matilda would cause a breeze to blow through her bedroom, even when the doors and windows were solidly closed. But one night Matilda went even further in her attempt to reach her owner; she brought in a ball and put it on the bed, not once but twice!

Matilda's owner woke up that night to the sound of a dog whimpering at the door. She looked out, but there was no dog. She returned to her bed to find a ball sitting on the end of it. Thinking her brother was playing a not-so-funny joke, Matilda's owner took the ball and tossed it out the back door. She returned to her bed, and so did the ball. A few minutes after she got back into bed, she felt pressure on the end of her bed, and there was the ball.

A few nights after that incident, Matilda's owner felt a breeze on her leg. As she got into bed in the dark, she felt something heavy at the end of the bed. She turned on the light but there was nothing visible on the bed.

Matilda's owner reported that she was still hearing and feeling Matilda months after she passed away. Maybe Matilda needed just one more game of toss before she went on to the next life.

Ghost dog barks at her family

What is a ghost dog to do when she wants to stay in touch with her earthly human family? For one Canadian Maltese/poodle cross named Brandy, you do what you did when you lived with them—bark. Brandy's owner said that Brandy barks in the morning at her and her husband to wake them up or just to talk. Brandy's family takes it all in stride. Her "dad" simply tells Brandy to lie down next to him, and he can feel her jump up near him.

Brandy died of complications from diabetes when she was almost eleven years old. But Brandy stays around her "mom" and "dad." She barks at her mom before the alarm goes off in the morning. Brandy also lets her dad know she's still around by giving him one sharp bark in his face, just like she did before she passed away. He tells her to lie down, and he can feel her as she does. Sometimes Brandy will bark at the back door as well.

Brandy has made a believer out of her dad, who had never experienced anything like this before Brandy came back to act as their unseen alarm clock. Apparently, Brandy can't bear to leave them behind. She's still part of their daily life.

Bull mastiff helps family say good-bye

Some dogs, like Jammer, help their families through the whole process of death, from the moments before to the return to an empty house to loving messages afterward to even helping their families find their new canine family members. Bull mastiff Jammer is a very special spirit. She helped her family every step of the way when it was her time to move to the Rainbow Bridge.

At the age of nine, Jam was diagnosed with a tumor on her heart. Her family made the decision that every pet owner dreads and scheduled Jam for her last vet visit. They took her to the vet's and let her out of the car. Her "mom" told Jam to take her time and let them know when she was ready to go inside. Jam sniffed some flowers as she walked around. After a few minutes, Jammer went to the door and looked back at her human family as if to tell them she was ready to go inside.

After seeing Jammer on her way, her owners went home, delaying their reentry to the house knowing that Jammer was not there. But they were wrong; Jam was waiting for them. After sitting in their car for fifteen or twenty minutes, Jam's owners went inside.

They had brought her collar home with them and placed it across a portrait of Jammer a friend had painted for them. Five minutes later Jam let her family know she hadn't really gone. They heard the metal part of the collar hit the picture glass. Looking at each other, the husband and wife knew their Jammer was still around, watching over them.

The next morning, Jammer's dad took the family's motorcycle to a friend for a road test. As he went up the hill, he saw Jammer's smiling face in the clouds. Then he heard her say, "Thank you, Dad. I love you," and she was gone.

But was she? Jammer was still looking out for her family as she guided them to the next dog to share their lives, Liberty. Three months after Jammer passed away, her owners got a call to come meet another bull mastiff, an eighteen-month-old female named Liberty. Jammer's mom said a little prayer for a sign if Liberty was supposed to join their family. Jammer was ready for her.

"We went and met Liberty and right before we left her owner said, "One of the things I just love about her is this patch of white on her chest." When she lifted her up and opened her paws, there was an angel with opened wings with a fuzzy face above it.

Jam was looking over us and found just the right girl for us and Liberty was sent to heal our hearts. Two years later she's still making us laugh."

Jammer's owner reports that she is still around, watching over all her earthly family. She feels Jammer from time to time and knows her canine angel is nearby.

Spirit dog communicates through his own offspring

Colonel Jackson, or "Jack" as he was called, was a loving golden retriever that lost his life to cancer as a young dog. Jack and his owner were inseparable. When Jack had to be put to sleep, his owner buried him in her rose garden. But Jack was not gone; he simply changed form.

Before Jack died, he sired a litter of puppies. Jack's owner got the only golden boy, and she named him Jeb. As a puppy, Jeb spent time lying on Jack's grave. But it was still a surprise to Jack's owner when Jack showed up in photographs of herself and Jeb in the yard. She has very clear photos of Jeb and her with a brightly lit orb floating nearby. She claims that she has over three hundred pictures with the light that have been checked by professional photographers for authenticity. She believes that the orb is Jack, watching over her and Jeb.

Random crows create controversy around dog's death

Crows were the messengers from the beyond for Australian Rhodesian ridgeback Sharna. Her family had never seen crows around their home until the day after Sharna's memorial was erected in the family's yard. The seven-year-old female had died after being bitten by a deadly paralysis tick. Sharna was gone physically, but her family believed that she spoke to them through the beaks of about fifteen crows that took up temporary residence at Sharna's memorial.

What's so unusual about seeing crows? Crows were rarely, if ever, seen near Sharna's home until the day after Sharna died. Then the murder of crows showed up and covered the veranda, trees, and yard. The crows spent most of their time over Sharna's memorial and watched her grieving owner, who felt that Sharna sent the crows to let her family know she was OK and watching over them. A week later, most of the crows moved on except for one that returns from time to time to remind Sharna's family that they are still loved and protected by one very devoted dog spirit.

Spirit dog gives blessing to owner's new spouse

The Lemp Mansion in St. Louis, Missouri, is known as one of the ten most haunted hotels in the United States. It is the permanent home to a number of human ghosts who still reside in the house where they died. The Lemp family was one of the founders of St. Louis's beer industry.

Regular tours directed by local mediums take visitors into the upper areas of the hotel and restaurant that are known to be haunted. During the late-night tours, visitors often feel cool drafts said to be caused by Lemp family members who have left their earthly bodies but not the mansion.

Mediums open and close the tours by passing on messages to the visitors from their loved ones who have died. Sometimes the messages and the ghosts can surprise even the tour guides. One of these unusual messages came from Weimaraner David, who managed to reach his former owner with a very important message and baffle the evening's tour guide and medium.

David's relationship with his owner was the epitome of the love between a boy and his dog, but David had died some years earlier from old age. His owner did not consider himself as being into "spooky stuff," but he had agreed to go on a Lemp Mansion ghost tour with his girlfriend a few nights before Halloween one year.

They were two of about thirty people on the tour. The guide talked briefly and then took the small crowd into the rooms known to be haunted. The rooms were fairly dark, but there was enough light to see and be seen. David's owner's girlfriend felt a large animal lean up against her leg. When she looked down, there was nothing there, except she could still feel what felt like a dog. The unseen dog stayed with her a few minutes and then left.

But David wasn't gone yet. He had one more thing to do that night.

The tour guide called the visitors together and took them back to the room where they could sit down and the medium could open the doors to the afterlife so loved ones could speak to the visitors. As the tour visitors waited for the medium to speak, she got an odd look on her face. She stumbled over the words, but the only name that kept coming out was "David." She said "David" wanted to let his—and this is where the medium really stumbled—"human" know he loved him and was watching him. After the medium relayed a few other messages, David's owner went up to speak to her. She was still somewhat nonplussed by the message. She admitted that "David" was not human and that confused her.

The girlfriend had been listening to David's owner and the spiritualist. She decided that now was the time to tell her boyfriend about her furry ghost experience. David's owner realized that his dog had touched his girlfriend and had spoken to him. It was only later that the owner and his family realized that the dog that loved him so much was giving his strong yet silent approval of the woman who would become his wife.

Animal communicator passes message of comfort from the afterlife

Piggy, a much-loved fawn pug, died only fifteen months after becoming part of a family. Piggy passed away on a Friday, and her owner spent the weekend crying and mourning her. But Monday morning Piggy sent a rainbow that touched her grave for a few moments. Piggy's owner was greatly comforted and knew that her pug was still nearby.

Sometime after that, Piggy's owner had a session with an animal communicator who shared a long and even more comforting message with her. The communicator described Piggy and then went on to tell her that Piggy would be with her forever. She also told her that Piggy felt her love every time the owner looked at her photograph.

The reading went on in great detail. Piggy's owner was amazed and deeply comforted by what she heard.

Piggy understands that I worry and she doesn't want me to worry about her, that she is fine. She said that Piggy can run fast and she doesn't hurt anymore, and she can see clearly now. She said that Piggy has found the man with the white hair that I sent to her to take care of her (I don't know who this could be unless it's my Grandpa). I told the AC [animal communicator] that sometimes when I'm sitting quietly on the back porch and I'm thinking about her, that I can sometimes still hear her little bark, and she said that Piggy heard me and that she's so happy, she's doing the bouncy dance (she used to bounce up and down on her front paws for me when she was happy) and barking and she's so happy that I understand. She and I spent a lot of time in our porch swing together. That was our special time together.

The animal communicator said that Piggy told her that she loves us and that we gave her something she hadn't ever had before, and that was a home. She wasn't sure what to think when she first came to be with us, but she felt loved. And she said that just as Piggy is on my heart (I have a pendant that my daughter gave me a week after Piggy passed away and it had "Piggy" on one side and the day of her death on the other), that I am on her heart (her little doggy tag had our name/number on it). She said that when Barney and Clyde Patches come running through the house for no reason, that that's Piggy herding "the boys" (we always have called them "the boys" and there's no way a stranger could know this) and that Piggy misses playing with the boys.

I had the AC ask about when Piggy died, did she hurt or suffer. She said no, she didn't suffer much, that her chest hurt, and sometimes how your body tells you to hang on, that she had to let go because it was so tight.

She said she was comforted that I was with her, but I wasn't; I was at work. When I told the AC this, she said that Piggy is insistent that I was with her and that I held her and told her I love her. She said she could hear my prayers, but it wasn't in words, it was in beautiful music, and the music was with her when she went over to Rainbow Bridge. When I got the call to go home and check on Piggy, I prayed all the way home. I got there and held her, I knew Piggy was gone, but I went ahead and took her straight to my vet (I guess I just wanted him to tell me for certain and hear the words).

When I got home with her, I just sat in the car for probably 45 minutes and held her and cried. The animal communicator said that Piggy could feel my tears and that she didn't want me to be sad anymore. I told her to tell Piggy that when I get to Heaven, I was going to run to Rainbow Bridge to see her first, and she said that Piggy would be there waiting for me, to help guide me over to Heaven, as others were there to help guide her over. She said that Piggy said she has all she wants to eat and drink, and she runs and plays in the greenest, prettiest grass that you've ever seen, and the sunshine is so bright and pretty, and the sky is the bluest blue anyone could imagine. Piggy said things are just the way that I told her they would be in Heaven.

The animal communicator said that she could see that Piggy and I were more like sisters than mother/ daughter (I always called her my "sidekick" because I took her everywhere I possibly could with me). She said that Piggy loved the pink dress and it made her feel very pretty. (Anytime I put a sweater or pretty collar on her, she would always "priss," and I had just gotten her a pretty pink polka dot harness dress. She got to try it on at home and wear it to the PugPalooza, a get-together especially for pug owners in May.)

The animal communicator also said that Piggy was laying her head over my heart like she always did and that she can feel my love for her (every afternoon when I came home and I picked her up, she would lay her head over on me, just at the heart). She said that Piggy comes to visit me in my dreams and she'll always be with me and wouldn't ever go away. She said Piggy also misses her Daddy, and that it made her sad when we had to leave every morning, but she always knew that we would come back later in the day (we were going to work) and she knew it was something that we had to do.

Piggy's owner realized that some people may not believe the depth and length of the animal communicator's message. But she believed and accepted the words.

"I don't know how you all feel about this, but the animal communicator said too much that there is no way she could know, so I choose to believe. It was extremely emotional for me and was a couple of hours before I could even talk about it. I know my Piggy can feel my love, and my heart overflows for her still today. I'll always miss her, but I take comfort knowing she knows how very, very much she was loved while I got to be her Momma."

However they choose to communicate, spirit dogs reach back from death, bringing love and life to the two- and four-footed family members they leave behind.

The Dog Ate My . . .

Contrary to the popular myth, dog does not eat dog.
—Proverb

"Sorry, ma'am, but the dog ate my homework." Ah, yes, the ever popular excuse from children who either forgot to do their homework or were just too lazy. While this excuse may sound like a joke, evidence shows that our best friend has eaten some very, *very* strange things indeed. At some point in history, a dog probably did eat a child's homework, and it soon became the stuff of legend.

The cause of this is a condition called pica—which is the desire to eat nonnutritional items. Humans and animals are known to suffer from pica, with female humans most frequently displaying the behavior during pregnancy. The cause is not entirely understood but is thought to be caused either by behavioral issues or by nutritional deficiencies. Puppies are more likely than adult dogs to chew things, just like human infants who are teething, but most puppies and babies grow out of it.

It is believed that animals are usually aware of what is lacking in their normal diet, and when these deficiencies are present, they are pushed to consume something containing the deficient substance.

Behavioral issues in dogs are a little more complex and could be caused by anxiety, stress, or even boredom. Some think that pica might be an attention-seeking behavior, triggered by a past interaction when the dog was caught eating a nonfood item. Whether the interaction was positive or negative, it may be that the animal is trying to repeat it, to gain the owner's attention. Whatever the cause, pica has led to dogs' consuming some very unhealthy and unusual objects.

Toys, balls, and balloons appear on the canine menu

Denise Allen of Texas had bought her dog, Timber, a dental chew toy wrapped in packaging that claimed the toy was safe. No warnings or calls for observation during use were printed on the wrapper, and so Allen thought everything was fine, until a one-inch-wide piece got lodged in the dog's intestines and caused a massive infection.

The spikes on the toy, designed to help clean plaque off a dog's teeth, probably contributed to the intestinal damage that ultimately led to the incurable infection. Vets attempted to save Timber with surgery, but instead all they found was the large piece of the chew toy.

Toys like this one do not show up on X-rays, which increases the risk to animals because diagnosis is harder than for an obstruction easily visible on an X-ray. Despite the lack of warning on the packaging, caution is always needed when giving these toys to dogs, and regular inspections should be made to be sure the toy is not damaged in a way that would allow a piece to come off and be swallowed.

Rope toy death a warning to all dog owners

The rope-type chew toys have also caused fatal injury to innocent pups. Merlin was a nineteen-month-old Portuguese water dog bought as a companion and family pet, to grow up with the family's two children. The rope toy he chewed on was made of many cotton and polyester threads, woven together into a rope and knotted at the ends.

Merlin, in his chewing, managed to pull off and ingest a number of these threads, which then became lodged in his gut. Merlin's family, the Weises, of Bainbridge Island, Washington, sought help when he became sick. Ultimately the threads caused perforations in his intestine and colon, and surgery was performed to remove the rope fragments that were so tangled they had to be cut up to get them out.

Despite the surgery, Merlin died just two weeks later. The Weises believe that this cannot be an isolated case and are concerned about the danger these toys pose to other dogs.

Would Victoria keep this a secret?

A springer spaniel named Taffy in Staffordshire, England, may well hold some kind of record for the volume of underwear that he has eaten. Prior to the surgical removal of his fortieth pair of underwear, he had already chowed down on three hundred socks, fifteen pairs of shoes, and a set of keys.

Taffy's owners, Sharon and Eubie Saayman, would find the eaten items "deposited" around the house on a frequent basis and did not notice any problems Taffy had in passing the items. Nature took its course and the things the dog consumed would move on. But the fortieth pair apparently got tangled and started to block the dog's intestines, causing him pain and prompting a trip to the vet. Taffy has since made a full recovery, and despite his bad habit is described as being a lovely dog.

Eggs-eptional circumstances cause for immediate surgery

A British spaniel named Moss chose a human toy to swallow—packaging and all. A British confection called Kinder Eggs consists of a chocolate egg shell that surrounds a plastic inner egg, which is normally yellow. Inside of this is a toy that the buyer assembles, and even when removed from the chocolate casing, the inner-plastic egg still tends to smell and taste of chocolate. The inner egg is about two inches long and an inch in diameter.

Moss chose to eat this egg, which caused concerns for his vet because of unknown factors. If he had not chewed up the toy and just swallowed the egg whole, he would be protected him from the sharp edges of the small toy inside. However, it would increase the risk of obstruction in his intestines when the whole egg passed out of his stomach. In the best-case scenario Moss would have completely chewed the toy and it would be in pieces small enough to pass through and safely out.

The vet chose to wait and see, telling Moss's owners to inspect the dog's feces to see if any brightly colored pieces of plastic were present, and warning them to be on the lookout for symptoms of blocked intestines, mainly, vomiting because the food consumed is unable to pass the obstruction.

Two days later Moss did indeed vomit, but as there was no undigested food, the vet was still unwilling to take further action, choosing to wait a few more hours. When more vomiting followed she called them back in for X-rays.

The X-ray showed the Kinder Egg in the dog's stomach and clearly showed the outline of the toy inside. The veterinary staff took guesses at what the toy was! According to the vet this kind of game in the operating room helps the staff cope with the stressful situations that they may come up against during surgery.

It was clear that surgical intervention was needed, and Moss was soon operated on to remove the large obstruction, which was easy to find in an otherwise empty stomach. The egg was given to the owners as a souvenir, and the nurse, while cleaning it up, couldn't wait to see what the toy inside the egg was—it was a space monkey.

Moss recovered well from his surgery, in part because the egg never left the stomach. Had it reached the intestines, it could have caused significantly more damage.

Blow-up dog toy has Yorkie fit to burst

Elaine Mather took her Yorkshire terrier, India, to a charity veterinary service in the United Kingdom when she stopped eating her food. X-rays and blood tests failed to show any possible cause for this symptom in the previously lively dog.

When Mather described a recent incident involving India's swallowing part of a rubber chew toy and vomiting it up, an obstruction was thought to be a possible cause for India's illness, and exploratory surgery was begun.

During the surgery the vet was surprised to find no less than eight colorful party balloons inside her stomach with very little damage to them. Mather does not know where the balloons came from, as they had none in their own home, but other than some weight loss, India suffered no real ill effects. A course of antibiotics was prescribed to prevent infection, but India made a full recovery.

Sesame Street character meets slobbery end

Jenny Biggs is mother to two—a young son and a boxer dog named Brandy, both of whom she spends her days picking up after. One day, however, she learned that playthings that are safe for a child are not necessarily safe for a dog, when her son's favorite Ernie toy disappeared.

Jenny was clued in to Ernie's fate when Brandy started

vomiting, and she took the dog to the vet. X-rays showed that the dog had swallowed the toy, and it was causing a severe blockage—a potentially life-threatening condition. Emergency surgery ensured that Brandy made a full recovery, and Ernie earned his place on Dr. Sandy Albright's wall of fame (for objects removed from a dog's stomach) at the Crossroads animal care facility in Cary, North Carolina.

Picky pooch prefers women's undergarments

For Deefer the bull mastiff, only women's underwear will satisfy his cravings. He started out his habit consuming socks and the remote control, but he soon moved on exclusively to women's underwear.

He racked up an impressive score card: twenty pairs of ladies' underwear in a one-year period. He coped with them just fine for the most part—passing them as nature took its course—until a pair got tangled up inside him and caused an intestinal blockage. Surgery was needed to remove the underwear meal, and the vet found that the pair was not alone! There were another two pairs inside him, yet to be passed naturally—and surprisingly pretty much undamaged by the dog's swallowing. Apparently he's not very careful when it comes to chewing his food.

Springer spaniel favors stones over biscuits

A case of confusion may be the reason a springer spaniel named Barney was filling his belly full of rocks at his home in England. While getting exercise outdoors, instead of returning with the sticks that were thrown to him during games of fetch, Barney turned his attention to eating up crab apples and rocks—lots of rocks.

He showed no symptoms of illness, but a rattling was heard coming from his stomach. Initially, eight-year-old Olivia Parkinson heard the strange noises, but her parents refused to believe her until they finally head it themselves.

Once at the veterinarian's office, they were able to see on the X-ray the large amount of rocks that poor Barney had eaten. The stones were too large for him to pass and, had it gone any longer, may have caused an obstruction, making him very sick. Surgery was performed to remove the six random rocks—each about an inch and a half in diameter—which Olivia later kept as souvenirs.

Barney, no longer trusted on walks, now wears a muzzle for his own safety.

Owner floored by dog's food choices

In Tennessee, when Bubba developed a case of pica, the cause was determined. The nonfood of choice for the mixed breed chow was the linoleum that covered the kitchen floor, and after eating a section of the linoleum, his owner, Melissa Kennedy, took him quickly to the vet for treatment.

Kennedy knew the risks the dog faced from the linoleum in his gut because she also is a vet, and she also knew the risks (and costs) of the surgery to remove the pieces. But for Bubba it didn't need to come to that; the linoleum was able to be removed through endoscopy.

The endoscopy also discovered a stomach infection with *Helicobacter* bacteria, a likely and frequent candidate for triggering pica in dogs. After a course of antibiotics, Bubba should be safe from eating the floor in the future or from craving any other strange and potentially dangerous dinners.

Wii shall overcome this obstruction

A missing Wiimote for a Nintendo game system went unnoticed until a three-year-old Labrador retriever became sick. The dog was taken to a vet in Colorado by the Becknell family after he began coughing up blood.

The vet could feel a foreign object during the examination, and an X-ray showed a rectangular object lodged inside the dog's stomach. The vet administered syrup of ipecac to induce vomiting, and gentle massaging of the dog's stomach while he was vomiting finally dislodged the remote, and it was expelled. It was instantly recognizable to the family as the son's Wii remote controller.

Surgery was avoided and the dog made a very rapid recovery once the control was removed from his stomach.

Hairbrush not a healthy snack for hungry hound

A hairbrush turned up as one of the most unusual objects that a Cardiff, Wales, vet had ever seen swallowed by a dog. Leo, a four-month-old Staffordshire bull terrier, had suddenly stopped eating, prompting his owner, Leanne Marston, to take him to a veterinarian to be checked out.

The vet, Deborah Mir, could feel a foreign object in the pup's stomach and could tell from the size that there was no way he could pass it—surgery would be necessary. The surgery was complicated by the hair from the brush. When the vet tried to remove the five-inch brush, it pulled the hair with it that was spread out through the dog's gut. It took a full five incisions to free up the hair so that the brush could be removed.

A rupture causing peritonitis cast doubt on the dog's recovery. However, a day later he was doing well, and his owners were ready to pick up Leo, back to his normal self.

No one saw him swallow the brush, but with four females in the household, there were likely to be plenty of them lying around.

Dog claims cleanest mouth around

In his seven years of life, a yellow Labrador named Bailey swallowed a wide array of objects from her menu of the unusual, including ten bars of Dove soap, almost all new and unused.

These would often make her vomit, producing, not surprisingly, bubbly vomit, which made sense when the soap was discovered missing. Bailey is not alone in her love of soap; many reports exist of dogs that vary in their preferred brand of soap.

Crayons too have graced Bailey's diet, but these nontoxic items caused much less of a fuss, or upset to her stomach. In fact they passed quite harmlessly to create a nice rainbow of feces. Not so harmless (because of the hard, potentially sharp pieces of plastic) but similar in results, are the marker pens she has eaten. Thus far she has practiced her bizarre habit without any ill effects.

Pair of tights prove to be a problem
for basset hound

Parsnip the basset hound was just seven months old when his habit of eating strange things started giving him problems. He attempted to add a handbag to his menu but was thwarted before he could do any damage. He also tried to eat the shoes of his owner's guests. He managed to take a couple of bites out of the shoes before they were rescued, and his owner said that he would chew on just about anything.

However, it was a pair of women's tights that finally got him into trouble. Owner Katie Phillips, of Telford, England, took Parsnip to the vet when he started experiencing digestive problems, and vet Barry Jacobs operated. During the surgery a pair of tights was discovered in one piece, without a single tear in them, suggesting that Parsnip swallowed them whole without so much as chewing, which seems quite an achievement in and of itself!

Thong poses throng of issues after dog eats it

A cocker spaniel named Arnie embarrassed owner Miriam Walters, in Sussex, England, when he had to have surgery to remove an intestinal blockage. He had a lengthy history of eating nonnutritional items—including socks and boxer shorts—and up until this point had passed them without incident.

He finally met his match when he consumed his owner's thong, which was removed just in time. The thong was becoming impacted, blocking his intestines—a little longer and he may have suffered more serious damage.

Eating bras doesn't bode well for dog's health

Not all underwear eaters were as fortunate as those mentioned so far. Nova, a young Weimaraner living in Holly Springs, North Carolina, died after swallowing a bra that she snatched out of her owner's gym bag. The thirteen-month-old dog suffered a great deal of damage to her esophagus and intestines when she ate the bra, and three surgeries were not enough to repair the damage and save her life. Complications took her ten days later.

Her owner, Crystal Sheppard, has since worked to set up a charity fund to help other owners who may not be able to afford the much-needed and often large vet bills that our dogs can leave us with.

Chain-chewing dog has change of heart

Eighteen-week-old Harley has displayed a taste for metal objects. The first time she exhibited this liking, she was seen by her owners chewing on her choke chain. But the next time they looked, the chain wasn't there. In fact, it was nowhere in sight.

Despite the husband's disbelief that such a small dog could swallow a chain like that, the Aldersons assumed the obvious and took the puppy to the vet in Cambridge, England, where it was confirmed that she had indeed swallowed the chain.

Surgery to remove the chain was performed before the chain could leave the stomach and cause damage to the intestines. The puppy actually attempted to eat the scissors that the vet had out while examining her before the surgery. Given her obvious addiction to all things metal, the Alderson family decided to throw away the choke chain.

Sticky gorilla spells big trouble for labrador

Reggie the black Labrador retriever worked long and hard in his home in Fremont, Ohio, to reach the tub of Gorilla Glue that was stored out of reach on a high shelf. His owner, Natalie Overmyer, thinks that Reggie would have had to jump multiple times to reach and retrieve the glue so that he could then consume a quarter of the tub.

He showed no ill effects to begin with, and seemed fine, in fact, for almost two weeks before he was taken suddenly ill. He was rushed into surgery after X-rays showed two large masses.

These masses were the glue that expanded like foam once it mixed with food and water and then hardened. The largest of the two was the size of a head of cauliflower. The glue is meant for bonding such things as wood, metal, and stone, and clearly is an unsafe item for dogs to consume.

Reggie made it through surgery well and fully recovered.

Staffordshire bull terrier has second thoughts after swallowing knife

Young Jake, a twelve-week-old Staffordshire bull terrier, was so small at the time that he performed his knife-swallowing feat that the seven-inch knife ran all the way from his pelvis to his throat. His owner, John Mallet, of Huyton, England, became worried when he started vomiting and standing with his paws on Mallet's chest—his head back, in an attempt to keep his body in a straight line.

X-rays showed the knife running from one end of the small dog to the other. The handle was in his pelvis; had it been the other way around, the risk would have been far more significant. Immediate surgery removed the kitchen knife and Jake was back on his feet a day later.

How he managed to swallow the knife is unknown, and his small size makes it all the more amazing that he did it and that he survived without more serious injury.

Extreme caution used in canine mishap

Kyle, another young staffie in the United Kingdom, foolishly attempted a similar trick. At just six months old, the young pup swallowed a fifteen-inch knife when he was only eighteen inches tall and eighteen inches long himself! He was taken to the vet when he began vomiting, and the examination showed no signs of a foreign object in the dog's body. When the vomiting didn't subside, an X-ray was taken, shocking the vet, who saw the fifteen-inch knife.

Proceeding with care during the hour-long surgery, the vet removed the knife, handle first, being careful to make sure that the knife blade did not further injure the dog on the way out. A week later Kyle was seen for a follow-up and was found to have some minor swelling from the surgery, but otherwise he was in good health and back to his normal self.

Skewered collie lucky to survive

Cassie the collie cross is lucky to be alive. For five months she walked around Tayside, Scotland, with a kebab skewer in her stomach, causing her pain. Owner Suzanne Weir took Cassie to the vet when she developed breathing problems, started losing weight, and a lump developed on her side. The vet thought she had either been shot with an air gun or she had a tumor; either way the prognosis was poor and Weir was expecting to soon have to put Cassie to sleep.

One Sunday evening, three inches of a wooden skewer were spotted sticking out of the dog's side. Weir pulled the rest out, a full seven inches of intact skewer, which she then took to the vet along with her dog. The twelve-year-old pooch was put on a course of antibiotics until the wound healed but was very soon back to her normal self and jumping around.

It is believed that Cassie swallowed the skewer at a party for Weir's three-year-old son, five months before. It wasn't long after that when the dog began to exhibit symptoms and lose weight. Over the following months the skewer worked its way out of the dog's stomach, causing a lump in its side before finally popping completely through.

Eye of the needle nearly causes canine calamities

Louie the beagle could have easily died and was lucky that his owner, Sue Mitchell, of Shifnal, England, saw him swallowing a needle. An object the size of a sewing needle might not have caused symptoms until peritonitis set in, but it was clearly visible on the X-rays that were taken as soon as he arrived for surgery.

"It's just one of those things that you do not expect to happen," Mitchell told BBC News. "You only have to turn away for a second." Luckily, Louie made a full recovery.

Dog chooses strange bedmates

At six months old, Saffy, a Yorkshire terrier living in St. Budeaux in Plymouth was as inquisitive as any puppy could be, befriending the dustpan and hand broom in the past, taking them with her to her bed. That was until owner Susan Natkaniec found her playing with a spool of blue cotton thread, without a needle attached.

At first Natkaniec assumed that there had been no needle in the spool from the start. But when Saffy started showing signs of distress—retching and pawing at her mouth—she decided to take her dog to the vet for safe measure. Turns out the poor puppy had accidentally swallowed the needle while playing, and it got lodged in the back of her throat.

As uncomfortable as that situation was for Saffy, removal was fairly easy for the attending vet, with little damage to the dog other than swelling and a sore throat—symptoms easily treatable with the proper medication. Saffy made a rapid recovery.

Jack Russell gets hooked on fishing

A ten-year-old Jack Russell terrier named Candy almost became the bait when she went fishing in Llanelli, South Wales, with Elwyn Thomas, her owner. As Thomas cast off, Candy jumped for and caught the bait. The fishing line snapped off close to the hook, and the dog swallowed the bait and the hook.

During their trip to the vet, the two-inch steel fishhook showed up on X-rays; however, the vet chose not to operate. Instead he decided it was safe to let nature take its course, partly because there was only a small amount of fishing line still attached to the hook. Instead he prescribed a soft diet, high in fiber, to help the hook pass quickly and safely. Banana sandwiches were recommended, and two days later the hook was passed. Candy, it seems, viewed this as an achievement and brought it to show her owners when it was over.

Needle finds way into poodle's brain

Knives aside, one of the scariest stories of swallowed objects would have to be the one of the needle that found its way into a poodle's brain. The poodle swallowed the needle with thread, luckily, still attached.

When swallowed, the needle went down the throat, through a space at the base of the skull, and into the tissues of the brain. The thread remained outside, and the vet determined that it could be removed by just pulling on the thread to bring it back out. The poodle made a full recovery, with no brain damage despite impaling her own brain with a needle.

An earily unpleasant snack

A mixed-breed Doberman pinscher and a German shepherd were observed attacking a young boy on a neighbor's driveway in Whittier, California. One of the dogs bit the boy's ear clean off and then swallowed it.

Animal control officers said the dogs were destroyed because they were so aggressive, but it was unknown which dog swallowed the ear. According to animal control officer Wendy Guerrero, the dogs' stomachs were emptied and the severed ear was found to be largely intact in the stomach of the Doberman. The ear was immediately wrapped and packed in ice before being sent to the hospital, where seven-year-old Brandon Olivas's ear was surgically reattached.

Eaten Super Bowl tickets something to bawl about

Buddy, a three-year-old Labrador retriever in Arizona, landed in the doghouse for a couple of days after decimating his owner's Super Bowl tickets that were delivered by a courier. The courier failed to follow the delivery instructions that were attached to the package and slipped it under the door instead of underneath the doormat.

The dog was able to get the tickets, tearing apart the packaging and the pair of tickets inside, which cost $900 each. Buddy's owner knew what Buddy was capable of and thought he had taken the appropriate steps to protect his valuable tickets by instructing the courier to leave the package under the doormat.

Some of the pieces were eaten, but more of them were well licked and chewed. Luckily for the owner enough pieces of the two tickets remained, and the ticket issuer was willing to give him replacements (ending poor Buddy's isolation in the backyard).

One-way ticket to the doghouse

A UK soccer fan faced a similar situation when his Japanese Shiba Inu, named JJ, ate his season tickets to the matches of his favorite team, Newcastle United. JJ had been named after England's famous midfielder, Jermaine Jenas.

"I'll be gutted if I can't get to matches. The only dribbling I'll see will be JJ." The avid soccer fan told BBC News that he was extremely upset. Luckily, the team offered him replacement tickets at a fraction of the original cost.

Pom-pom–loving pug pigs out

A poor pug was found to be supporting the family's school team in a most unusual way. The owners didn't realize that she had eaten a pair of the cheerleading pom-poms until they began to pass through her little body in a natural way.

Thankfully the owners were good sports about the whole ordeal. "Our school colors are maroon and white and there was the pom-poms coming out," the owner told MSNBC. "My husband said, 'Look, she's in the school spirit!'"

Knockoffs no problem for cheap leather and coin lover

Sherman the cairn terrier has already eaten a couple of thousand dollars' worth of leather in the form of handbags, wallets, shoes, belts, and even journal covers. He doesn't discriminate either; he has been known to lunch on his owners' and their guests' goods at any given time.

His owners accidentally left a bag of rolled pennies on the floor by the door, which they had planned to take to the bank later that week. But when they heard some rustling around, they went to check on the dog and saw him scarfing down as much change as he could. They ordered him to stop but that just made him eat faster! In all, he managed to eat twenty-eight coins before they could pull him away.

The owners called their local vet and found out that zinc, when consumed in large quantities, can cause a type of anemia that can be fatal if not treated within forty-eight hours. They were told to sit tight and wait. And so, for thirty-six hours, they scooped poop and examined what was there—doing the same thing when Sherman eventually started vomiting more coins. But time was running out and he was in danger, so with six pennies still inside, they rushed to the clinic.

Thankfully, for Sherman's sake, the coins were removed after several attempts with endoscopy rather than surgery, but still the bill was large. An extra six cents cost the owners a total of $743.59.

The street sweeper ate my dog

Finally, mention should be made of a very unfortunate dog named Zoe, which rather than eating something unusual, was *eaten* by something unusual in Missouri. The Great Pyrenees disappeared inside the machinery of a street sweeper after she ran away from her owner, Gene Fee, toward the machine.

Fee saw the big white dog disappear and went home, having no hope of seeing Zoe again and fearing that she surely had died inside the rumbling contraption. However, the operator, John Reutter, realized what had happened and stopped the machine to look inside. To his delight, there was Zoe—trapped in a strange location but safe and unharmed nonetheless. He immediately called for help.

Ten minutes, three maintenance vehicles, and six workers later, the adventurous Zoe was free. The crew called her owner, and the two were happily reunited. Just goes to show that despite all the things that we see our faithful friends eating, every once in a while we see the world bite back!

Resources

Thanks and credit to the range of valuable sources from around the world without which researching this compendium of wacky dog stories would not have been possible:

ABC Local
ABC News
BBC News
customs.gov.au
The Daily Mail
Fox News
The Independent (United Kingdom)
K9 Magazine
Knox News
MSNBC
news.yahoo.com
The New York Times
Pet Friendly Magazine
Rocky Mountain News
The Sun (United Kingdom)
The Times of London

About the Author

Ryan O'Meara is the founder and managing director of K9 Media Ltd., Europe's most prominent pet publishing company. He began his career with animals at the age of sixteen working as a dog training apprentice in Derbyshire under the tutelage of one of the United Kingdom's most well-known kennel owners.

In 1994 he went on to become a professional trainer and worked with more than one thousand dogs over the course of five eventful years, achieving numerous accolades and becoming one of the youngest handlers ever to qualify for and compete in the British Spaniel Championships.

In 1999 O'Meara established the company he now runs, which publishes the United Kingdom's first dog lifestyle publication, *K9 Magazine,* and operates a network of more than thirty-five pet-related media brands with a global audience of more than 6.3 million pet lovers. Along with his role as K9 Media's managing director, O'Meara is also editor in chief of *K9 Magazine.*

In 2006 O'Meara became a behavioral assessor on the BBC Three television show *Dog Borstal.* In 2007 he was behind the launch of DogsBlog.com, one of his proudest accomplishments, which is the United Kingdom's national dog adoption and rescue Web site that has helped thousands of shelter dogs find new homes. His most recent endeavor was launching *Pet Friendly Magazine* in 2008.